IMAGES
of America

PHENIX CITY

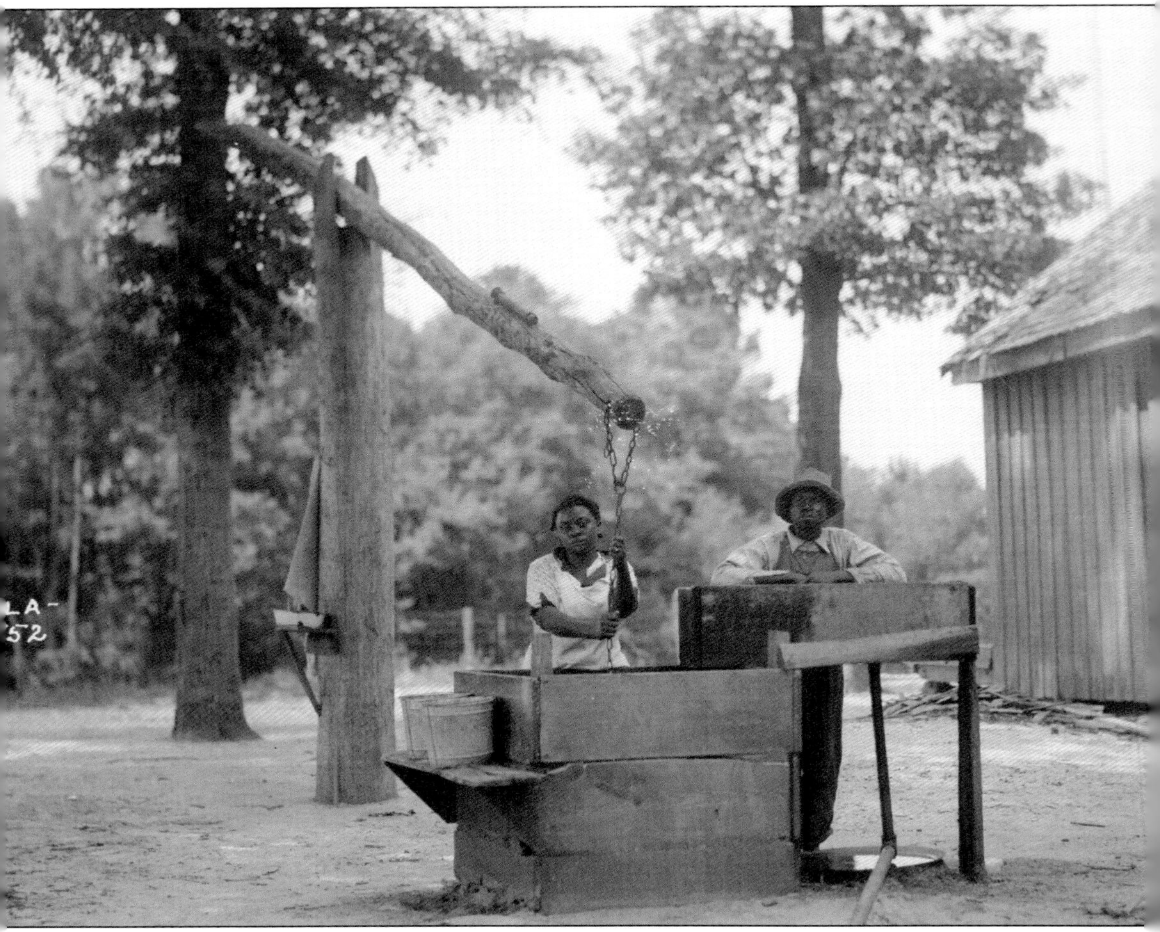

Cliatt Plantation Sharecroppers, Cottonton, Russell County, Alabama. Two unidentified sharecroppers work the well on the Cliatt plantation. (Courtesy Library of Congress.)

On the Cover: "Dinner-Toters" are seen standing at the mill entrance, 1913. After the dinners are delivered, the toters help tend the machines. Toting dinners allowed families to earn additional income and served as a form of on-the-job training. (Courtesy Library of Congress.)

IMAGES
of America

PHENIX CITY

John Lyles

ARCADIA
PUBLISHING

ISBN 978-0-7385-8569-7

Published by Arcadia Publishing
Charleston, South Carolina

Printed in the United States of America

Library of Congress Control Number: 2009940681

For all general information contact Arcadia Publishing at:
Telephone 843-853-2070
Fax 843-853-0044
E-mail sales@arcadiapublishing.com
For customer service and orders:
Toll-Free 1-888-313-2665

Visit us on the Internet at www.arcadiapublishing.com

To Nichole, Collin, Nicholas, and Abigail

CONTENTS

ACKNOWLEDGMENTS

There are several people whose time, energy, and talent allowed me to present this book. Specifically, I wish to thank Dennis Jones, Sean Driggers, Mike Bunn, Gloria Battle, Dalton Royer, Gisle Remy, Kenneth Thomas Jr., Freda Page, Fr. Tom Weise, Margaret Wilson, Harvetta Jackson, Greg Schmidt, Charlotte Sierra, Sister Cecelia, and Johnnie Warner for their commitment and contributions towards preserving Phenix City's history. Any omissions are a function of the mind and not the heart. Much is owed to all.

The research process involved many institutions as well. Without their efforts in collecting and making available historical and archival sources, none of this would be possible. My sincere regards to the staffs of the Alabama Department of Archives and History, Atlanta History Center, Auburn University Archives and Special Collections, Chattahoochee Valley Community College Library, Columbus State University Archives, Columbus Black History Museum, the Columbus Museum, Columbus Public Library, Franchise Missionary Baptist Church, Library of Congress, Mother Mary Mission, Phenix City Public Library, St. Patrick's Church, and the W. S. Hoole Special Collections Library.

Finally, to my wife, Nichole, thank you for your love and encouragement.

INTRODUCTION

Phenix City, Alabama, located at the headwaters of the Chattahoochee River, was officially created on February 19, 1889. Like the river, Phenix City can trace its story farther in time and space. From pre-Colonial times to now, the current of history has cascaded down rocky shoals to wider, slower flows prior to its arrival at Phenix City. Native American contact and conflict, territorial settlement, statehood, the expansion of slavery, the Civil War, emancipation, and Reconstruction are but a few currents that preceded the official existence of Phenix City, but their legacies informed its history. At once a separate fluid entity and dependent upon a complex and diverse network of tributaries, Phenix City's is an account of a single city and of locations such as Fort Mitchell, Coweta Town, Seale, Summerville, Girard, Lively, Knights Station, Brownville, Fort Benning, and Columbus. Each tributary has deposited its silt and shaped the flow of Phenix City's narrative.

The city has a rich and distinguished past centered on its Native American heritage; reliance on cotton; roles as the Alabama suburb of Columbus, the site of the last major battle of the Civil War and the seat of government for Russell County; proximity to Fort Benning; and reputation as "sin city." Here I present a small fraction of that record.

This book is not intended as a formal or comprehensive history of Phenix City; rather, it is a collection of images accompanied by interesting and historical accounts that give meaning and context. Not everyone will be happy with this version; it neither celebrates nor condemns but merely documents. Presented chronologically, the book allows the reader to sense the ebbs and flows, the continuity and fractures in Phenix City's tale.

One of the main purposes of this text is to raise awareness for the preservation and accessibility of historical and archival data. Historical research is dependent upon the critical evaluation of primary sources, which offer a contemporary view of a particular event. Diaries, journals, correspondence, photographs, maps, government documents, oral histories, objects, and artifacts serve as the raw materials needed to interpret the past. In many cases, they serve as the only remaining evidence, without which the record is left uncertain or lost. When used along with previous interpretations by historians, primary sources provide the means necessary for historical analysis.

During my research, it became painfully obvious that the state of historical preservation in Phenix City is lacking. No sizeable collection of manuscript materials exists. Over half a dozen newspapers printed in Phenix City have been identified, with no surviving copies located. The few collections available are in private hands. History, therefore, becomes a function of not what you know but whom you know. The documentation of the local African American experience is nearly totally void. Whether a product of neglect, failure to see any value in history, or a lack of trust, the end result is a permanent loss of valuable chapters in Phenix City's story. I urge all individuals and institutions with historical materials to consider donating them to an appropriate repository for future generations to study and enjoy.

One

Territorial and Formative Years 1680–1839

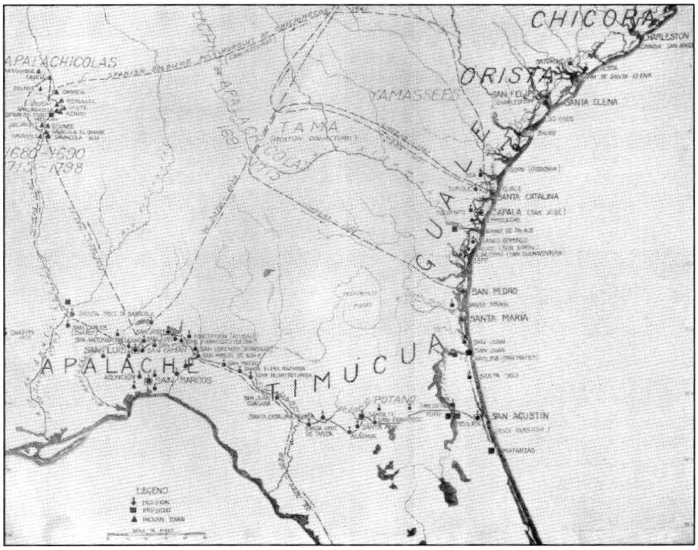

Map of Georgia Country in Spanish Days. This map details the missionary and military activity of the Spanish in the "Georgia Country" from 1680 to 1798. "Georgia Country" is a reference to the land contested by Spain and England during Colonial times. Spanish missions, presidios, and expeditions as well as Native American towns are indicated. The area of Apalachicola encompasses modern day Russell County, Alabama. (Courtesy Columbus Public Library.)

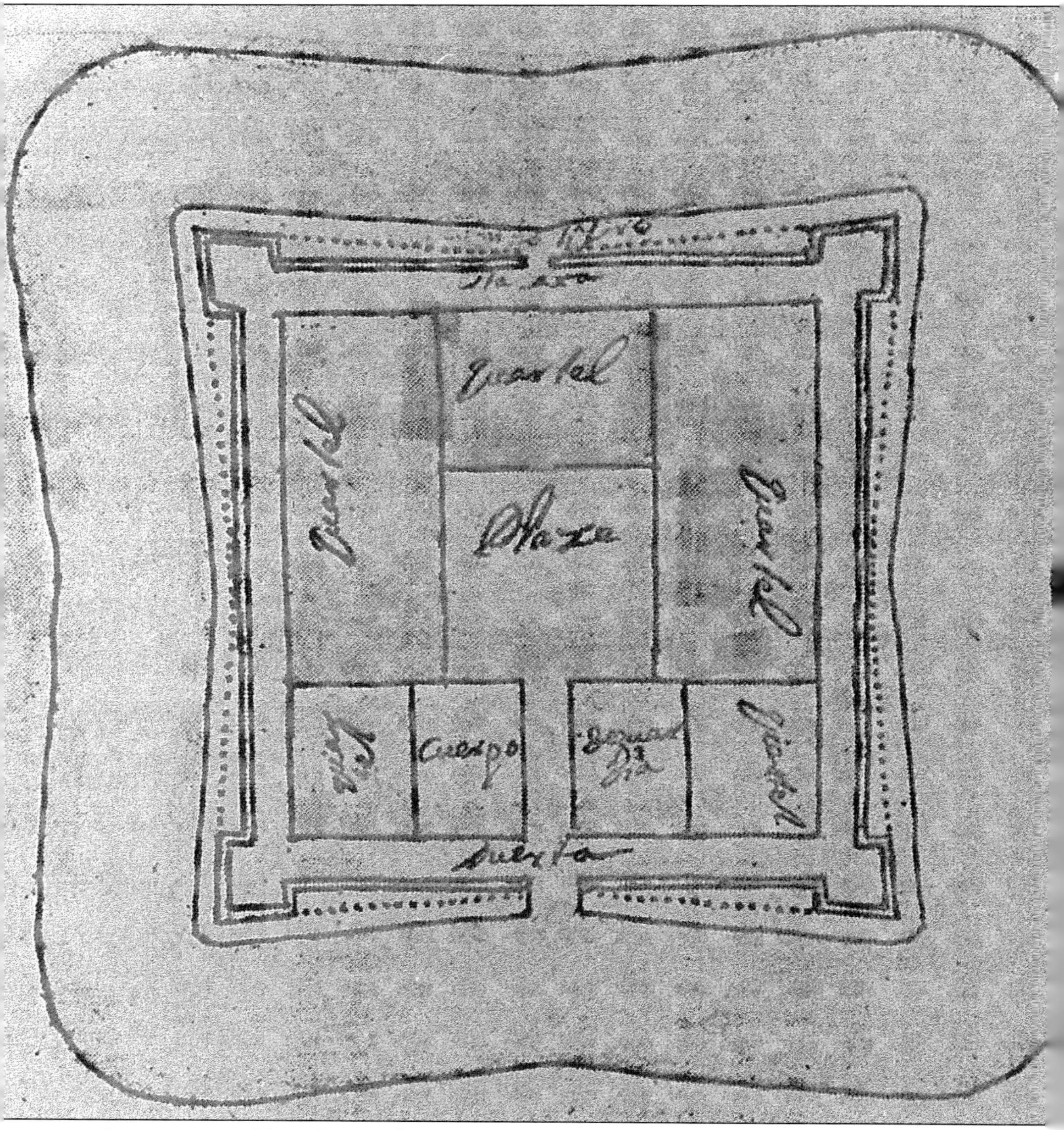

APALACHICOLA FORT. Located near Holy Trinity, the square, palisaded fort was built in 1689 by Spain. Don Diego de Quiroga y Lasada, governor of Florida, ordered the construction of the military and religious outpost as an attempt to gain influence among the Lower Creek Indians and to check English advancements in the territory. Unsuccessful in both regards, the Spanish razed the fort after little more than one year of occupation. (Courtesy Columbus Museum.)

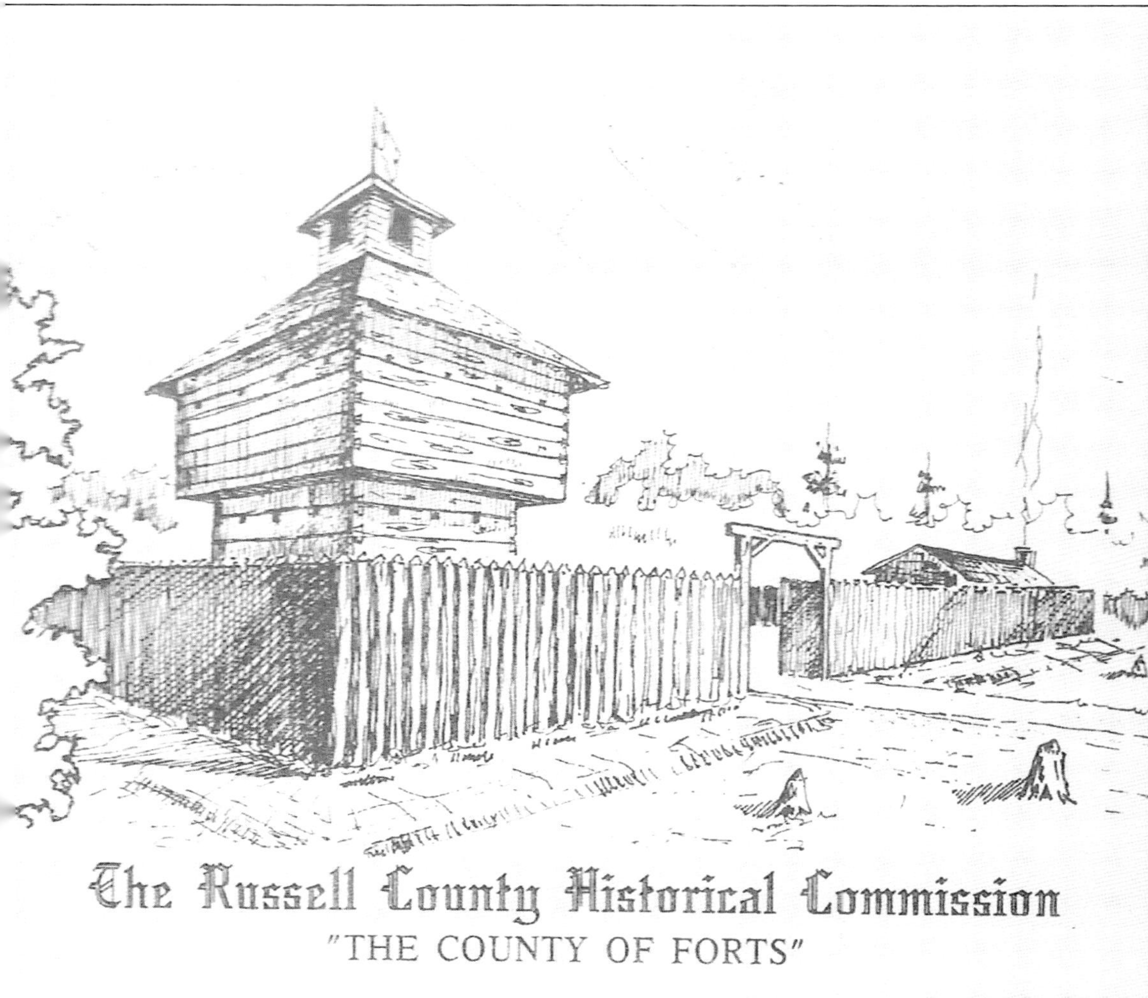

Fort Mitchell. Constructed by the Georgia Militia under the command of Gen. John Floyd, Fort Mitchell served as the center of United States–Creek Indian relationships from 1813 to 1837. The "strong stockade fort defended by blockhouses" served as a base of operations and haven during the Creek War (1813–1814). Strategically located at the head of a federal road, the fort played a major role in frontier relations with the establishment of the Creek trading house or factory (1817) and the Creek Indian agency (1820). Fort Mitchell was named in honor of Georgia governor David Brydie Mitchell. (Courtesy Chattahoochee Valley Community College.)

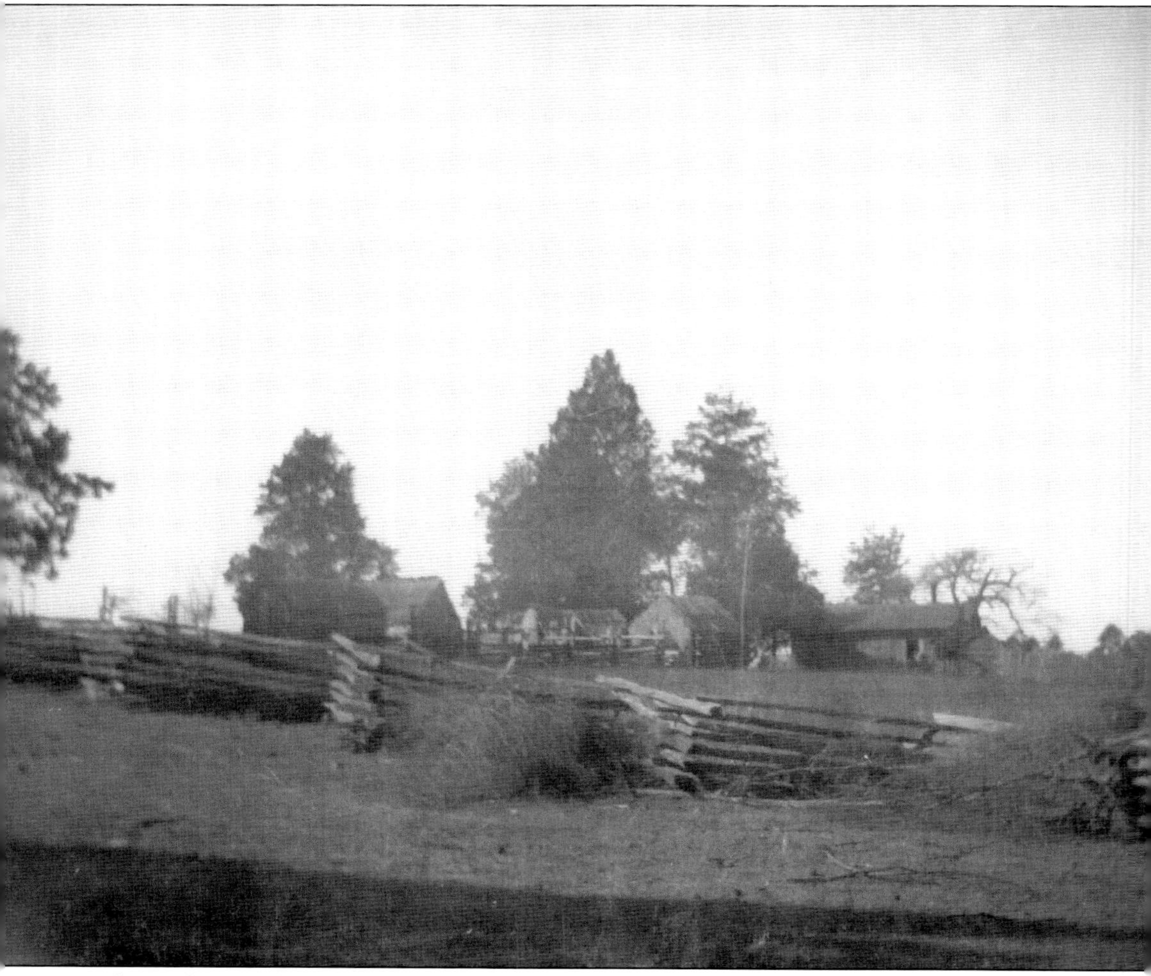

Creek Indian Agency near Fort Mitchell. This 1915 view shows the remains of the agency. Col. John Crowell's office was located beyond the outbuildings. The Creek agency at Fort Mitchell was a gathering point for forced removal to Oklahoma. (Courtesy Chattahoochee Valley Community College.)

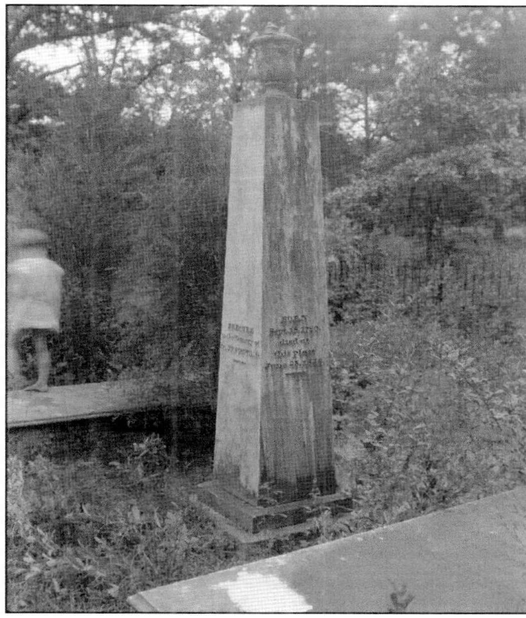

John Crowell. A North Carolina native, John Crowell arrived in Alabama in 1815. He was Alabama's first territorial delegate to Congress. Crowell also served as Indian agent at Coweta from 1821 until the Creek Indian's removal in 1836. (Courtesy Library of Congress.)

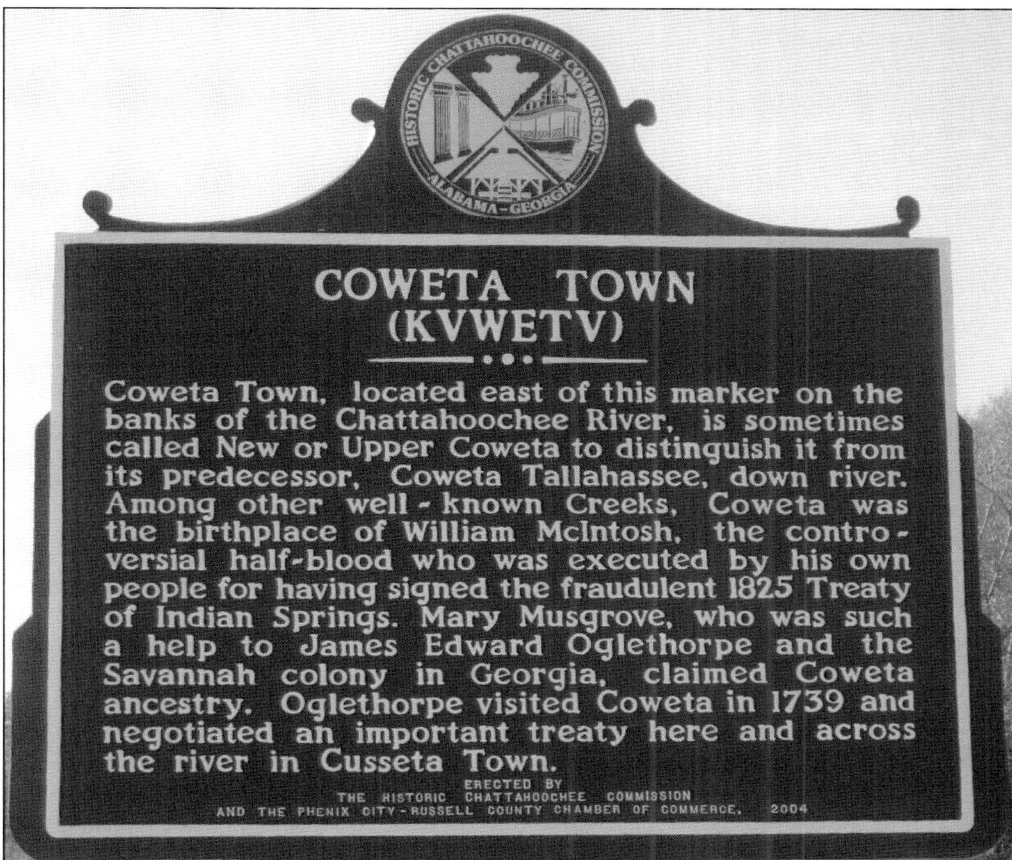

Coweta Town. Coweta served as the political capital of the Lower Creek Nation. (Courtesy Columbus Public Library.)

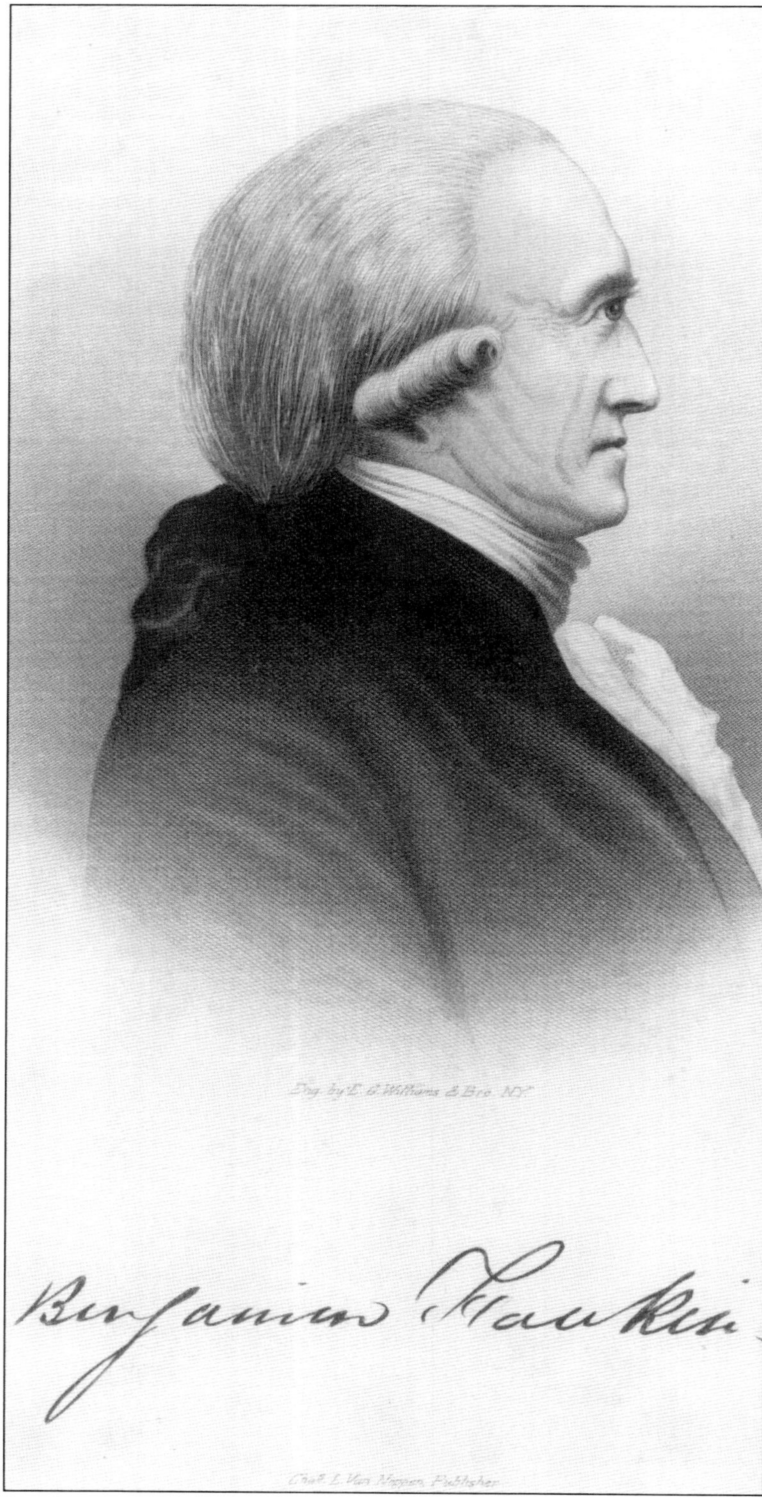

Benjamin Hawkins. A diplomat and agent to the Creek Indians, Benjamin Hawkins (1754–1816) was appointed as Indian agent for all the tribes south of the Ohio River by President Washington in 1796 and held the office until his death in Crawford County, Georgia, on June 6, 1818. An advocate of the "civilization" of the Creeks, Hawkins believed the adoption of yeoman farming best allowed the Creeks to assimilate to white society. He negotiated a number of treaties with the Native Americans and accompanied official surveys for the state of Alabama. (Courtesy Columbus Public Library.)

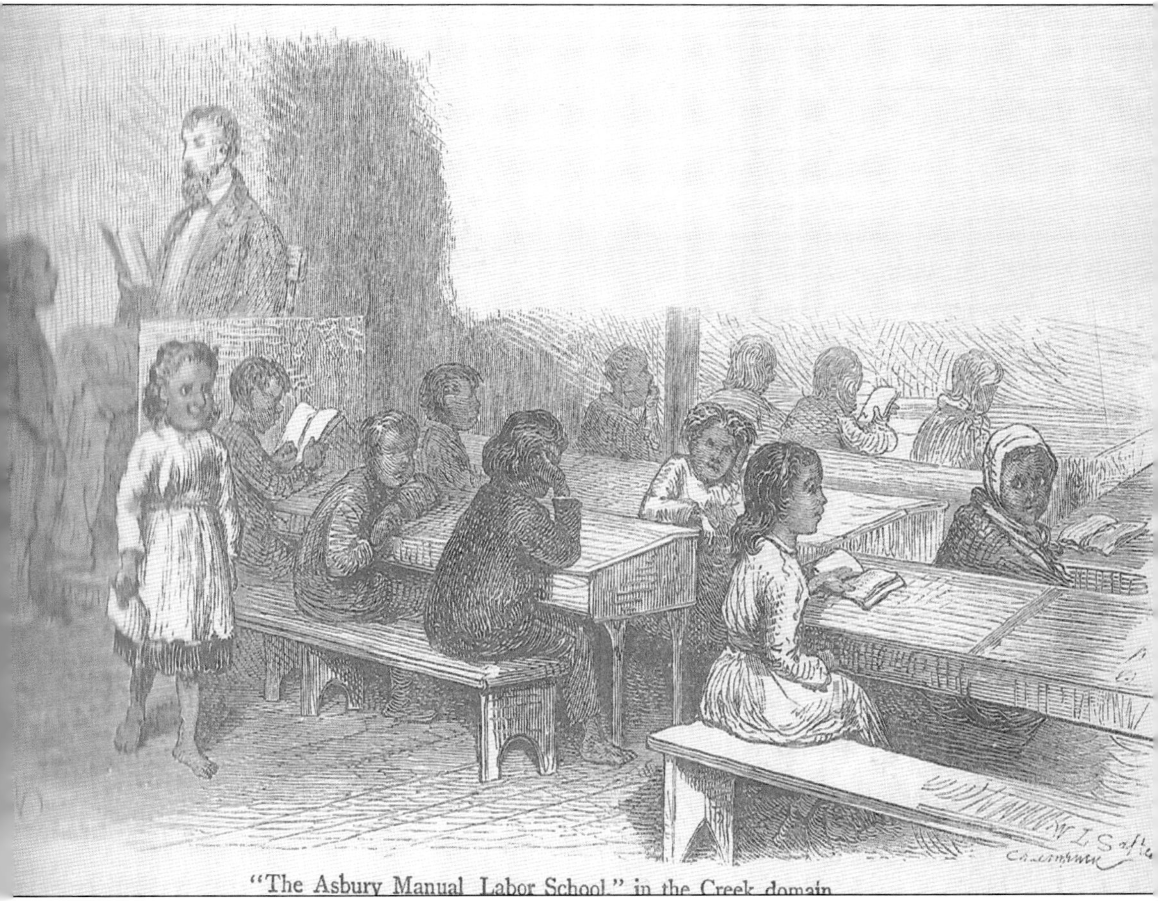

"The Asbury Manual Labor School," in the Creek domain

ASBURY MISSION AND MANUAL LABOR SCHOOL. In 1821, William Capers, a Methodist missionary, negotiated with the chiefs to open two mission schools within the Creek Nation. Capers planned to construct one school at Tuckabatchi and another at Coweta. Only Asbury, at Coweta, was built. Located a mile north of Fort Mitchell, Asbury opened with 12 students and remained active until 1829. (Courtesy Columbus Public Library.)

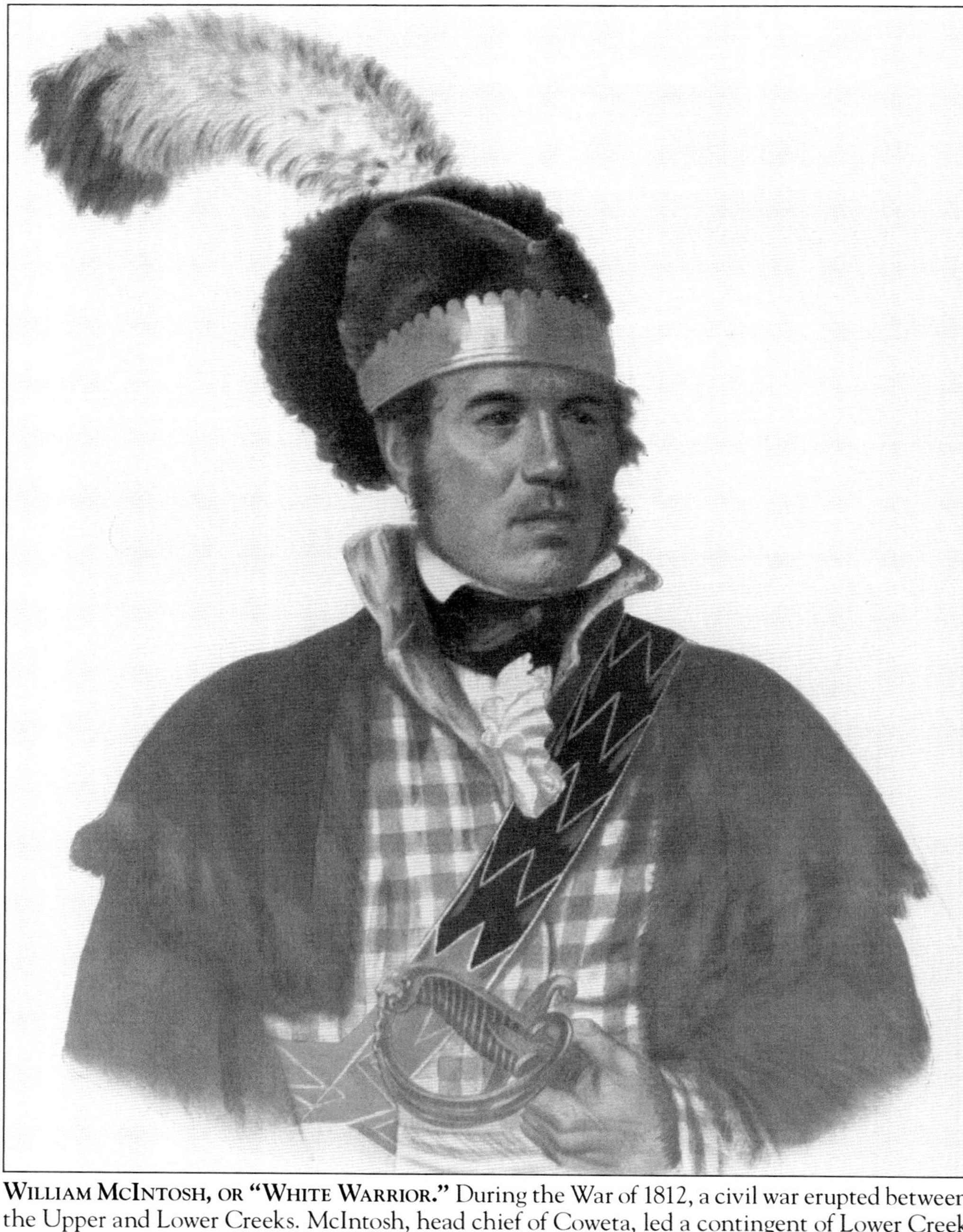

William McIntosh, or "White Warrior." During the War of 1812, a civil war erupted between the Upper and Lower Creeks. McIntosh, head chief of Coweta, led a contingent of Lower Creek forces and quelled the Creek War, also known as the Red Stick Rebellion. McIntosh supported the United States' position of acculturation, and he ceded Creek territory by signing the Treaty of Indian Springs in 1821. On April 30, 1825, the Law Menders and Red Stick leader Menawa assassinated McIntosh as retribution for signing the treaty. The Treaty of Indian Springs was rejected as fraudulent by both the Creeks and the U.S. government and replaced by the 1826 Treaty of Washington, allowing the Creeks to keep about 3 million acres in Alabama. (Courtesy Columbus Public Library.)

MENAWA, OR THE GREAT WARRIOR. Menawa was one of the principle leaders of the Red Sticks during the Creek War. After the war, Menawa continued to resist the encroachments of settlers, refused to sanction cessions of territory, and opposed compulsory emigration of his people. On April 30, 1825, he led a party of 200 warriors that assassinated William McIntosh. (Courtesy Columbus Public Library.)

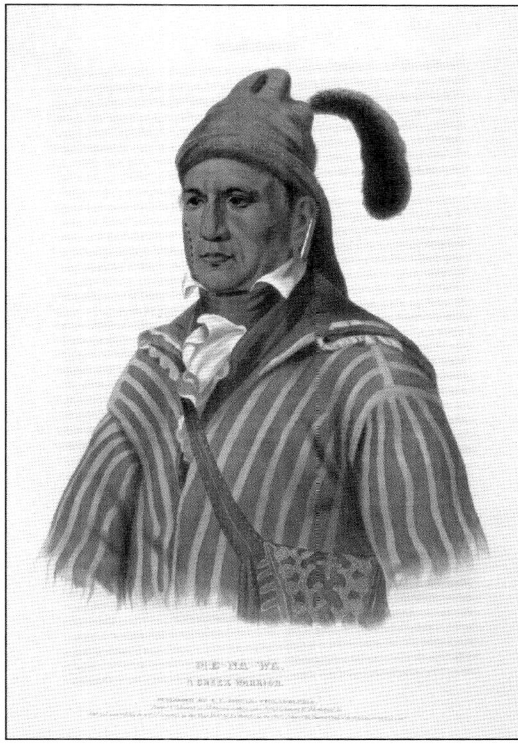

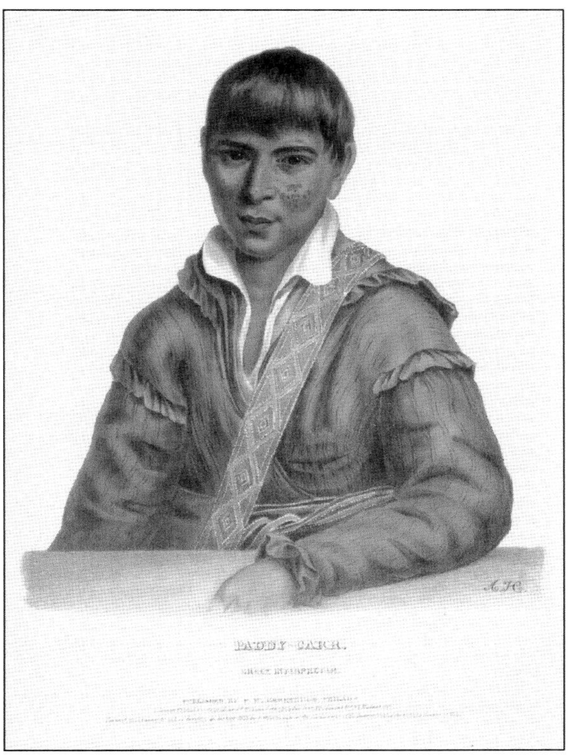

PADDY CARR. Born near Fort Mitchell, Alabama, Paddy Carr was taken into the family of John Crowell, the Indian agent at Fort Mitchell. Intelligent and skilled with languages, Paddy served as a principle guide and interpreter for the Creeks. He acted as translator for the Creek chiefs when they protested the Treaty of Indian Springs. (Courtesy Columbus Public Library.)

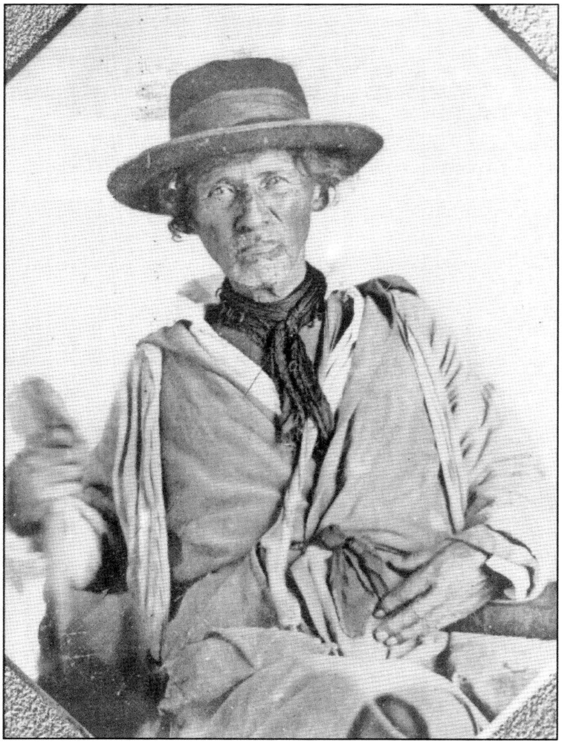

Timpoochee Barnard, 1826. Yuchi leader Timpoochee Barnard allied his warriors with American forces during the Creek War (1813–1814). On August 9, 1814, Barnard signed the Treaty of Fort Jackson, which effectively ended the war, as "Captain of Uchees." The terms of the treaty ceded 23 million acres of Creek land in Alabama and Georgia to the U.S. government. Barnard is buried at Fort Mitchell. (Courtesy Columbus Public Library.)

Dueling Grounds. The grounds around Fort Mitchell served as a frontier courtroom. Numerous duels occurred to settle quarrels. (Courtesy Chattahoochee Valley Community College.)

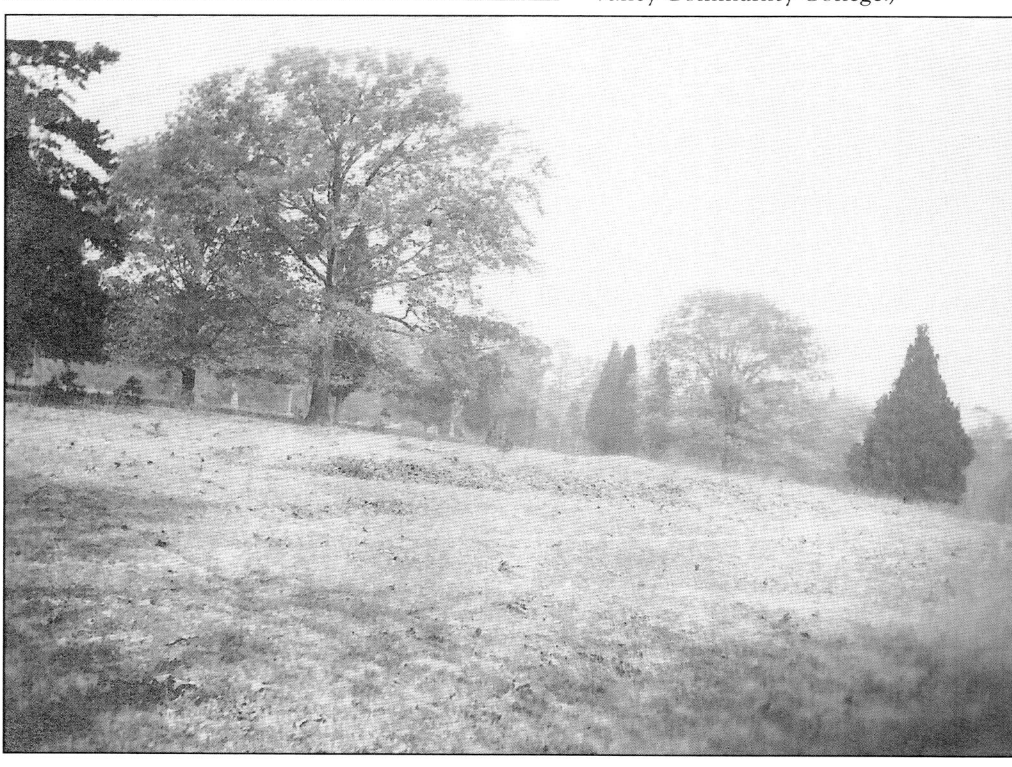

BARKLEY MARTIN LETTER, 1831. The settlement of Russell County is part of the larger story of growth in the Alabama Territory during the 19th century. It is a tripartite story of white settlers, African slaves, and the Creek Nation. Prior to its creation as a county in December 1832, settlers had long been acquiring and cultivating its lands, exacerbating frontier tensions in the process. Warning of a "rebellion of the slaves, aided by the Indians," Martin's letter makes plain the discontent and hostility that permeated frontier settlers and settlements. (Courtesy Columbus Public Library.)

At the request of the commanding officers who visited Fort Mitchell on the 4th inst. did I with them wait on the commanding officer of the United States Troops stationed there, to know the grounds upon which the communi ation refered to was made to Gen. Woolfolk, and from the circumstances that transpired on Sunday last, do think, that Lieut. Clay was justifiable in giving notice to Gen. Woolfolk, and I do believe that the town of Columbus and the frontier se'tlements would do well to direct their attention to th means & measures that would repel any thing like a rebellion of the slaves, aided by the Indians.

BARK EY MARTIN.

Columbus, Oct 5, 1831

SETTLERS HEADSTONES, 1830S. These headstones are of two early Russell County settlers and are thought to predate the relinquishment of Creek lands. (Courtesy Chattahoochee Valley Community College.)

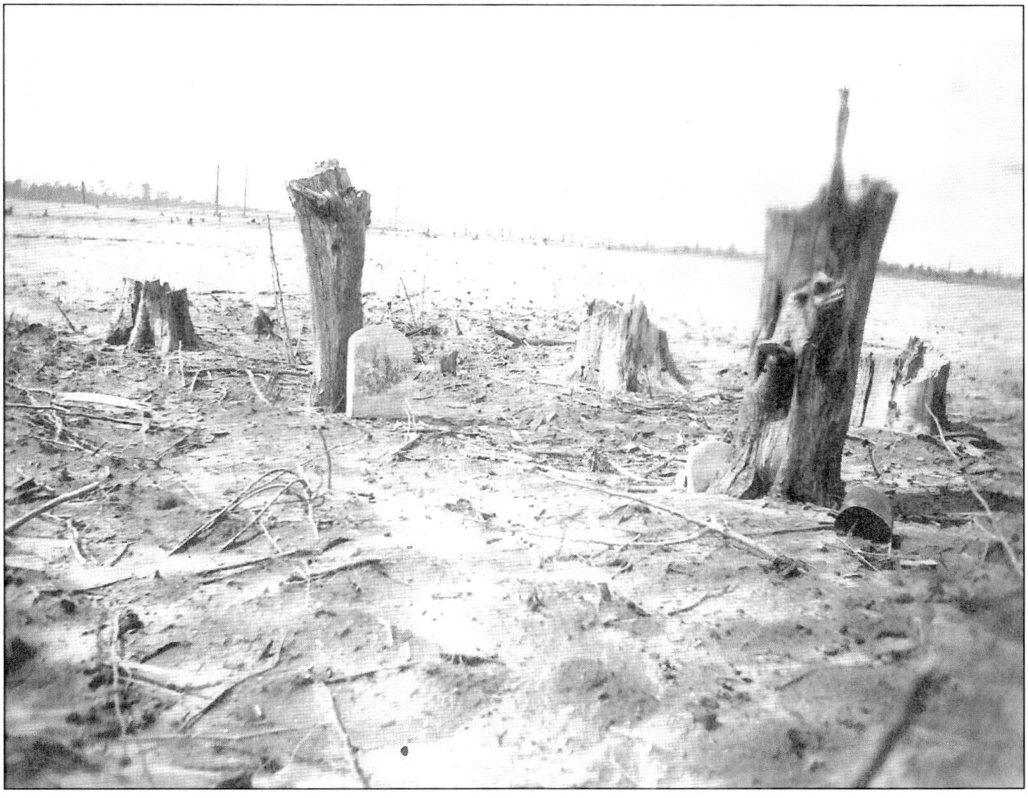

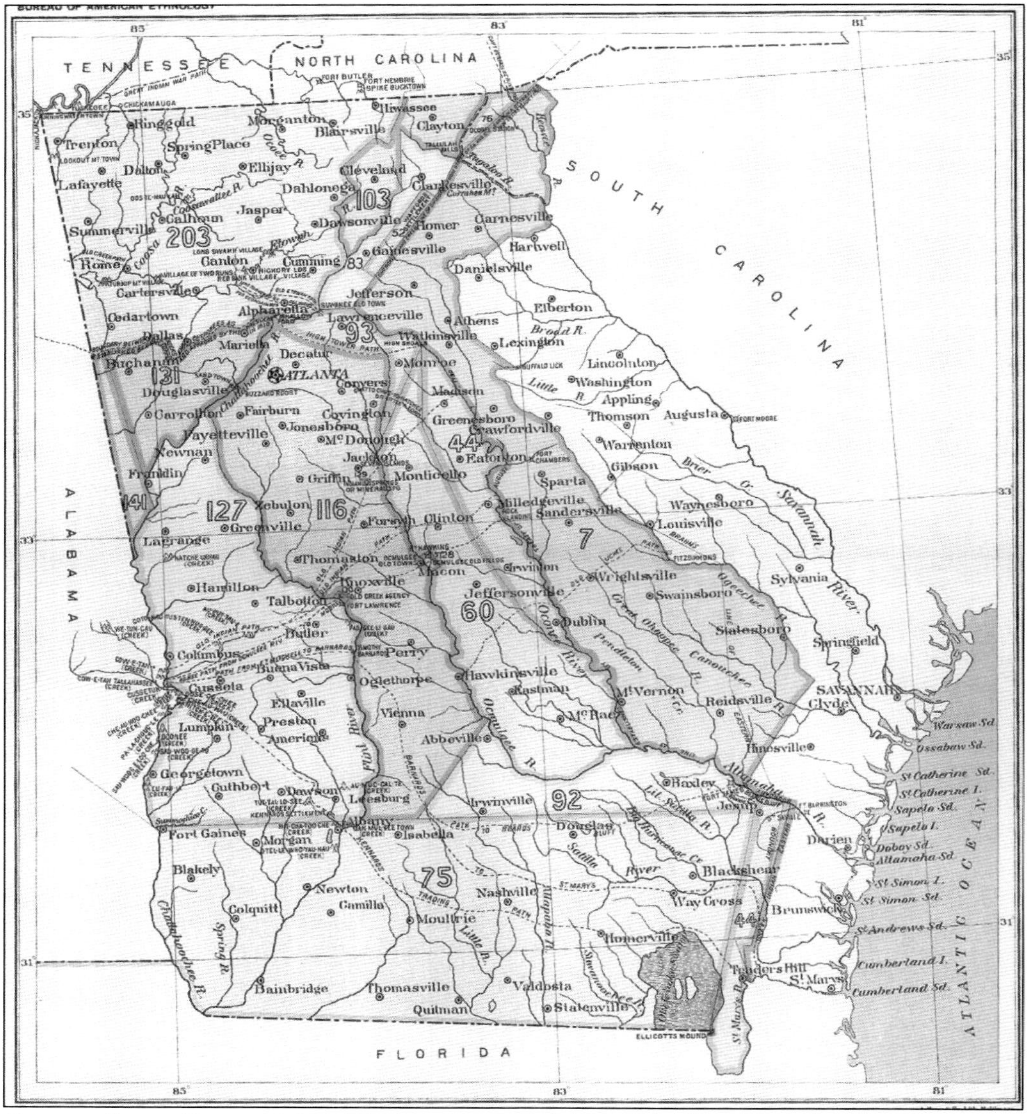

Georgia Land Cession Map. The Treaty of Washington (1826) settled the dispute between the United States and the Creek Nation over the legality of the Treaty of Indian Springs. The Washington treaty effectively voided the Indian Springs treaty and ceded to the United States all the land belonging to the Creeks east of the Chattahoochee River. By 1828, many Creeks were removed from Georgia, and the state legislature had established the frontier town of Columbus. (Courtesy Columbus Public Library.)

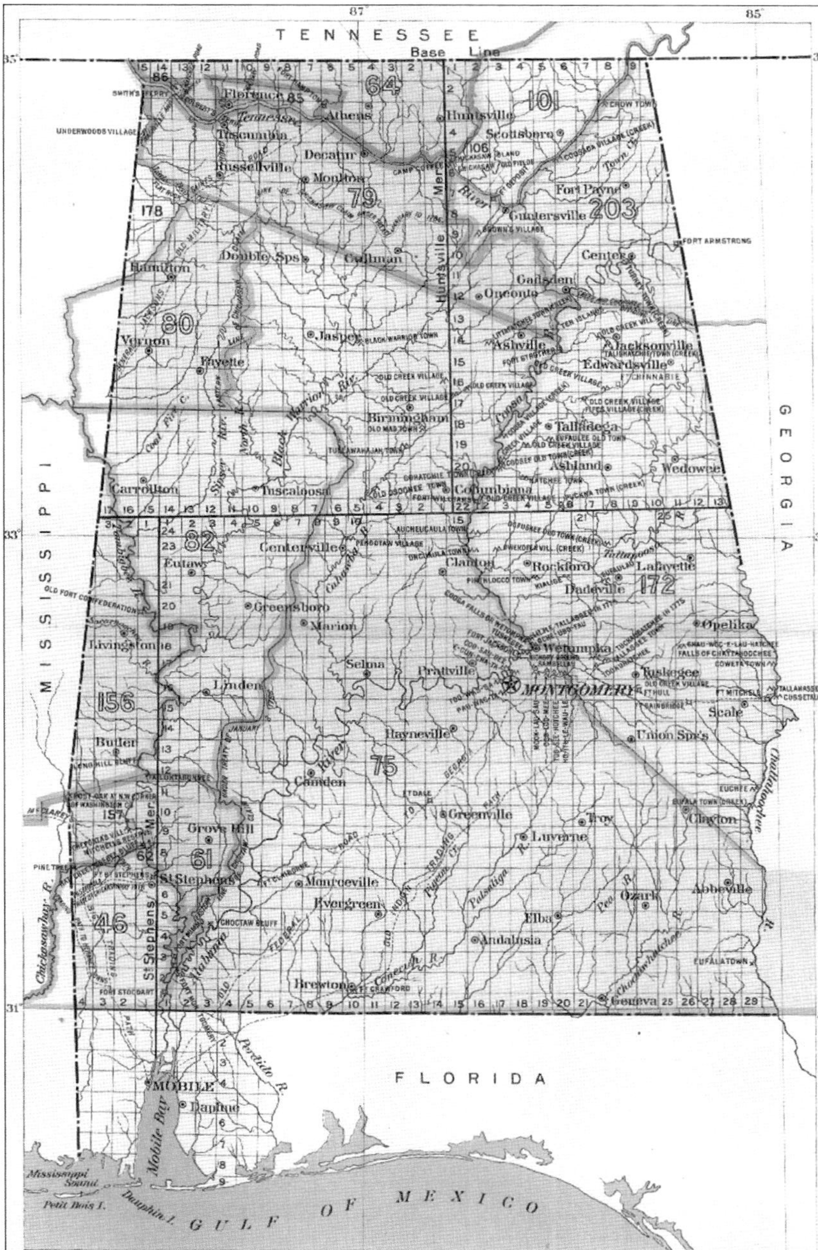

Alabama Land Cession Map. In 1832, the Creek Indians signed the Treaty of Cusseta. The treaty required that the Creek Nation relinquish all tribal land east of the Mississippi River, including territory in Alabama. Although Creek chiefs and heads of families were granted rights to, respectively, one section and one half-section of land of their choosing, the Creeks found themselves overwhelmed by squatters. The treaty also specifically allotted Benjamin Marshall one section of land, to include his improvements on the Chattahoochee River. Marshall's section, or reserve as it was known, would eventually become the town of Girard. (Courtesy Columbus Public Library.)

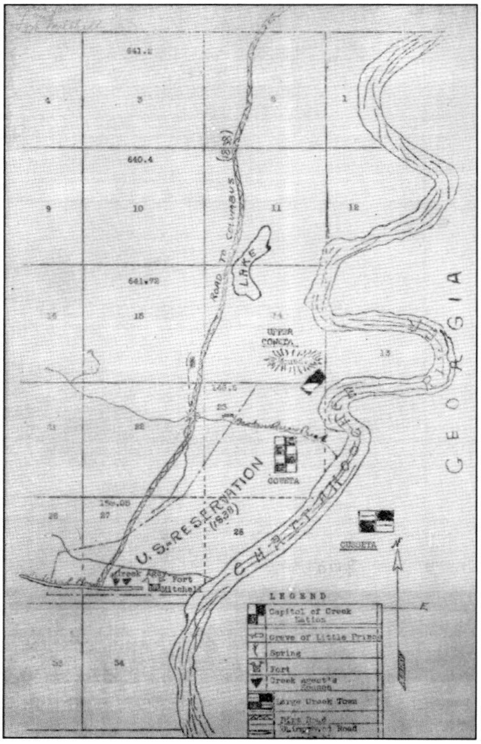

DETAIL MAP OF COWETA TOWN AND FORT MITCHELL. This drawing of the U.S. reservation details the locations of Fort Mitchell and the Creek agency in relation to the Coweta and Cusseta towns of the Creek Nation. (Courtesy Chattahoochee Valley Community College.)

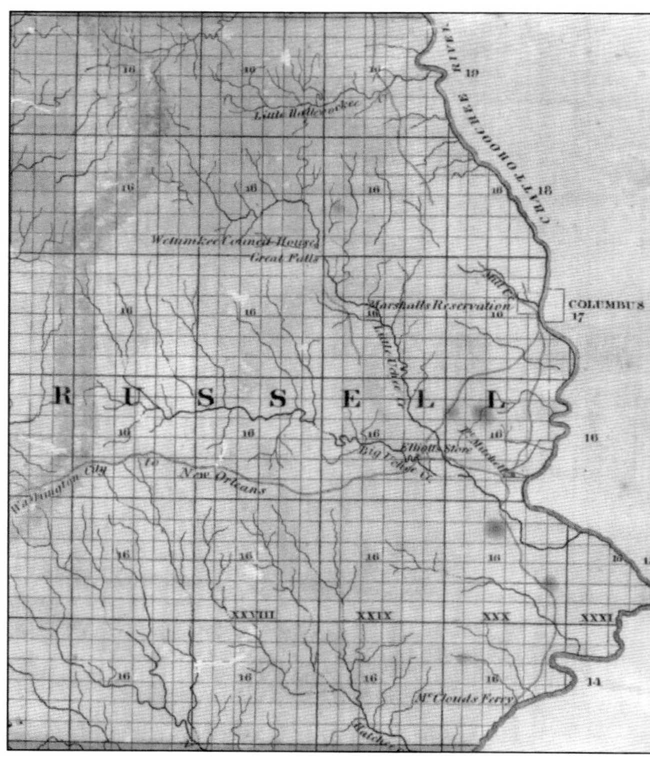

DETAIL VIEW OF RUSSELL COUNTY FROM JOHN LATOURETTE'S MAP OF ALABAMA, 1837. Following the Treaty of Cusseta, the Alabama legislature quickly divided the ceded Creek territory into counties. Russell County was created on December 18, 1832. Hardeman Owen, Thomas Martin, and Anderson Abercrombie were appointed commissioners. Russell County is named in honor of Gilbert Christian Russell, commander of the 3rd U.S. Infantry Regiment during the Creek War. (Courtesy Columbus Public Library.)

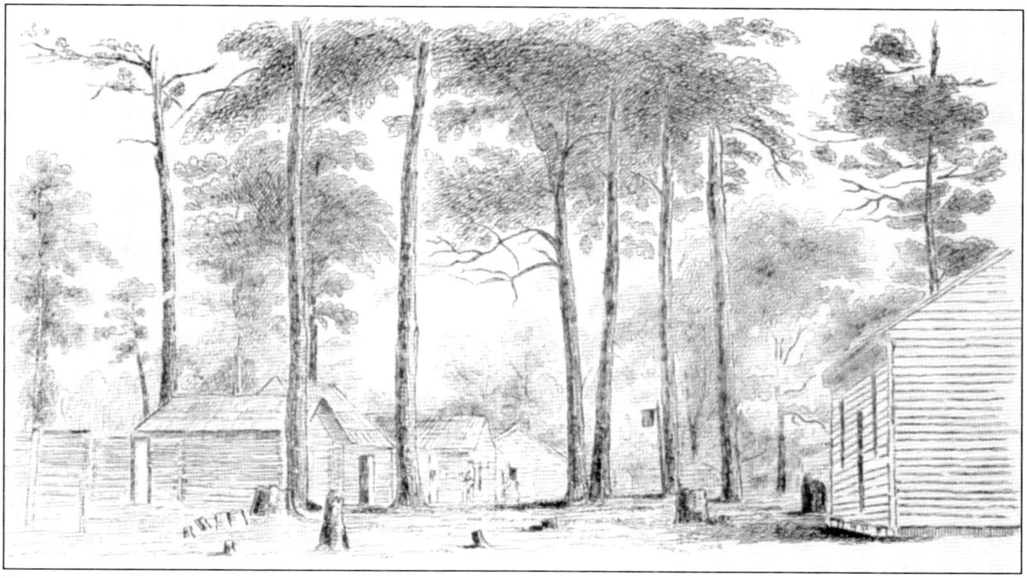

EMBRYO TOWN OF COLUMBUS ON THE CHATTAHOOCHEE, 1828. This Basil Hall sketch of Columbus shows the frontier village prior to it becoming a trading and manufacturing town. In 1832, Daniel McDougald and Robert Collins ventured to establish industry on the Alabama side of the river and purchased Benjamin Marshall's reserve. The two speculators intended to harness the power of the falls for milling and manufacturing purposes. The next year, apprehension grew in Columbus when it was learned that Russell County's seat of government would be located on the opposite bank. Girard was viewed as the first movement at establishing a rival town. (Courtesy Columbus Public Library.)

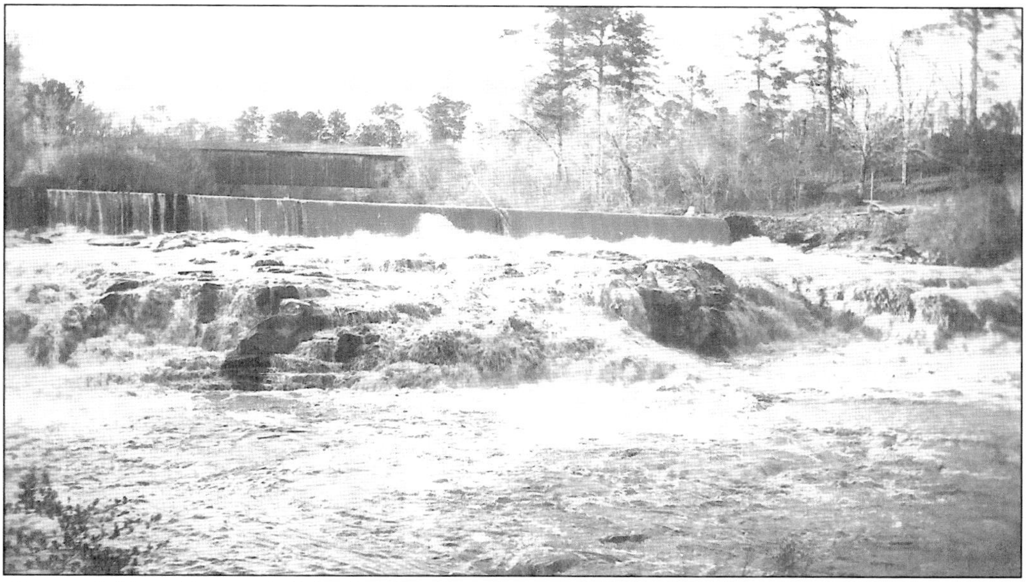

MOFFITT'S MILL. Removal of the Creek Indians hastened the arrival of settlers such as Capt. Henry Moffitt, who purchased the Russell County property and constructed a mill at the Wetumpka Council House site of the Lower Creek Indians in 1836. Moffitt's Mill is now located in Lee County. (Courtesy Chattahoochee Valley Community College.)

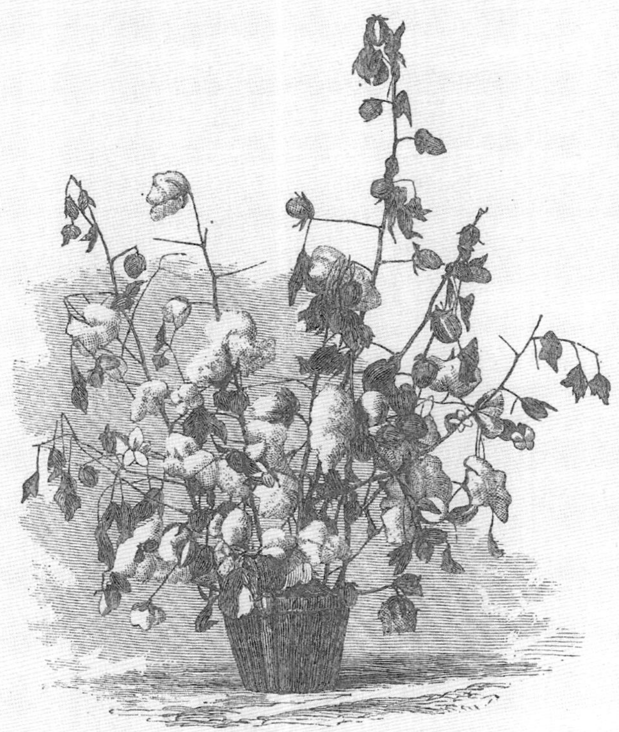

The Cotton-Plant.

COTTON KINGDOM. Cotton transformed the frontier into functioning communities. This cotton kingdom built upon the labor of black slaves dominated Russell County's economy. The labor requirements for cotton cultivation were high, and slavery became indispensable to cotton production. (Courtesy Columbus Public Library.)

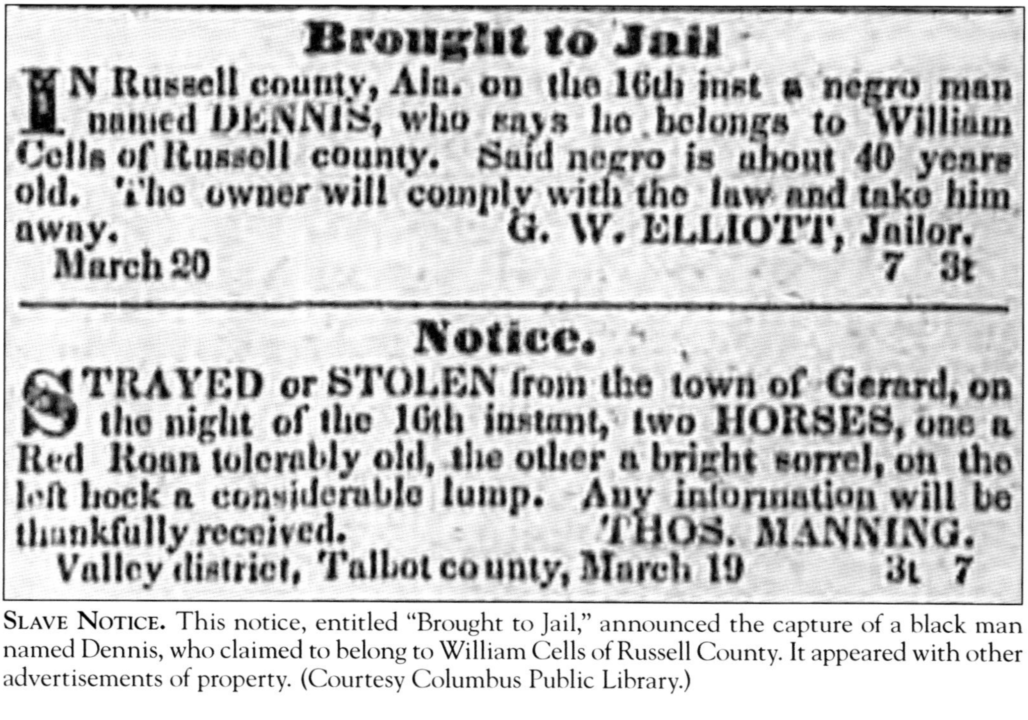

Brought to Jail

IN Russell county, Ala. on the 16th inst a negro man named DENNIS, who says he belongs to William Cells of Russell county. Said negro is about 40 years old. The owner will comply with the law and take him away.
G. W. ELLIOTT, Jailor.
March 20 7 3t

Notice.

STRAYED or STOLEN from the town of Gerard, on the night of the 16th instant, two HORSES, one a Red Roan tolerably old, the other a bright sorrel, on the left hock a considerable lump. Any information will be thankfully received.
THOS. MANNING.
Valley district, Talbot county, March 19 3t 7

SLAVE NOTICE. This notice, entitled "Brought to Jail," announced the capture of a black man named Dennis, who claimed to belong to William Cells of Russell County. It appeared with other advertisements of property. (Courtesy Columbus Public Library.)

Two

Antebellum Days 1840–1860

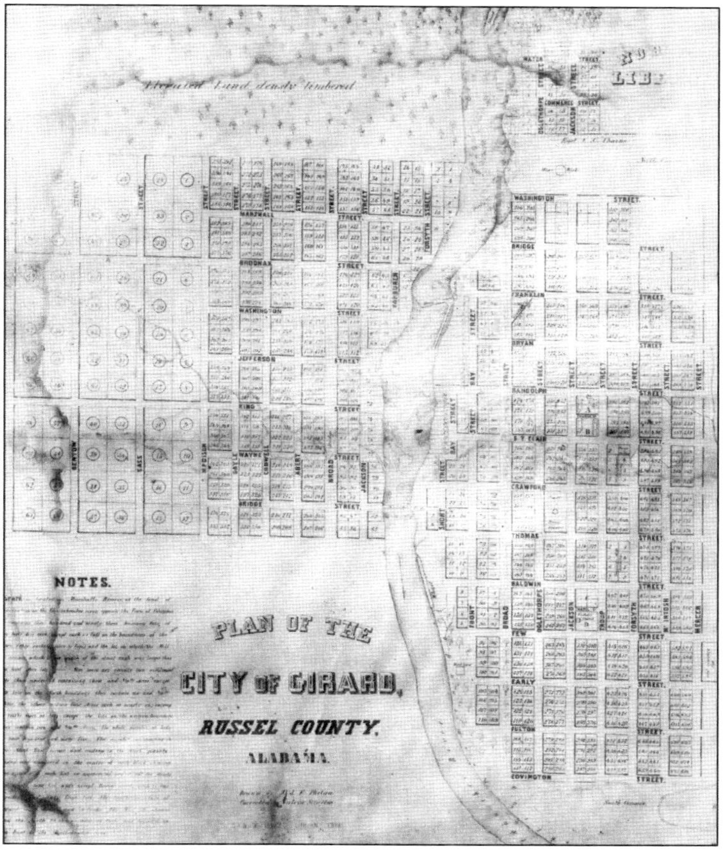

Plan of the City of Girard, Russell County. Girard was located on Marshall's Reserve at the head of navigation on the Chattahoochee River opposite the town of Columbus. Girard was laid out with 72 settlement lots and 393 business lots. (Courtesy Columbus Public Library.)

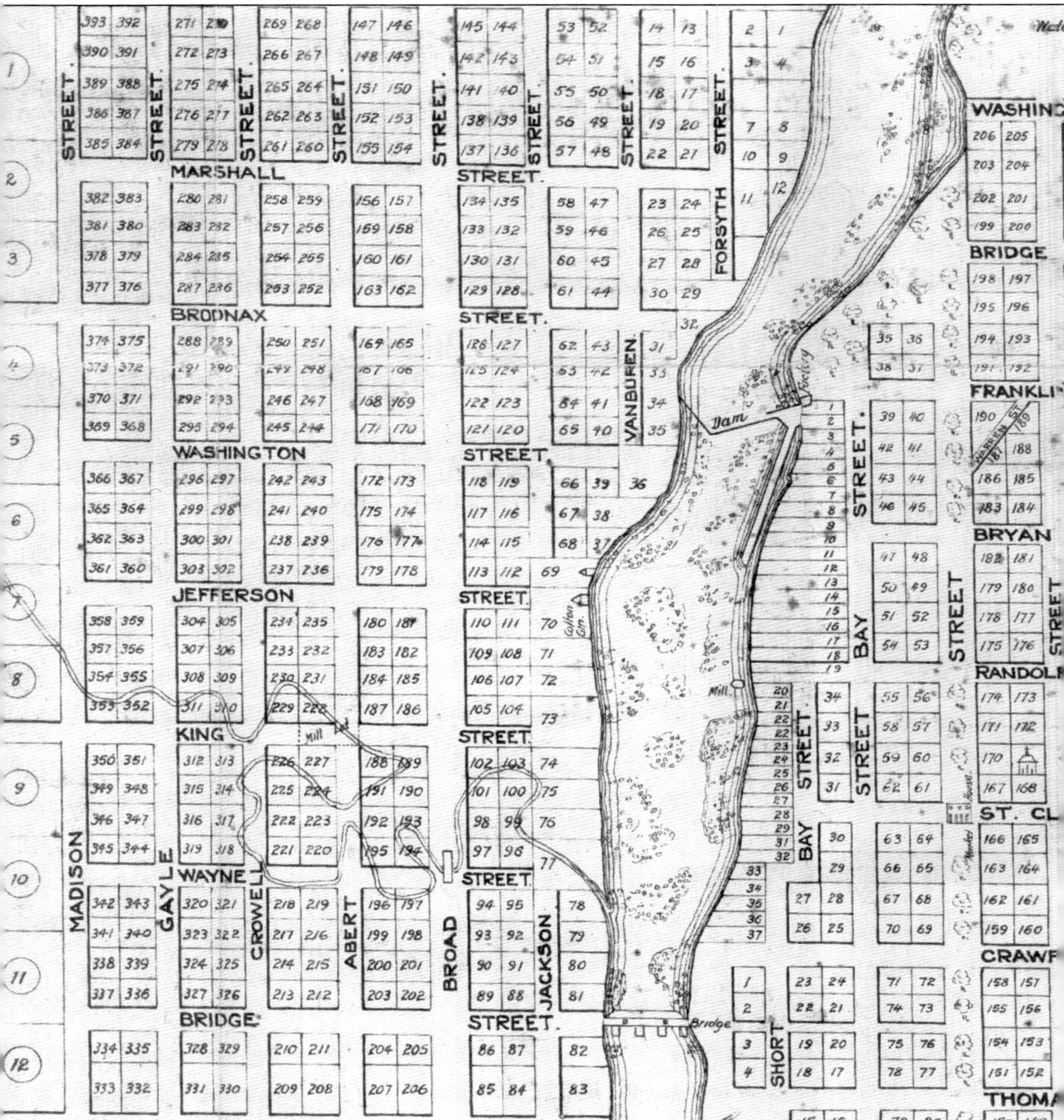

Plan of the City of Girard, Russell County, a Detail View. The map provides evidence that Girard had harnessed the power of the Chattahoochee River. Two cotton gins located on lots 69 and 70 are indicated. However, in 1859, Girard's ability to harness this power was rendered void by the U.S. Supreme Court. In adjudicating a border dispute between Alabama and Georgia, the court ruled, "So far as this line runs along the western bank of the Chattahoochee River . . . it runs along the western bank at high water mark, using high water mark in the sense of the highest line of the river's bed. Or, in other words, the highest line of that bed, where the passage of water is sufficiently frequent to be marked by a difference in soil and vegetable growth." In short, the power of the river belonged to Georgia. (Courtesy Columbus Public Library.)

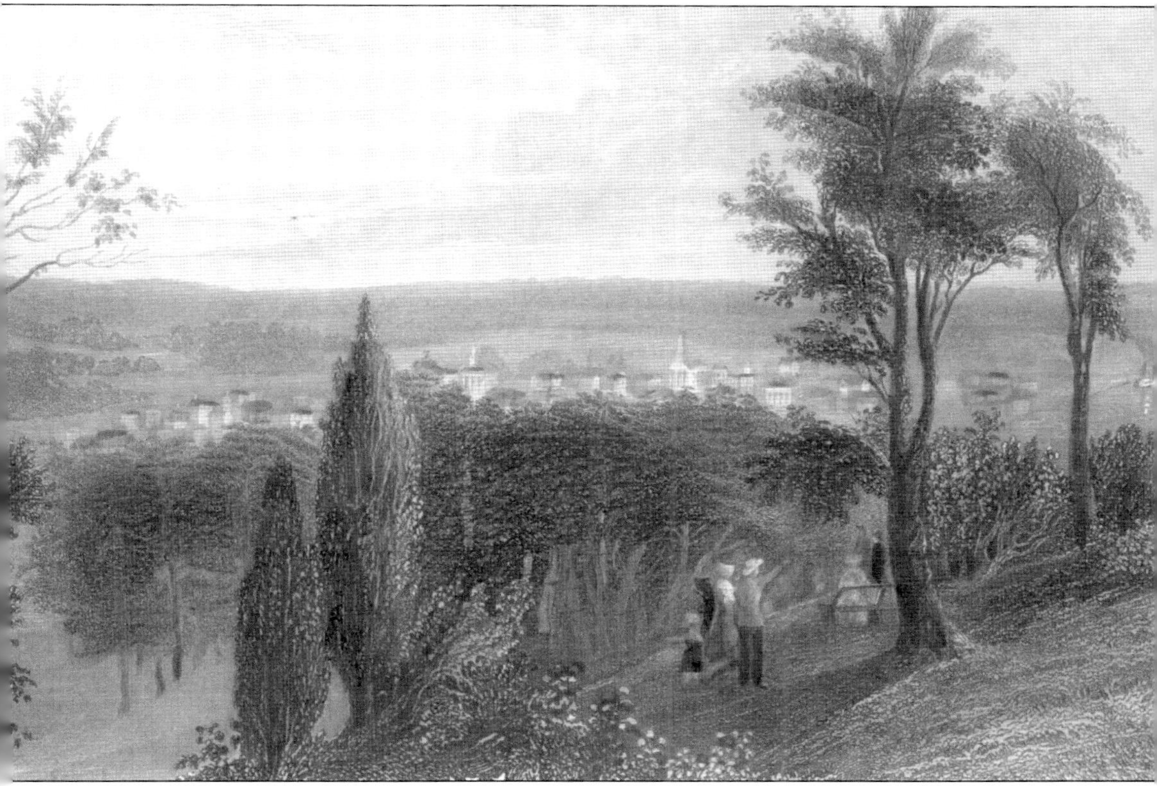

View of Columbus from Alabama Hills, 1841. This highly romanticized view of Columbus not only illustrates its burgeoning skyline across the Chattahoochee but also highlights the virgin landscape of Girard. The view is probably from the hills near the Girard Cemetery along Sand Fort Road. (Courtesy Columbus Museum.)

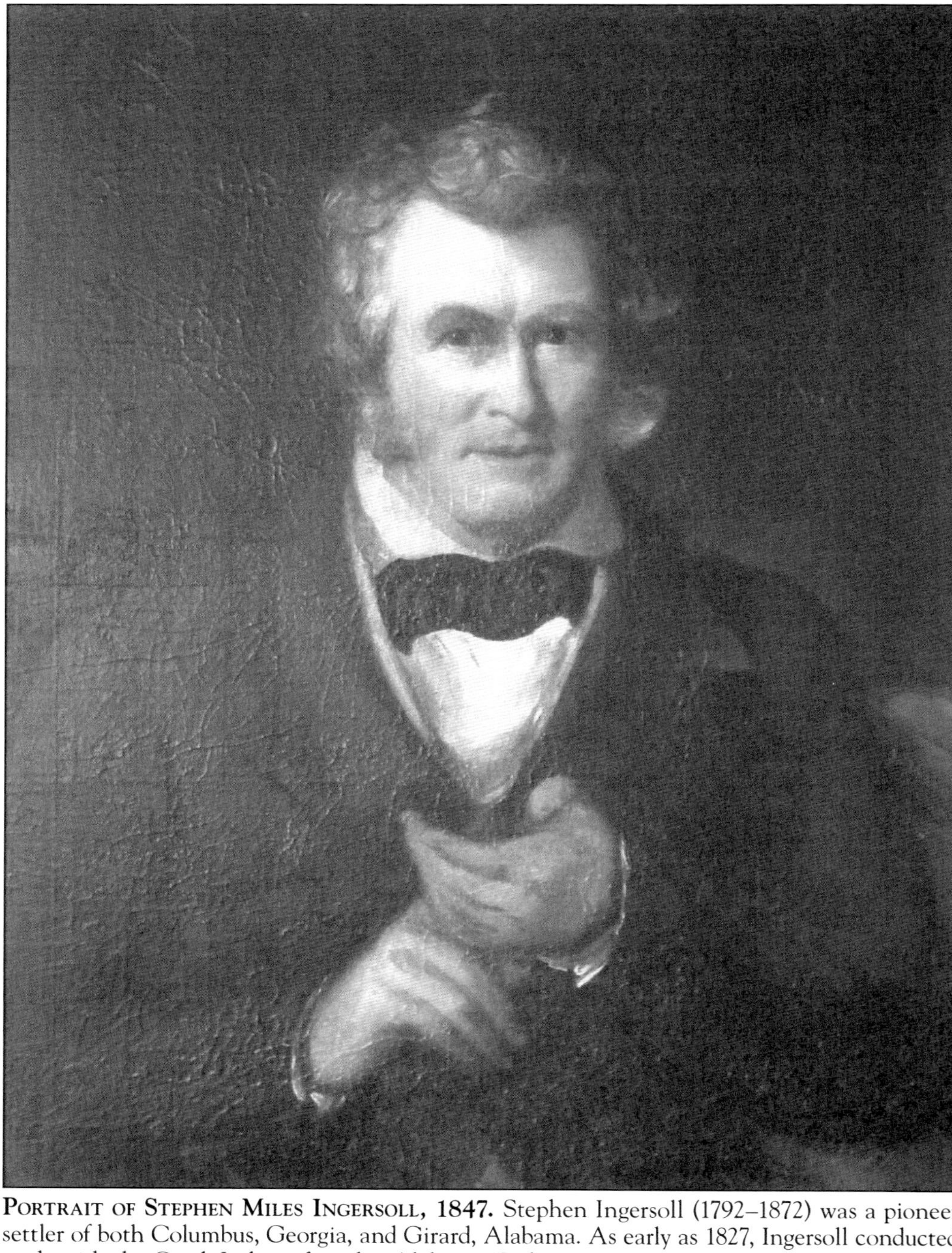

PORTRAIT OF STEPHEN MILES INGERSOLL, 1847. Stephen Ingersoll (1792–1872) was a pioneer settler of both Columbus, Georgia, and Girard, Alabama. As early as 1827, Ingersoll conducted trade with the Creek Indians from his Alabama "Indian Store" and operated a mill in Georgia. A substantial landowner, Ingersoll sold a portion of his pasture land to Eagle Mills in 1860. Eagle Mills obtained the property to provide housing for its operatives. The mill village became Brownville. (Courtesy Columbus Museum.)

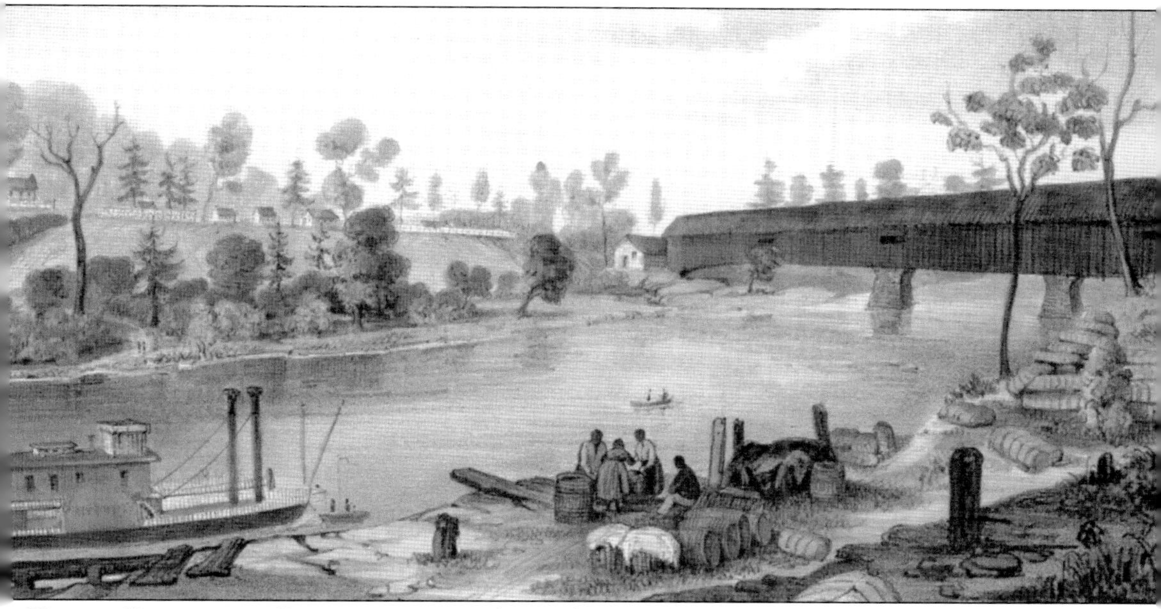

View of Girard from Columbus, 1838. John Godwin settled in Girard in 1832. Accompanied by Horace King, a bridge builder and slave, Godwin built most of the early bridges across the Chattahoochee River. He constructed and operated a sawmill on Holland Creek and contracted to build the new Russell County Courthouse at Crawford. Pictured is the original bridge constructed by Godwin and King. (Courtesy Columbus Museum.)

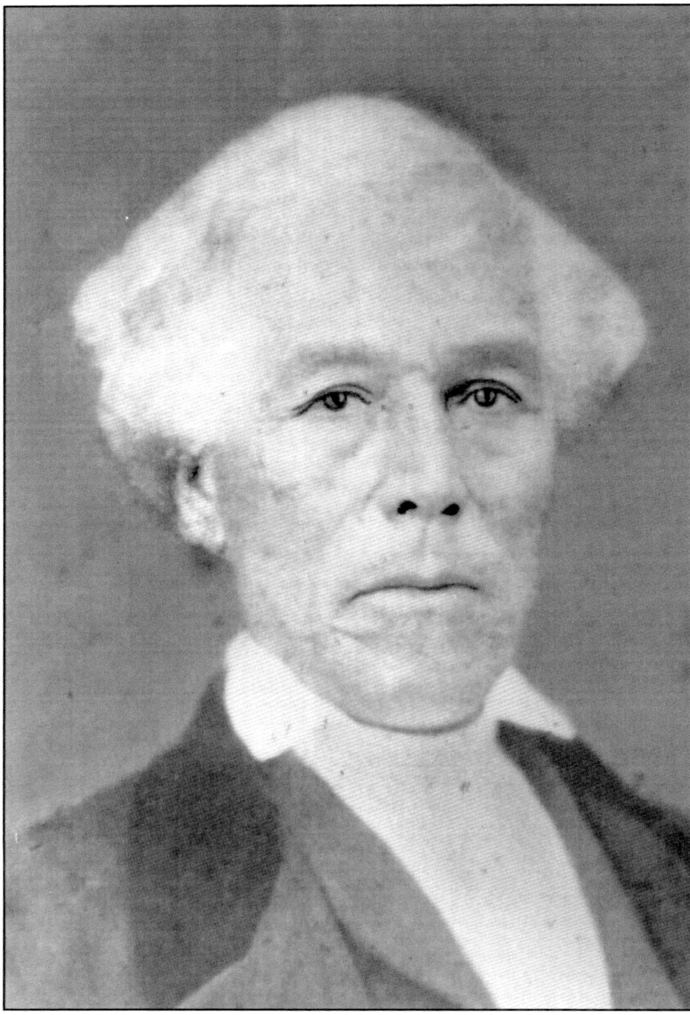

Horace King, Master Bridge Builder. In 1832, Horace King arrived in Girard, with his master John Godwin, to construct the first public bridge across the Chattahoochee River. The 560-foot span provided the region easy access to the Columbus markets. King and Godwin would build many of the important structures in the region, including both bridges across the Chattahoochee. King was manumitted in 1846. From the 1830s to the 1880s, he became the most respected bridge builder in Alabama and Georgia. (Courtesy Columbus State University Archives.)

Dillingham Street Bridge. Horace King rebuilt the lower bridge at Dillingham in the late 1860s. He also supervised the 1858 construction of the upper bridge at Fourteenth Street. (Courtesy Columbus Public Library.)

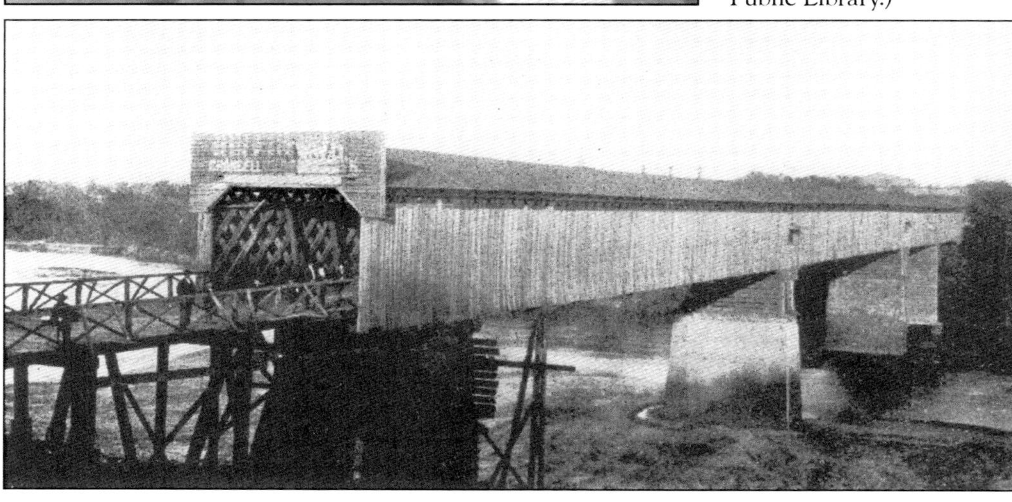

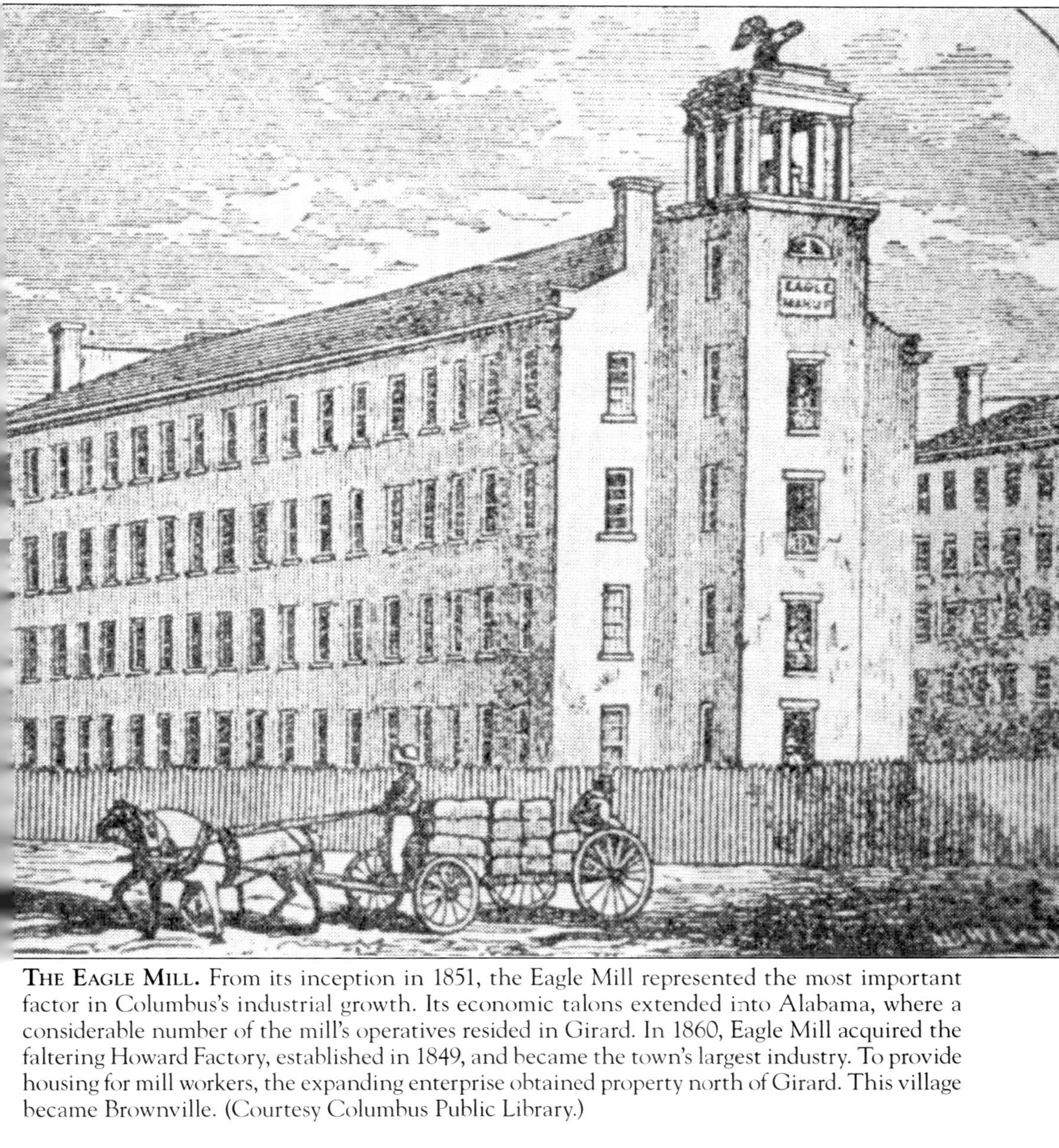

THE EAGLE MILL. From its inception in 1851, the Eagle Mill represented the most important factor in Columbus's industrial growth. Its economic talons extended into Alabama, where a considerable number of the mill's operatives resided in Girard. In 1860, Eagle Mill acquired the faltering Howard Factory, established in 1849, and became the town's largest industry. To provide housing for mill workers, the expanding enterprise obtained property north of Girard. This village became Brownville. (Courtesy Columbus Public Library.)

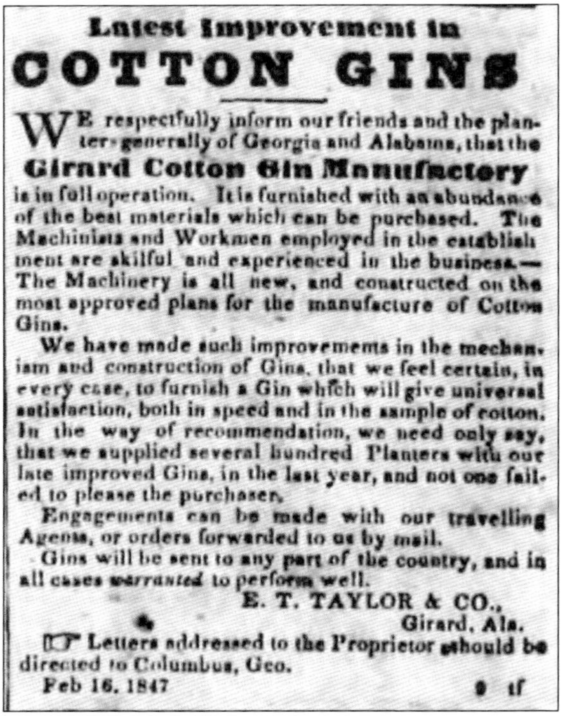

Latest Improvement in

COTTON GINS

WE respectfully inform our friends and the planters generally of Georgia and Alabama, that the

Girard Cotton Gin Manufactory

is in full operation. It is furnished with an abundance of the best materials which can be purchased. The Machinists and Workmen employed in the establishment are skilful and experienced in the business.—The Machinery is all new, and constructed on the most approved plans for the manufacture of Cotton Gins.

We have made such improvements in the mechanism and construction of Gins, that we feel certain, in every case, to furnish a Gin which will give universal satisfaction, both in speed and in the sample of cotton. In the way of recommendation, we need only say, that we supplied several hundred Planters with our late improved Gins, in the last year, and not one failed to please the purchaser.

Engagements can be made with our travelling Agents, or orders forwarded to us by mail.

Gins will be sent to any part of the country, and in all cases *warranted* to perform well.

E. T. TAYLOR & CO.,
Girard, Ala.

☞ Letters addressed to the Proprietor should be directed to Columbus, Geo.

Feb 16, 1847 9 tf

Cotton Gin Advertisement. E. T. Taylor announced the latest improvements in cotton gins in this 1847 advertisement for the Girard Cotton Gin Manufactery. Cotton gins operated by using a series of circular saws attached to a rotating cylinder. The teeth of the rotating saws pulled the cotton fiber through a wire grate and separated the seed. By 1850, most plantations had their own gins. (Courtesy Columbus Public Library.)

Cliatt Antebellum Gin House, Around 1840. L. A. Cliatt, of Cottonton, constructed a cotton-ginning warehouse in 1840. The warehouse is open on three sides and originally contained an attached cotton press. The process of cleaning cotton, separating seeds, and packing the cotton into bales occurred at the gin house. (Courtesy Library of Congress.)

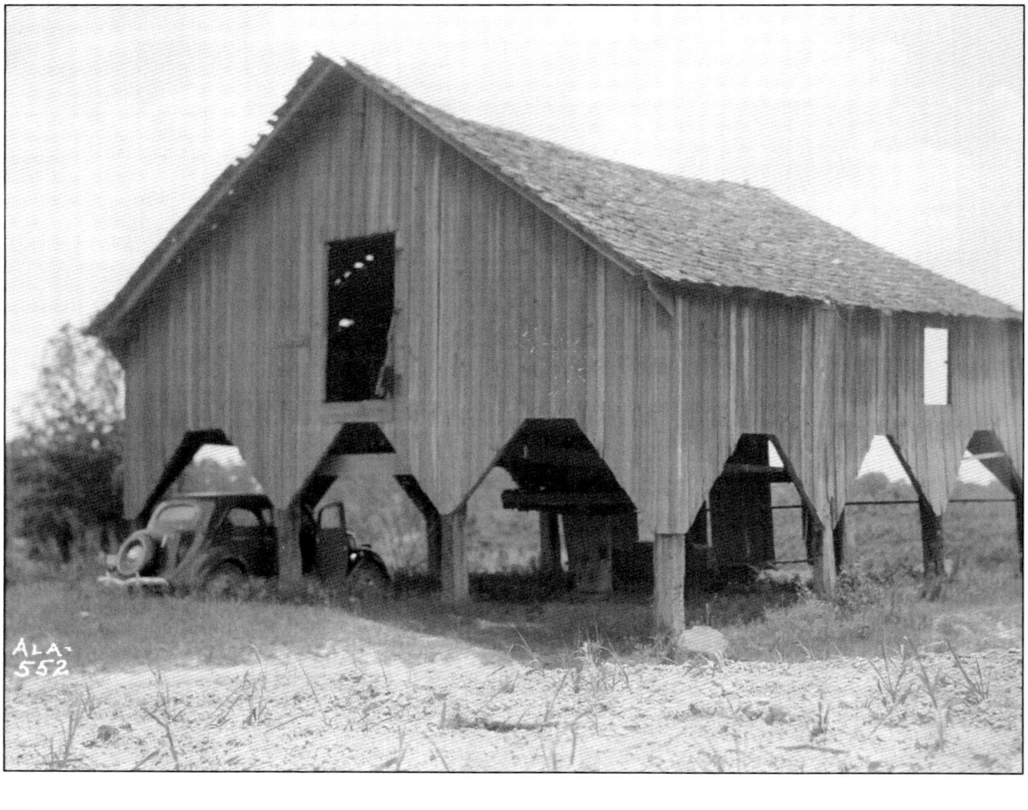

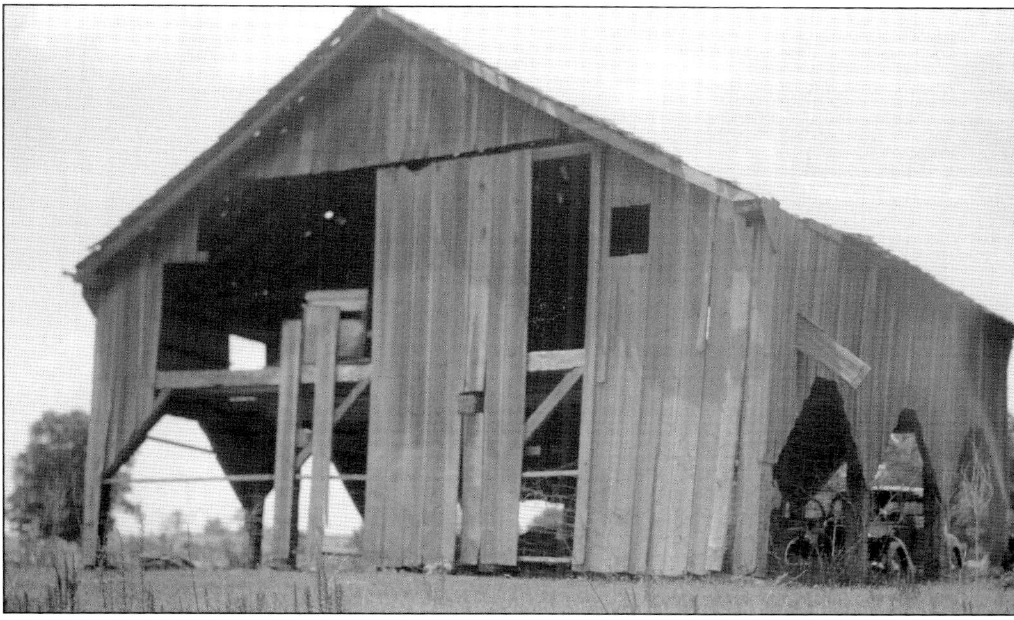

CLIATT GIN HOUSE, AROUND 1840. Another view shows L. A. Cliatt's cotton-ginning warehouse. For planters, gin houses offered an additional source of income by charging a commission to gin cotton for neighbors. (Courtesy Library of Congress.)

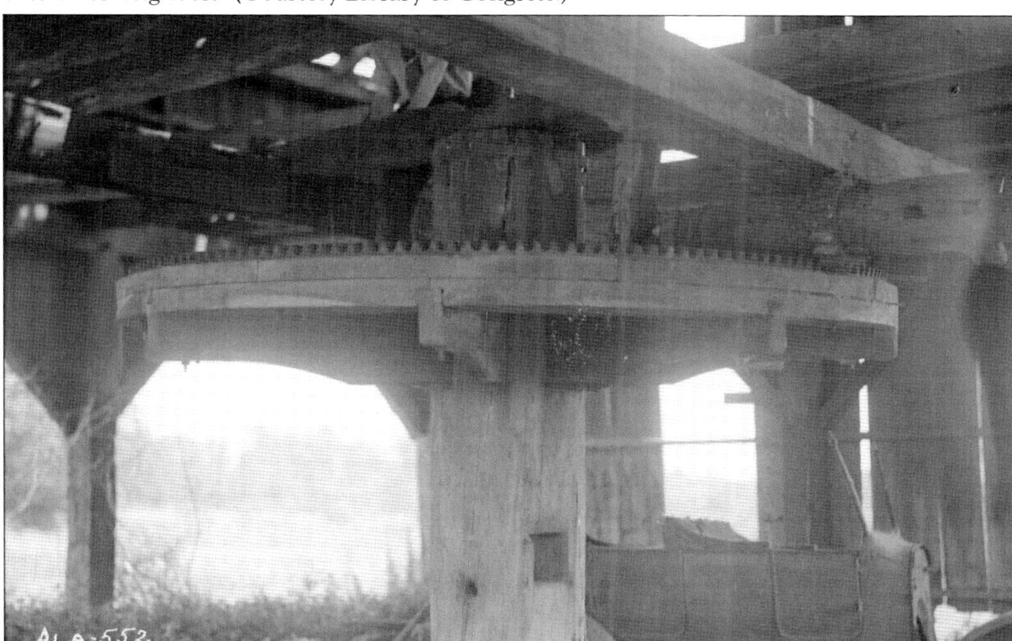

CLIATT ANTEBELLUM MULE COTTON GIN GEAR, AROUND 1840. Pictured is the gear of an antebellum mule-powered cotton gin. The cotton was ginned on the floor above. The mortise is visible, but the drive arm that allowed two mules to be used is missing. This gin produced an estimated five bales every 10 hours. The mules would be changed more frequently. (Courtesy Library of Congress.)

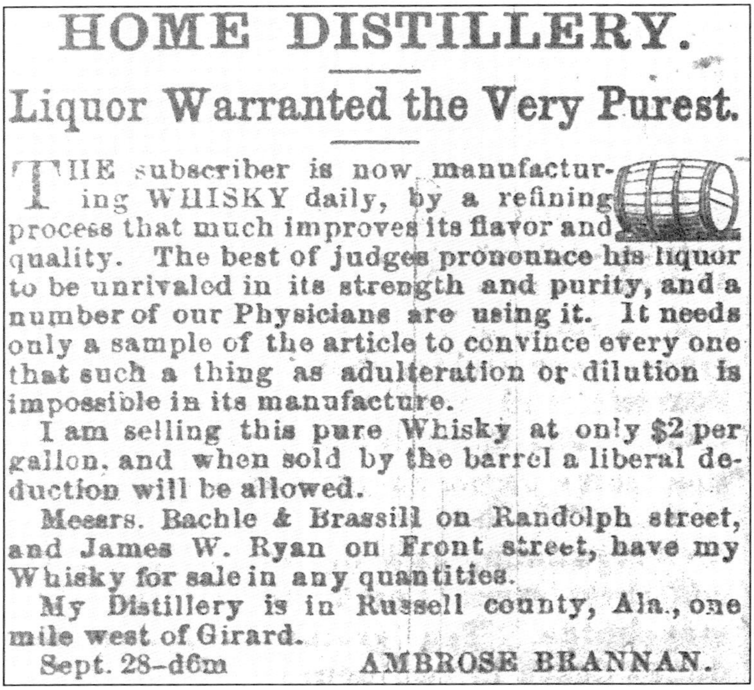

HOME DISTILLERY.

Liquor Warranted the Very Purest.

THE subscriber is now manufacturing WHISKY daily, by a refining process that much improves its flavor and quality. The best of judges pronounce his liquor to be unrivaled in its strength and purity, and a number of our Physicians are using it. It needs only a sample of the article to convince every one that such a thing as adulteration or dilution is impossible in its manufacture.

I am selling this pure Whisky at only $2 per gallon, and when sold by the barrel a liberal deduction will be allowed.

Messrs. Bachle & Brassill on Randolph street, and James W. Ryan on Front street, have my Whisky for sale in any quantities.

My Distillery is in Russell county, Ala., one mile west of Girard.

Sept. 28–d6m AMBROSE BRANNAN.

Homemade. Cotton was king, and manufacturing in antebellum Russell County revolved around it. Ambrose Brannon, however, operated a whiskey distillery that provided a ready cash market for corn and fruit products. (Courtesy Columbus Public Library.)

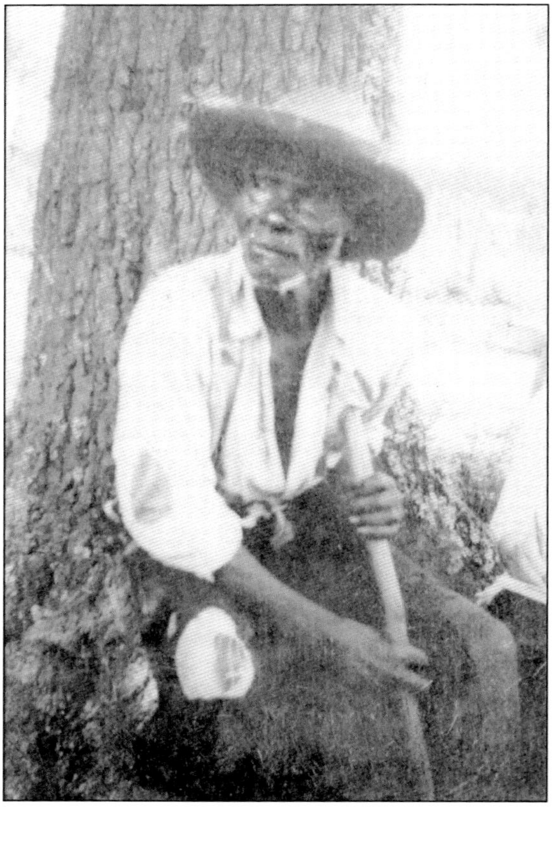

"Uncle" Orv, a Slave. Slavery expanded in Russell County to satisfy the demand of commercial agriculture, specifically the production of cotton. Slave labor was determined by gender, age, and physical strength. As a young child, Orv tended livestock and maintained the yard around the house. Between ages 8 and 12, he hoed weeds along with the women in the field. Orv graduated to more strenuous work as a plow hand by his mid-teens. A small number of slaves acquired trade skills, and others were employed in industrial settings. In Hurtsboro, slaves operated Joel Hurt's lumberyard. (Courtesy Chattahoochee Valley Community College.)

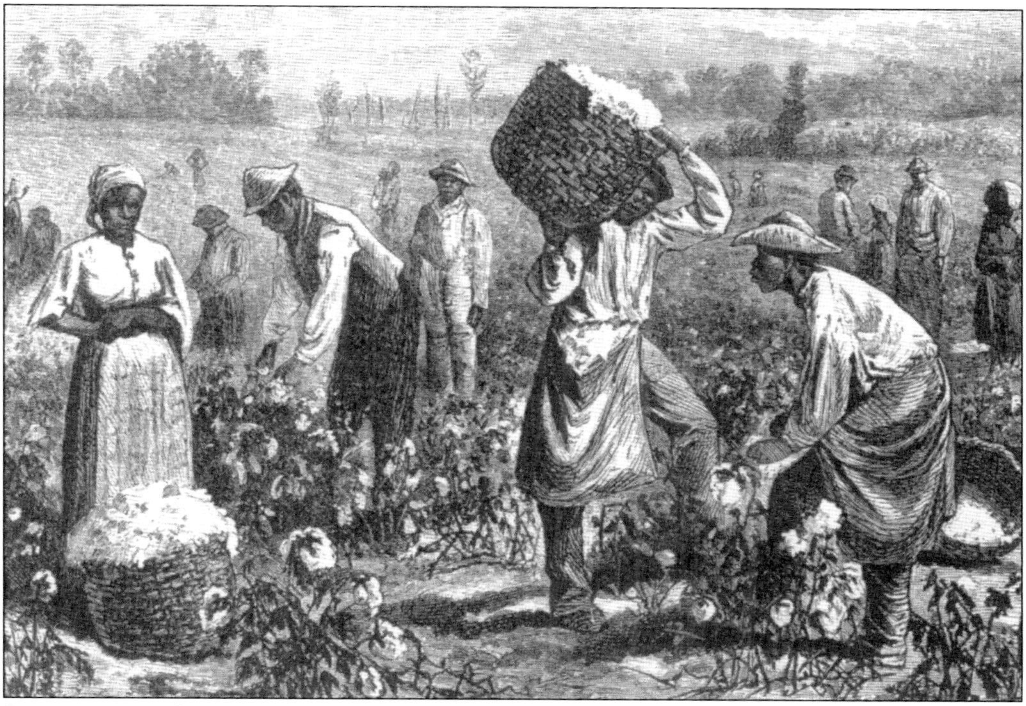

SLAVES IN THE COTTON FIELD. Russell County had a black majority from about 1836 through the end of the 19th century. As early as 1840, there were approximately 14,000 people living in Russell County, and 54 percent were African American slaves. Over the next two decades, Russell County's slave population increased to 58 percent of the total population, or 15,638 bondsmen. The slave population was largely due to cotton culture. Although only 10 percent of the county's population owned slaves in 1860, probably one in every three households included a slave owner. (Courtesy Columbus Public Library.)

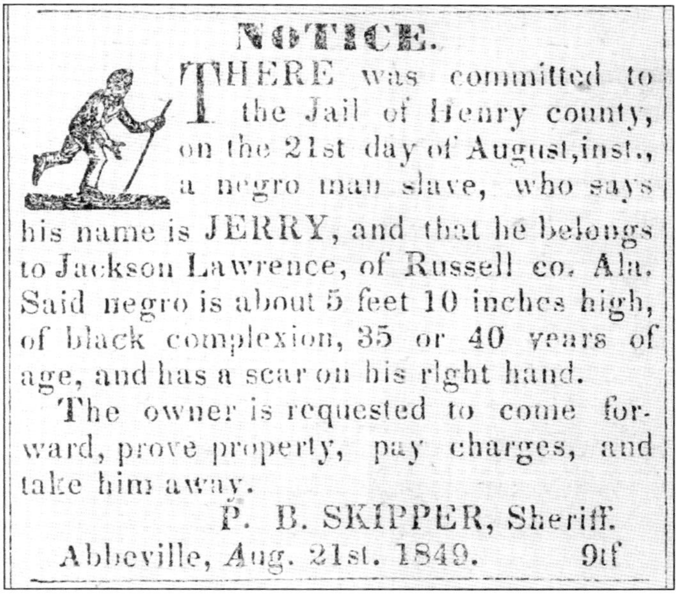

NOTICE.

THERE was committed to the Jail of Henry county, on the 21st day of August, inst., a negro man slave, who says his name is JERRY, and that he belongs to Jackson Lawrence, of Russell co. Ala. Said negro is about 5 feet 10 inches high, of black complexion, 35 or 40 years of age, and has a scar on his right hand.

The owner is requested to come forward, prove property, pay charges, and take him away.

P. B. SKIPPER, Sheriff.

Abbeville, Aug. 21st. 1849. 9tf

RUNAWAY SLAVE NOTICE, 1849. Abbeville, Alabama, sheriff P. B. Skipper placed notice of the capture of Jerry, an African American man. Slaves rarely protested their condition violently; resistance took a more passive form. Common acts of resistance include flight, feigning illness, working slowly, and breaking tools. (Courtesy Columbus Public Library.)

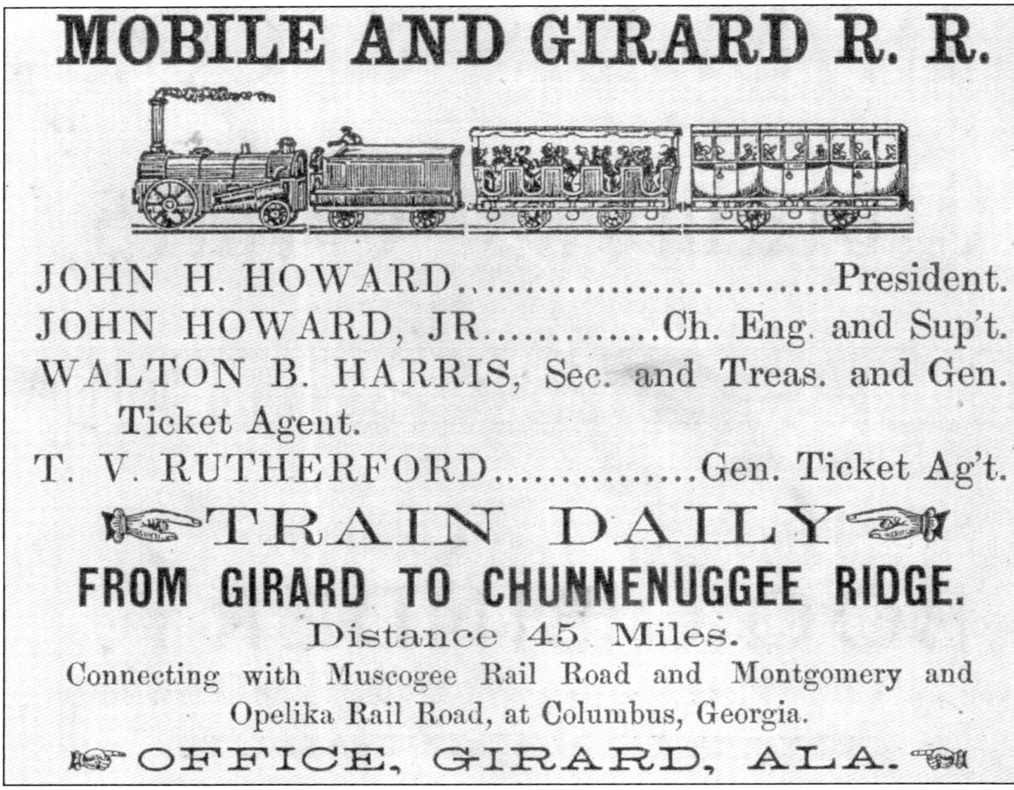

MOBILE AND GIRARD ADVERTISEMENT. The Mobile and Girard Railroad Company was established January 25, 1845, as the Girard Railroad Company. The initial line consisted of 7 miles of track from Girard in the direction of Crawford. The Girard Railroad's goal was to connect with either the navigable waters of Mobile Bay or the railroad from Montgomery. In 1854, the Girard line officially became the Mobile and Girard Railroad Company. (Courtesy Columbus Museum.)

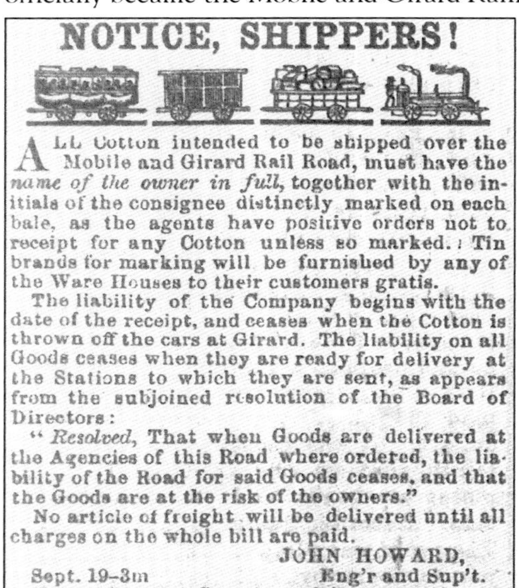

NOTICE, SHIPPERS!

ALL Cotton intended to be shipped over the Mobile and Girard Rail Road, must have the *name of the owner in full*, together with the initials of the consignee distinctly marked on each bale, as the agents have positive orders not to receipt for any Cotton unless so marked. Tin brands for marking will be furnished by any of the Ware Houses to their customers gratis.

The liability of the Company begins with the date of the receipt, and ceases when the Cotton is thrown off the cars at Girard. The liability on all Goods ceases when they are ready for delivery at the Stations to which they are sent, as appears from the subjoined resolution of the Board of Directors:

"*Resolved*, That when Goods are delivered at the Agencies of this Road where ordered, the liability of the Road for said Goods ceases, and that the Goods are at the risk of the owners."

No article of freight will be delivered until all charges on the whole bill are paid.

JOHN HOWARD,
Eng'r and Sup't.
Sept. 19–3m
Union Springs Gazette and Troy papers copy

MOBILE AND GIRARD ADVERTISEMENT TO SHIPPERS. In this advertisement, Supt. John Howard highlights the complexity of the cotton trade. The successful completion of the cotton trade involved the transport, insurance, and market arrangements of cotton. Cotton factors, commission merchants, brokers, warehouse men, shipping merchants, insurance agents, and banks played integral commercial roles. Howard makes plain the railroad's role in the affair was limited to shipping. (Courtesy Columbus Public Library.)

Three
War and Reconstruction 1861–1877

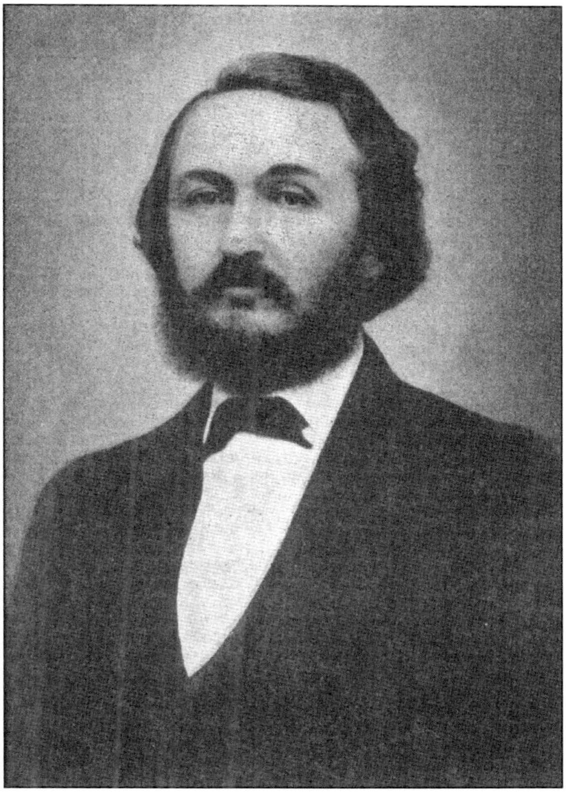

Robert A. Hardaway. A resident of Russell County for many years, Robert A. Hardaway served with the U.S. Army during the Mexican-American War but did not see combat. He later served as superintendent of the Mobile and Girard Railroad. At the outbreak of the Civil War, Hardaway resided in Macon County, where he purchased his father's plantation. He began the war as commander of an Alabama artillery battery recruited from Russell, Macon, and Tallapoosa Counties and was present in over 40 engagements. (Courtesy Columbus Public Library.)

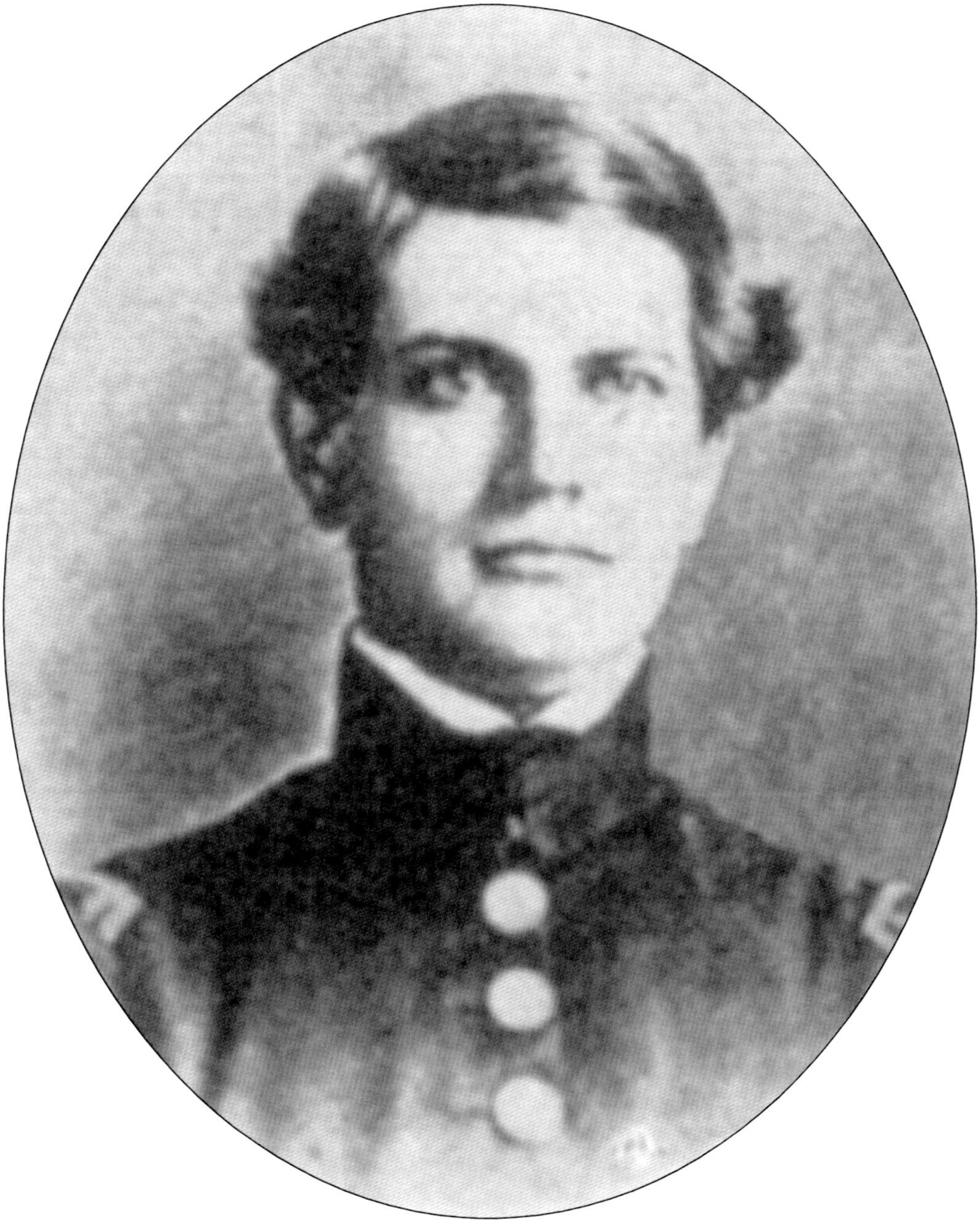

James Cantey. Elected colonel of the 15th Alabama Infantry, James Cantey answered the Confederate States of America's call for secession. The 15th Regiment organized and trained at Fort Mitchell in the summer of 1861 and moved at once into Virginia under the command of Maj. Gen. Thomas J. "Stonewall" Jackson. Appointed brigadier general on January 8, 1863, Cantey transferred to Mobile, Alabama, and raised a brigade from three Alabama regiments and one Mississippi regiment. Cantey surrendered at Durham Station, North Carolina, on April 26, 1865. After the war, he returned to his plantation until his death at Fort Mitchell in 1874. (Courtesy Columbus Public Library.)

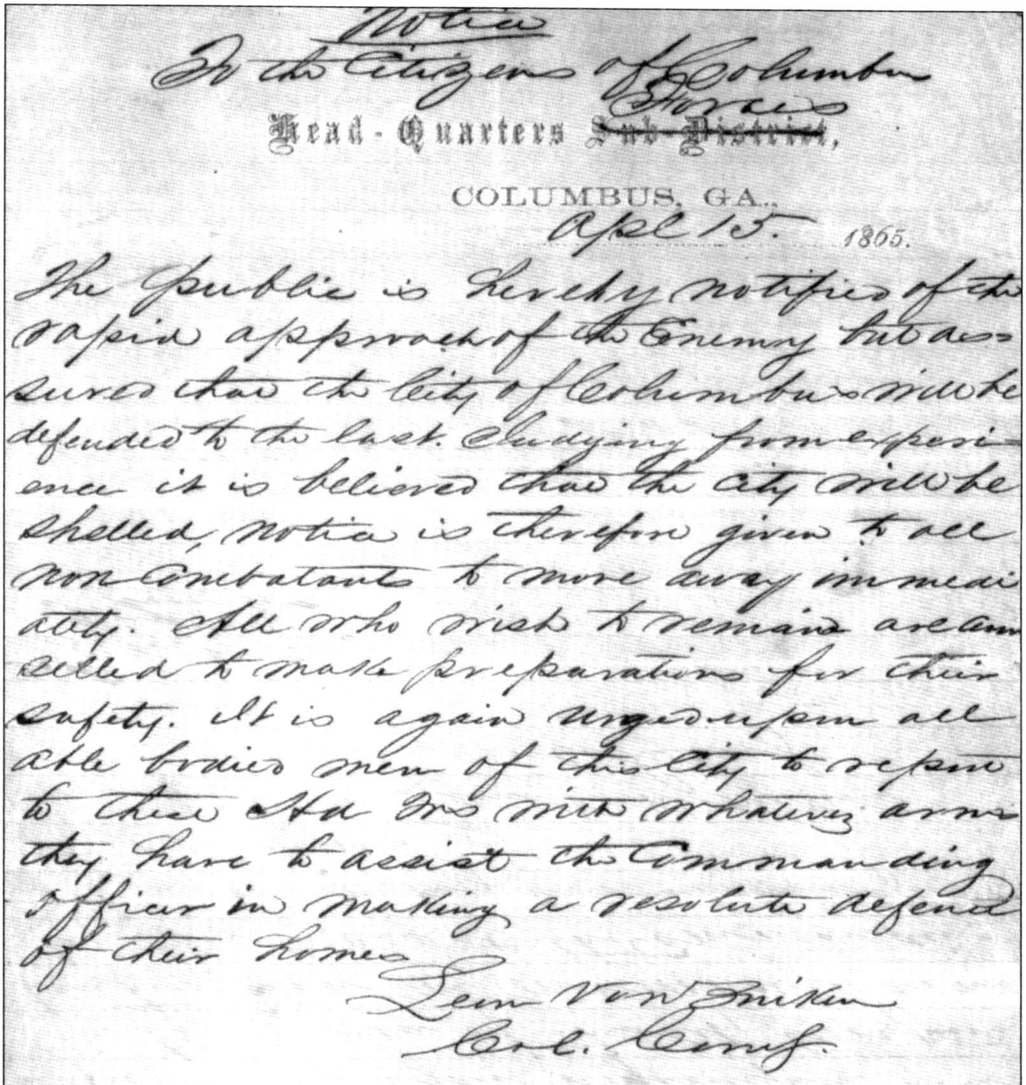

Notice

To the Citizens of Columbus

Head-Quarters ~~Sub-District~~ Forces,

COLUMBUS, GA., Apl 15. 1865.

The Public is hereby notified of the rapid approach of the Enemy but assured that the City of Columbus will be defended to the last. Judging from experience it is believed that the city will be shelled, notice is therefore given to all non combatants to move away immediately. All who wish to remain are counselled to make preparations for their safety. It is again urged upon all able bodied men of this city to report to these Hd Qrs with whatever arms they have to assist the Commanding Officer in making a resolute defence of their homes

Leon Von Zinken
Col. Comd.

Insert
3 times

Von Zinken Letter. Col. Leon Von Zinken, garrison commander at Columbus, penned this proclamation warning the citizens of Columbus to evacuate the city in advance of the approaching Federal forces. Von Zinken promised "that the city of Columbus will be defended to the last." (Courtesy Columbus State Archives.)

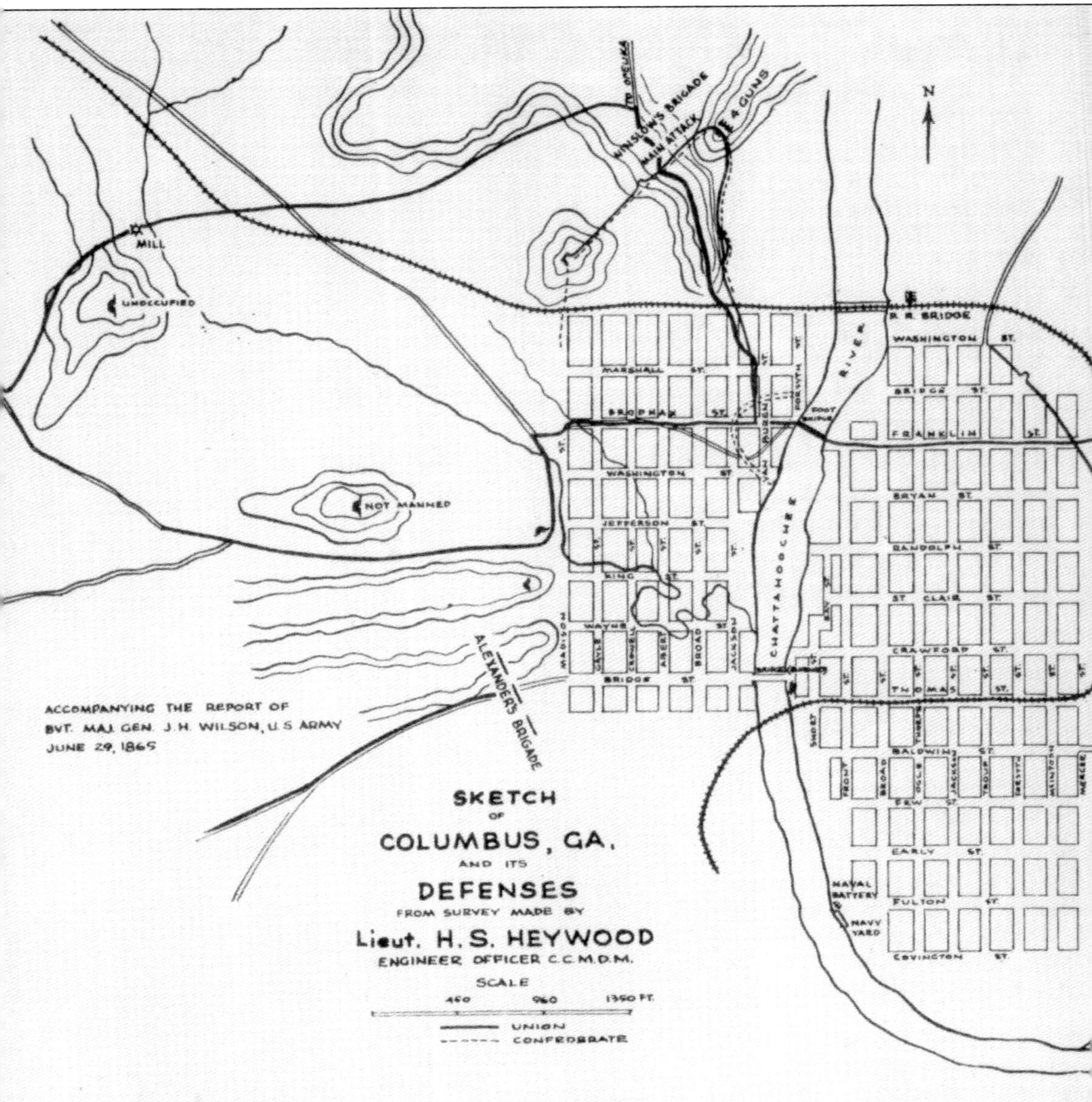

SKETCH OF COLUMBUS, GEORGIA, AND ITS FORTIFICATIONS FROM SURVEY MADE BY LT. H. S. HEYWOOD, 1865. The Battle of Girard, also known as the Battle of Columbus, took place on Easter Sunday, April 16, 1865. The defenses of Columbus were concentrated on the Alabama side of the Chattahoochee River and extended from Holland Creek to the high ground along Summerville Road. Confederate general Howell Cobb commanded the forces defending Girard and Columbus. He decided to concentrate his defenses on the upper and railroad bridges and ordered the removal of planks from the Dillingham Bridge and the Clapps Factory Bridge north of the city. (Courtesy Columbus Museum.)

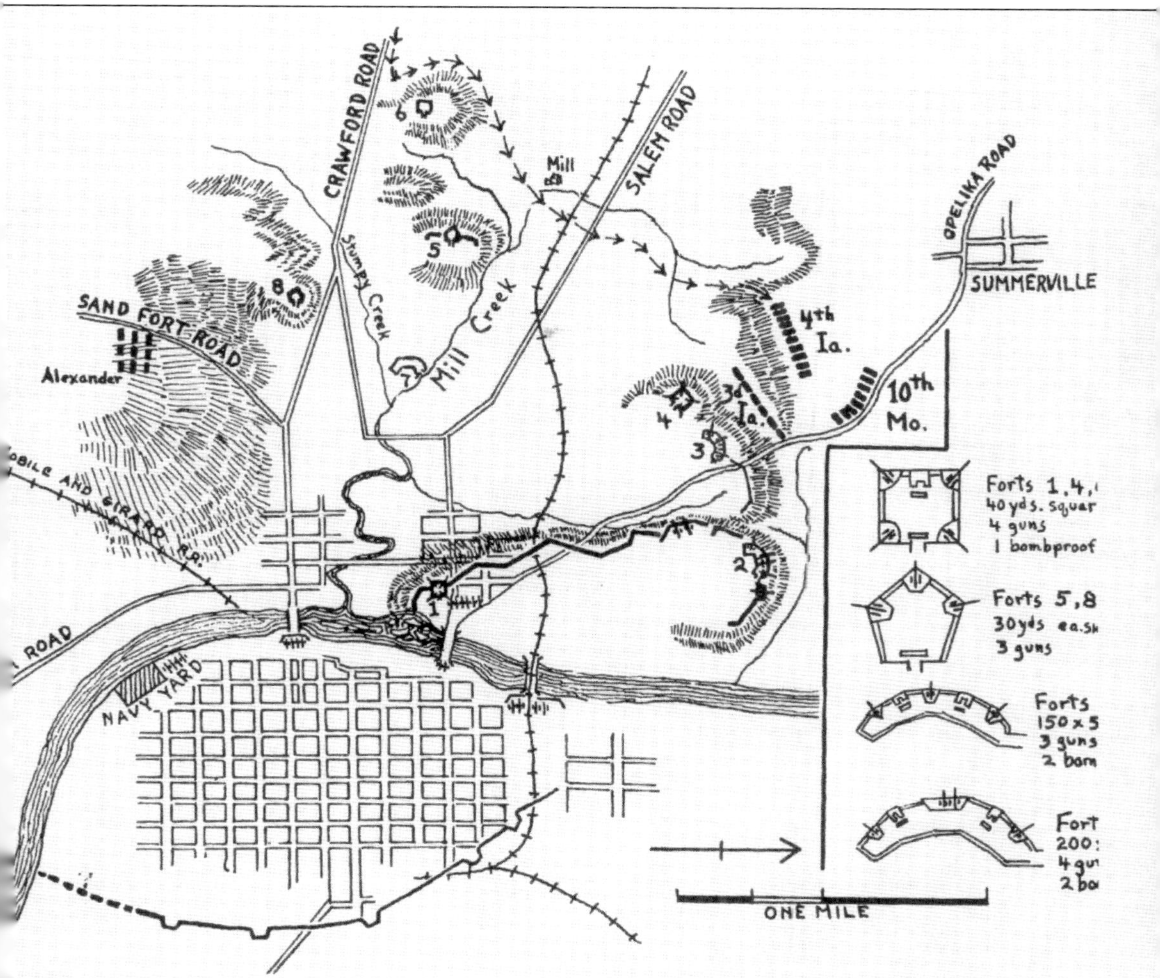

Sketch of Columbus, Georgia, and Its Fortifications. This view provides a westward perspective of the fortifications of Girard and Columbus. The first Federal units arrived in Girard via Crawford Road and drove toward the Dillingham Bridge. The Iron Works Battalion fired at the bridge, and the advance Federal guard withdrew. (Courtesy Columbus Museum.)

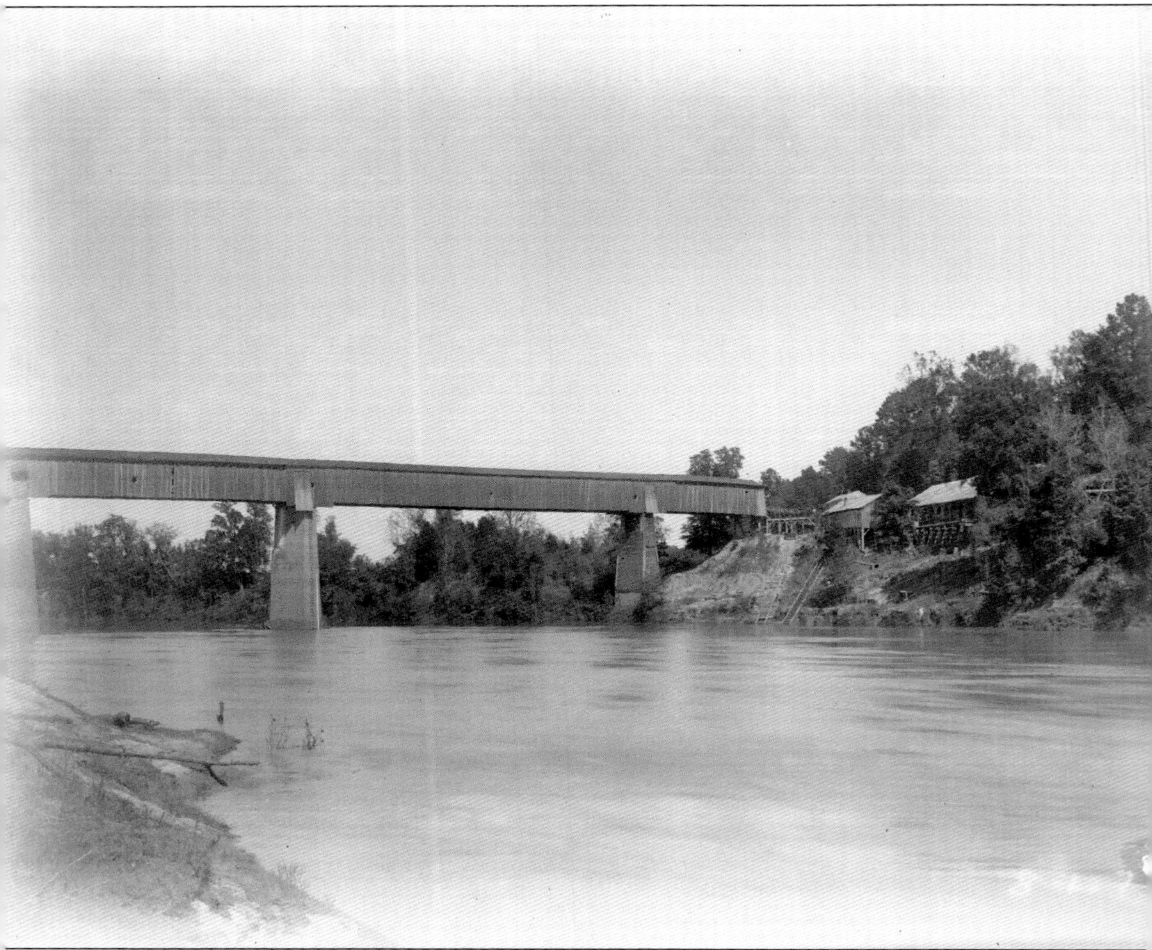

Covered Bridge, 1891. Union general James H. Wilson determined to attack down Summerville Road and capture the upper bridge under cover of darkness. The night attack caused confusion on all sides. Believing the Federals had breached the lines, Wilson released his reserves. Thinking the advancing column to be retreating Confederates, the rebels allowed them to cross the bridge. Built in 1858 by Horace King, the upper bridge stood until a 1902 flood carried it away. (Courtesy W. S. Hoole Special Collections Library.)

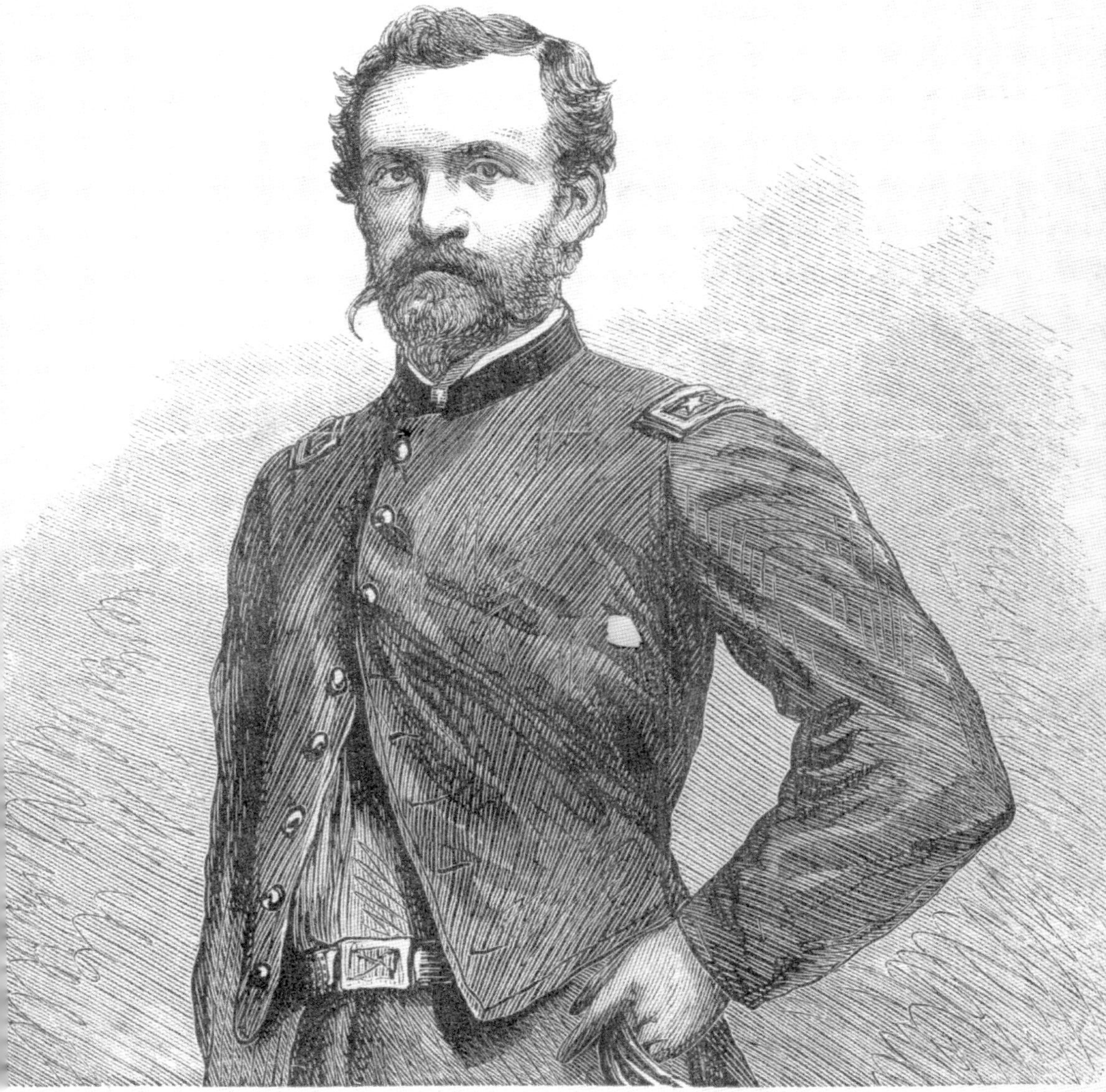

JAMES H. WILSON.

Gen. James H. Wilson. James H. Wilson (1837–1925) served as a Union general during the Civil War. Initially a topographical engineer, Wilson joined the cavalry in 1864. In March 1865, he was sent with more than 13,000 horsemen through Alabama and Georgia to destroy the South's military infrastructure. That May, his cavalrymen captured Confederate president Jefferson Davis. (Courtesy Columbus Public Library.)

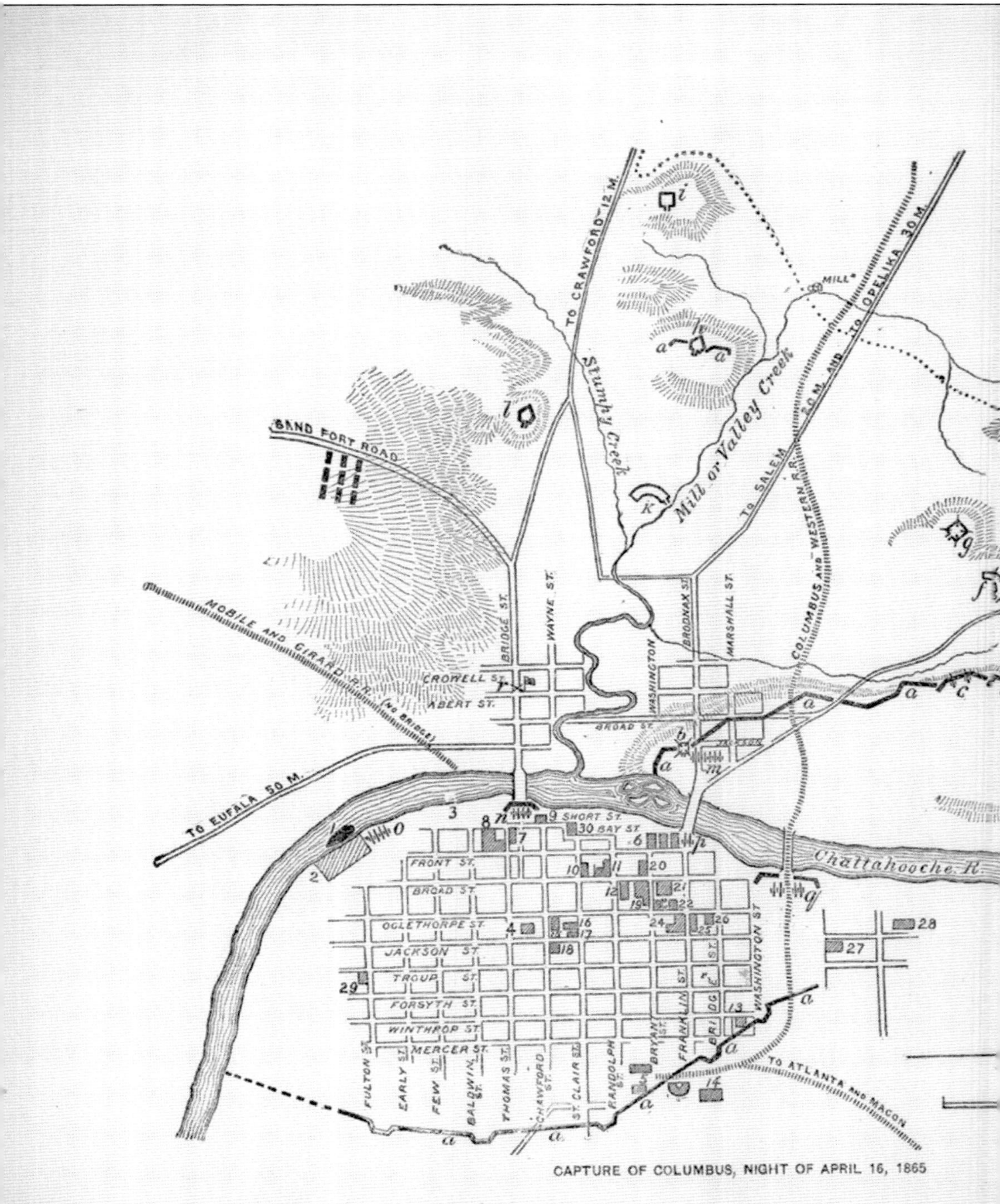

Capture of Columbus, Night of April 16, 1865. "My Forces captured this place [Columbus] by a most gallant attack 10 o'clock last night, losing 25 men killed and wounded, and captured about

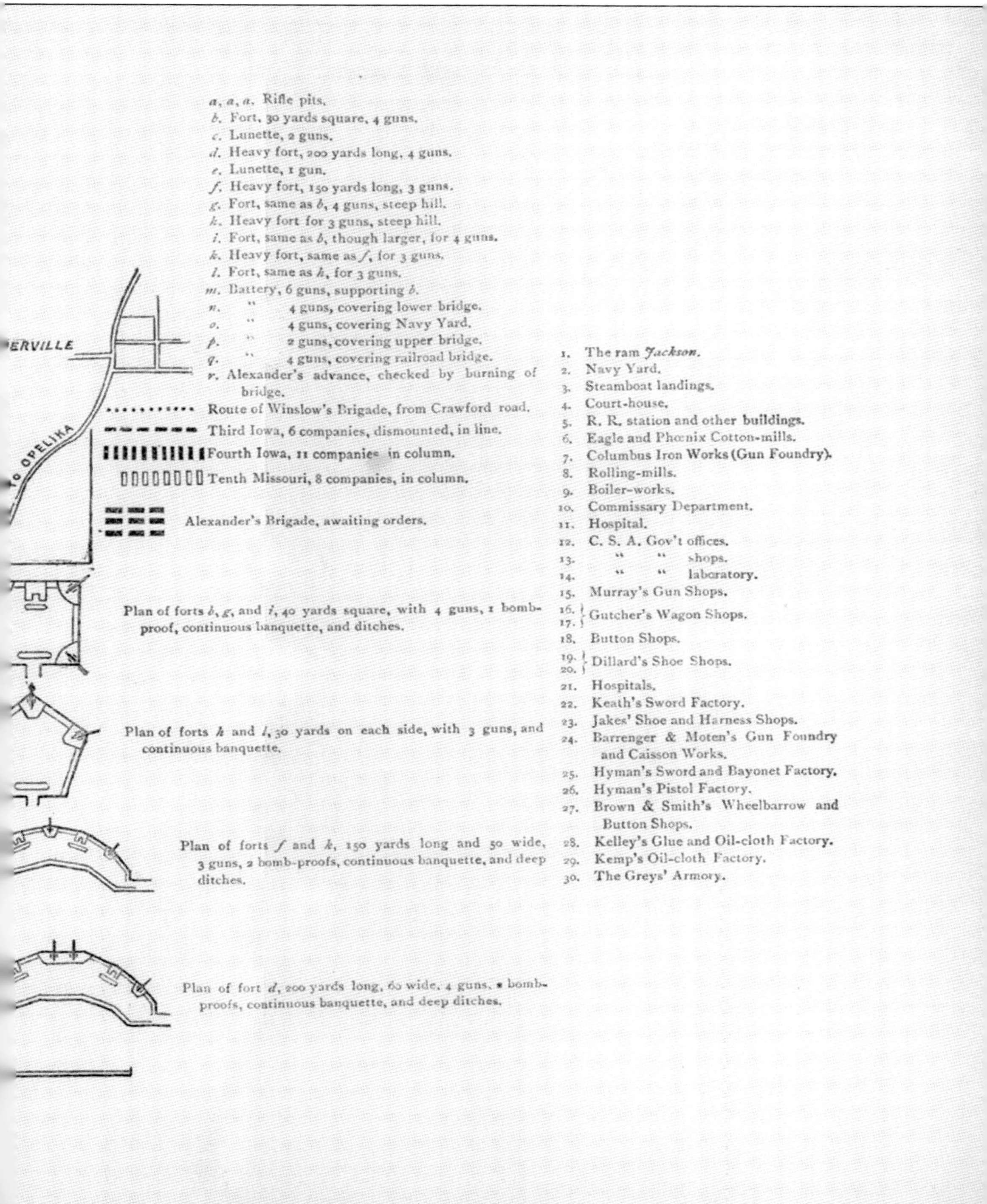

1500 prisoners, 24 field guns, and 1 gunboat carrying six 7-inch rifled pieces," Wilson reported to Maj. Gen. Edward Canby on April 17, 1865. (Courtesy Columbus Public Library.)

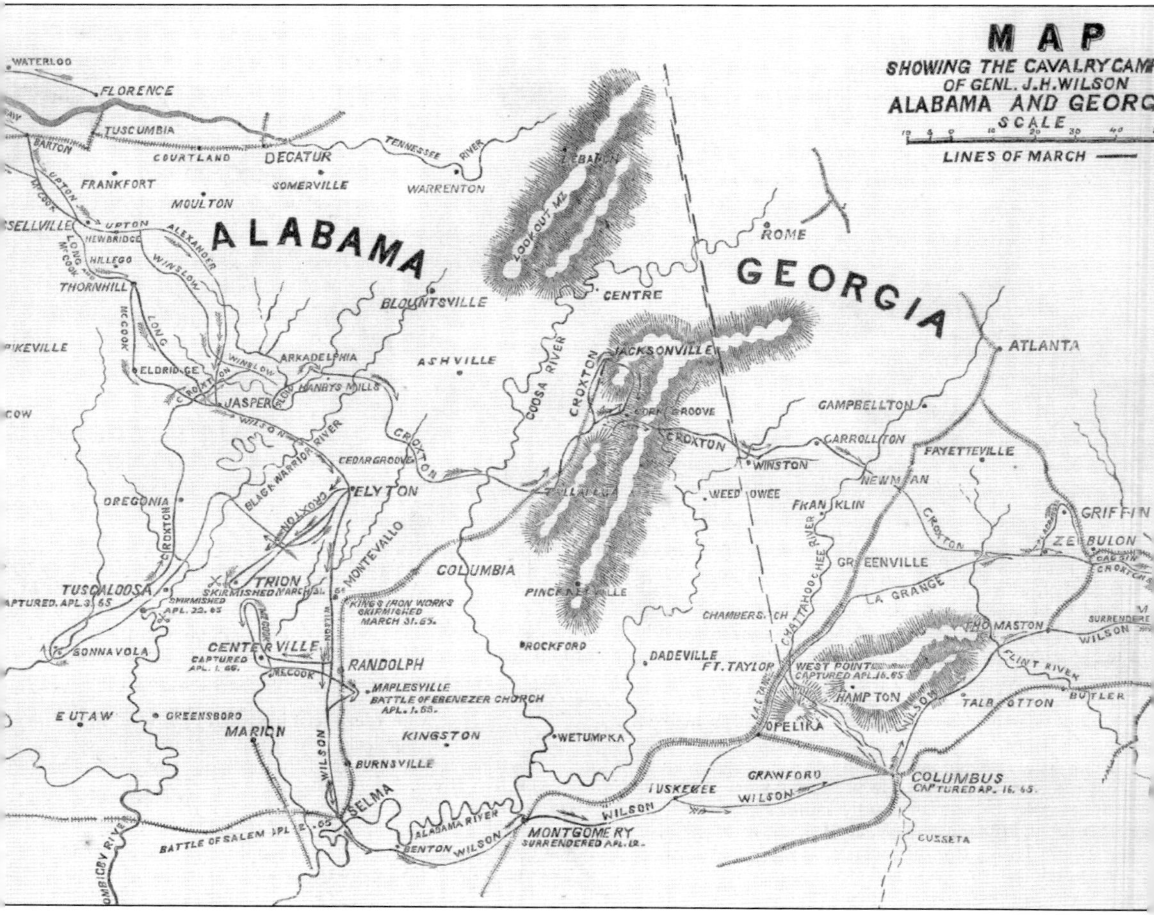

MAP SHOWING THE CAVALRY CAMPAIGN OF GEN. J. H. WILSON, ALABAMA AND GEORGIA, 1865. Wilson's raid was a cavalry operation through Alabama and Georgia in March and April 1865. Brig. Gen. James H. Wilson led his Union army cavalry corps on an expedition to destroy Southern industrial capacity. (Courtesy Columbus Public Library.)

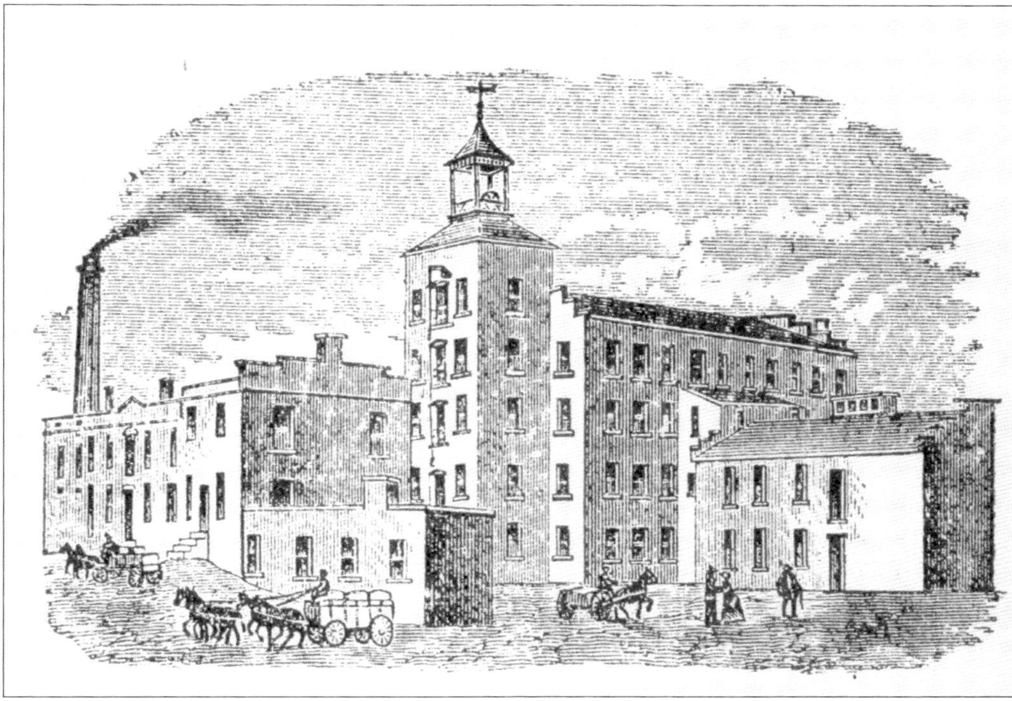

Muscogee Mill No. 1. By 1866, George Parker Swift and his son George Parker Swift Jr. chartered the Muscogee Manufacturing Company on the site of Coweta Falls Mill, previously owned by John J. Grant and destroyed by General Wilson's Union troops. Critical to the early resurgence of industrial production was the abundant and cheap supply of white labor in the city and especially across the river in Girard. (Courtesy Columbus Public Library.)

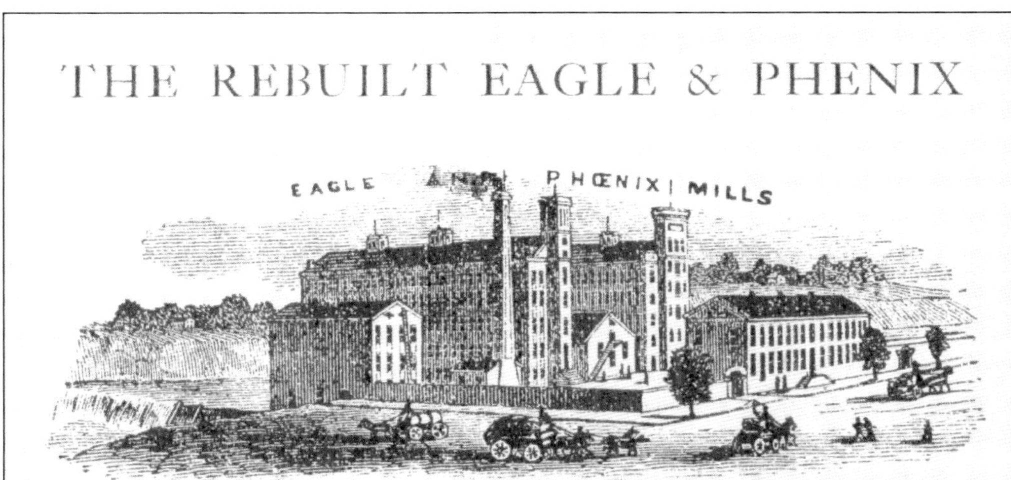

Eagle and Phenix Manufacturing Company. During the Civil War, Eagle Mills manufactured a variety of goods that supported the Southern war effort. In April 1865, Union general James Wilson ordered the destruction of the Eagle Mills complex following the capture of the city. (Courtesy Columbus Public Library.)

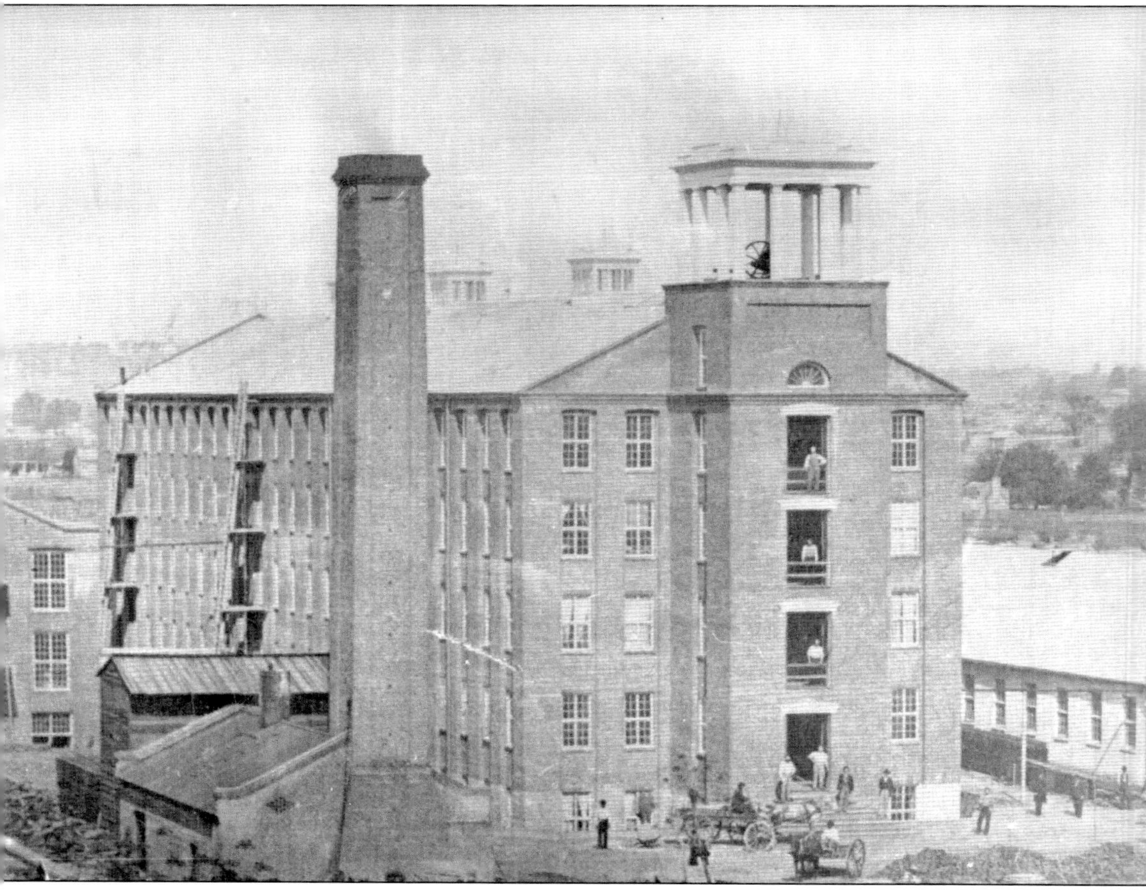

The Eagle and Phenix Mill No. 1, Around 1869. Resurrection of Eagle Mills was swift and sustained. Mill No. 1 was rebuilt in 1868 with more production capacity than both the original Eagle and Howard factories. Two years later, a larger Mill No. 2 was completed. Mill No. 3 debuted in 1878 with the combined production capacity of Mills No. 1 and No. 2. The Eagle Mill added "Phenix" to its title to symbolize its rising from the ashes like the mythical bird. (Courtesy Columbus State University Archives.)

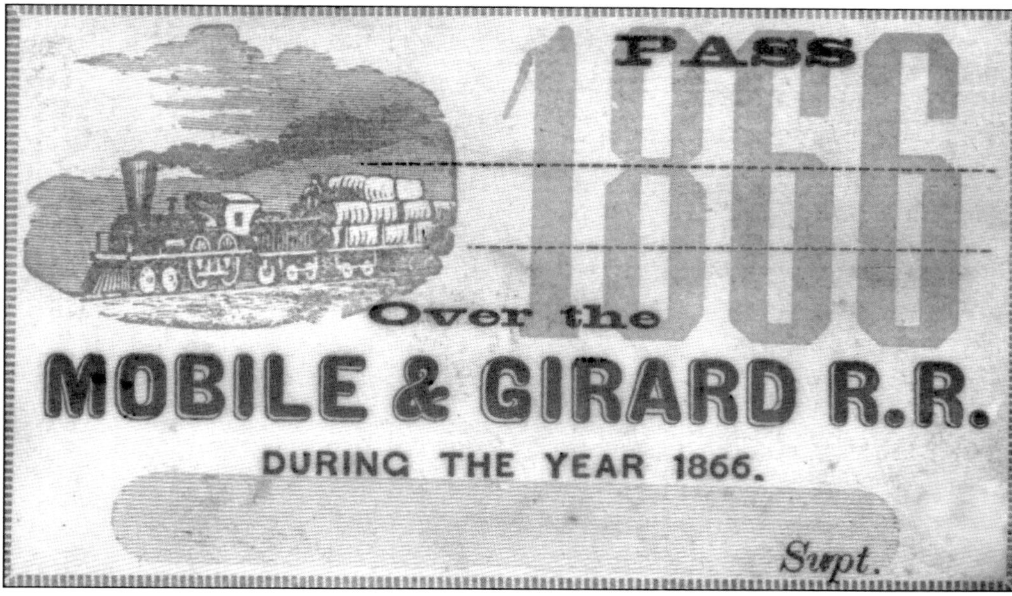

MOBILE AND GIRARD RAILROAD PASS, 1866. The Mobile and Girard emerged relatively unscathed from the Civil War. A bridge over the Chattahoochee River near the Dillingham Bridge was completed on January 1, 1869. Construction of the Mobile and Girard line to Troy, Alabama, commenced after the war and was completed in 1870. Late in the 1870s, financial trouble emerged that led to an eventual sale to the Central Railroad and Banking Company of Georgia. (Courtesy Columbus Museum.)

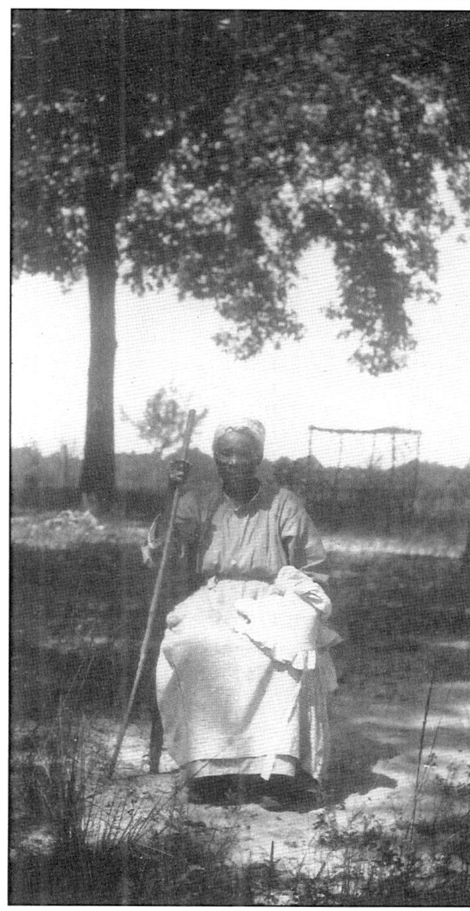

SLAVERY TO SHARECROPPING. The decades following the Civil War were difficult years for farmers in Russell County. Former slaves and landless whites needed access to land and compensation for their labor, but cash-strapped landlords could not offer wages. As the *Russell Register* proclaimed in 1876, "There is not one man in five hundred who can carry on a cash business." The concept of sharecropping, or the crop lien system, was adopted. Sharecropping offered poor whites a means to eke out a living; it gave freed blacks some semblance of the independence and the opportunity to become a proprietor; and it returned the planters' plantations to productivity. (Courtesy Chattahoochee Valley Community College.)

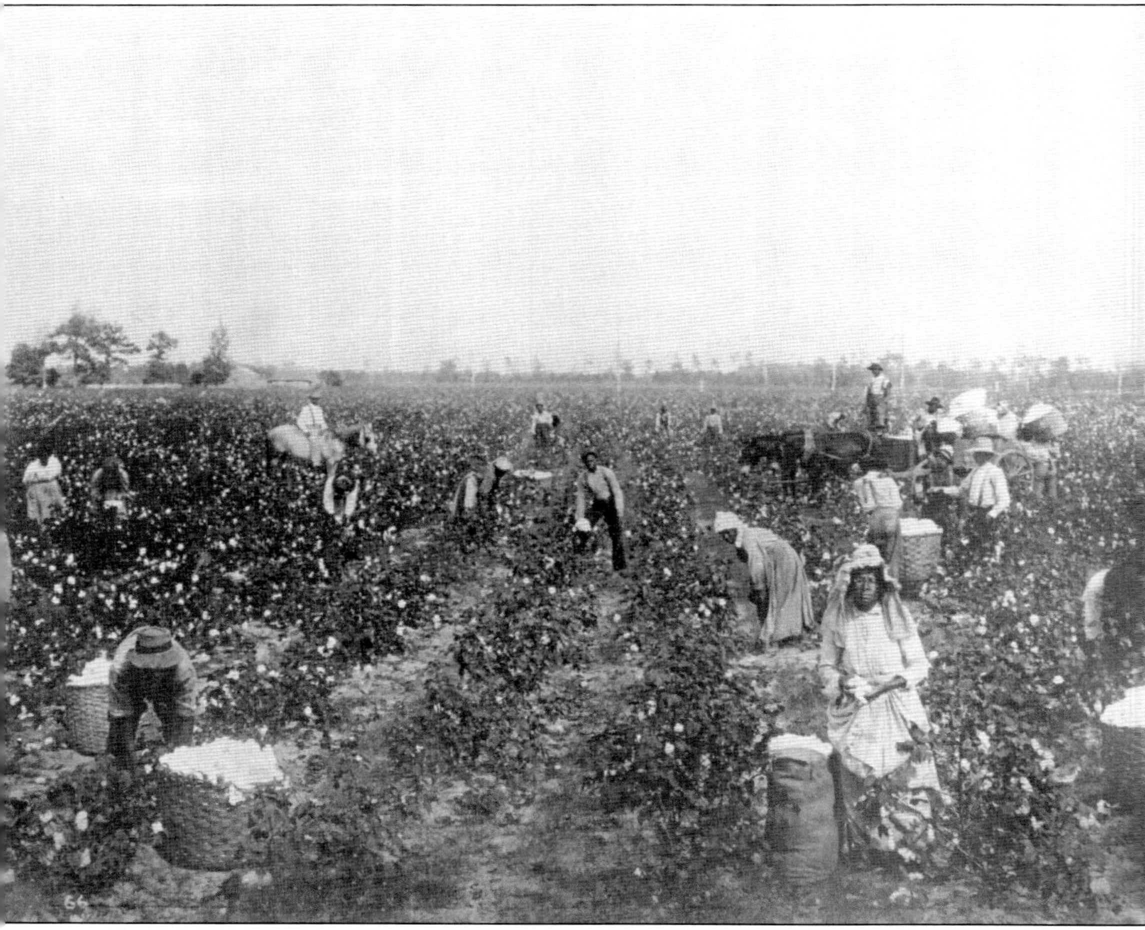

FIELDS OF COTTON. The sharecropping system was simple. The landowner would furnish the land and supplies. The sharecropper received an advance of food, clothing, seed, implements, and livestock to subsist on until the sale of the crop. The landlord held lien against the future production to secure the debt for subsistence, supplies, and land. At harvest, the landowner took his share plus interest. Anything left over constituted the sharecropper's earnings for the year. More often than not, sharecroppers could not pay off what they owed and fell into debt. (Courtesy Columbus State Archives.)

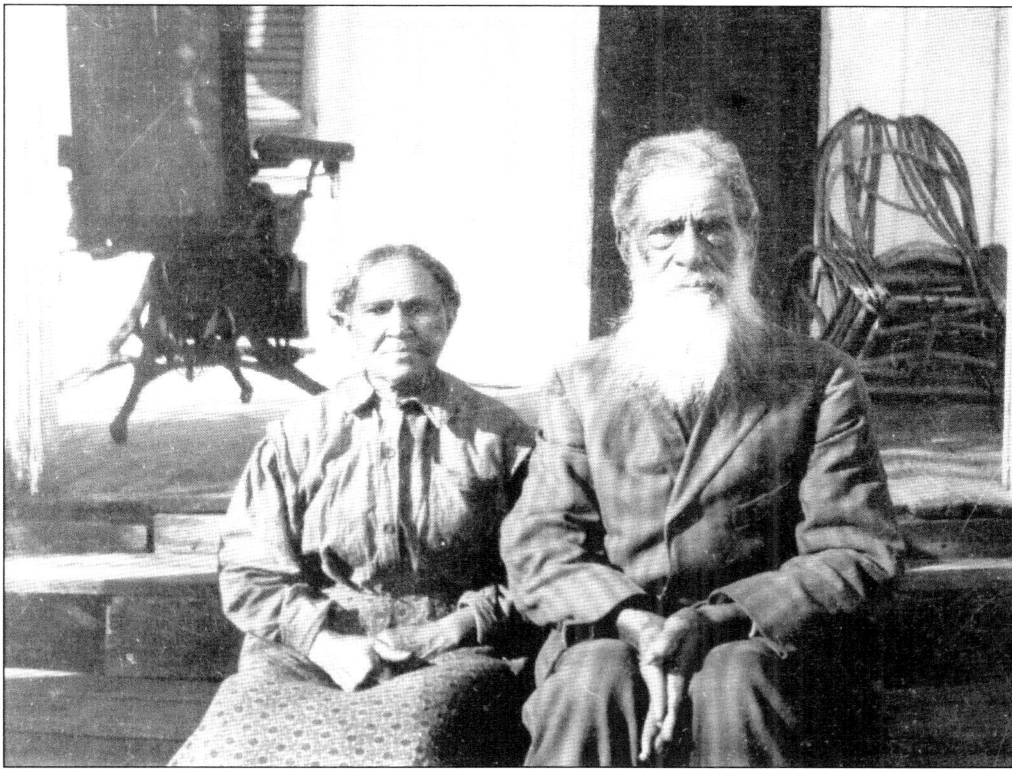

WINTER CANTEY AND WIFE FANNIE. After the Civil War, with the protection of the 13th, 14th, and 15th Amendments and the Civil Rights Act of 1866, African Americans enjoyed a brief period when they were allowed to vote, participate in the political process, acquire land, seek their own employment, and use public accommodations. Opponents, however, soon rallied against the former slaves' freedoms and found a means to limit their mobility through Jim Crow laws. Winter Cantey was the slave of Gen. James Cantey. (Courtesy Chattahoochee Valley Community College.)

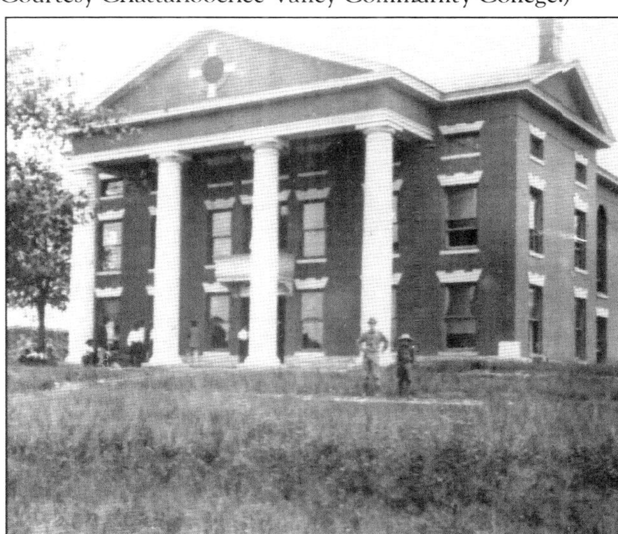

RUSSELL COUNTY COURTHOUSE, SEALE. In 1866, the creation of Lee County from the northern portion of Russell hastened the need to relocate the county seat from Crawford to a more central location. Crawford and Girard, both border towns, were viable locations as were Silver Run (Seale) and Sand Fort. Though centrally located Silver Run won out, political maneuvering prevented the immediate transfer of records from Crawford. Brownville now lay in Lee County. (Courtesy Chattahoochee Valley Community College.)

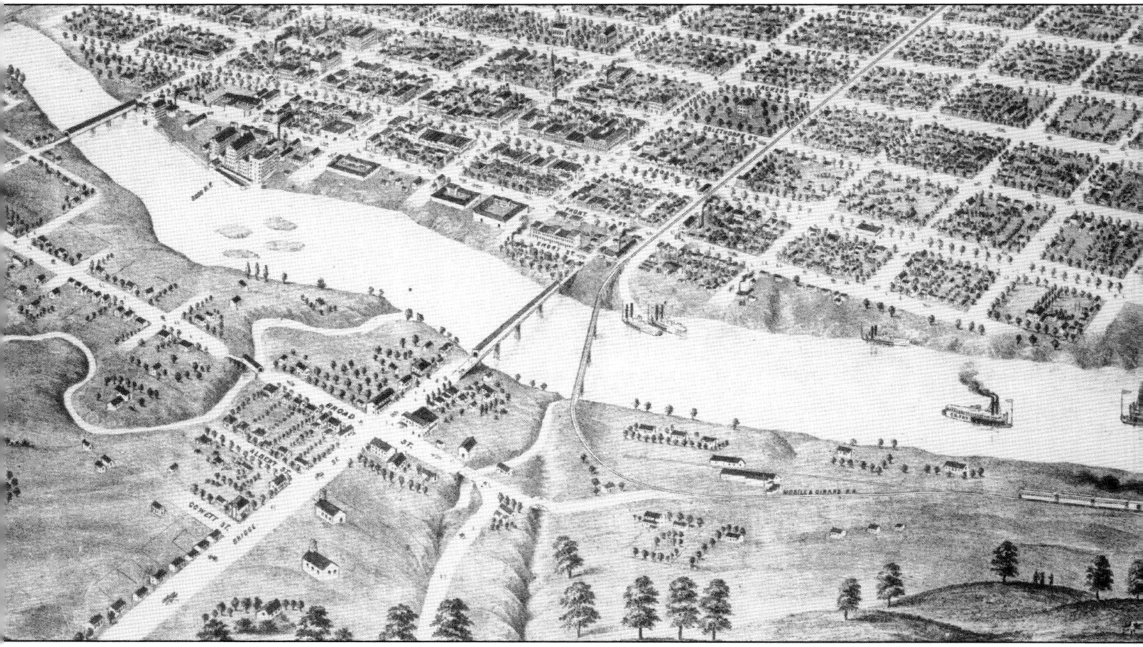

Bird's-Eye View of Columbus, 1872. Columbus's industry recovered much quicker than Reconstruction legends would have people believe. By 1870, over 100 manufactures were in full operation. However, a survey of Girard revealed a quiet town. (Courtesy Columbus Public Library.)

Four

Emergence of a New South
1878–1919

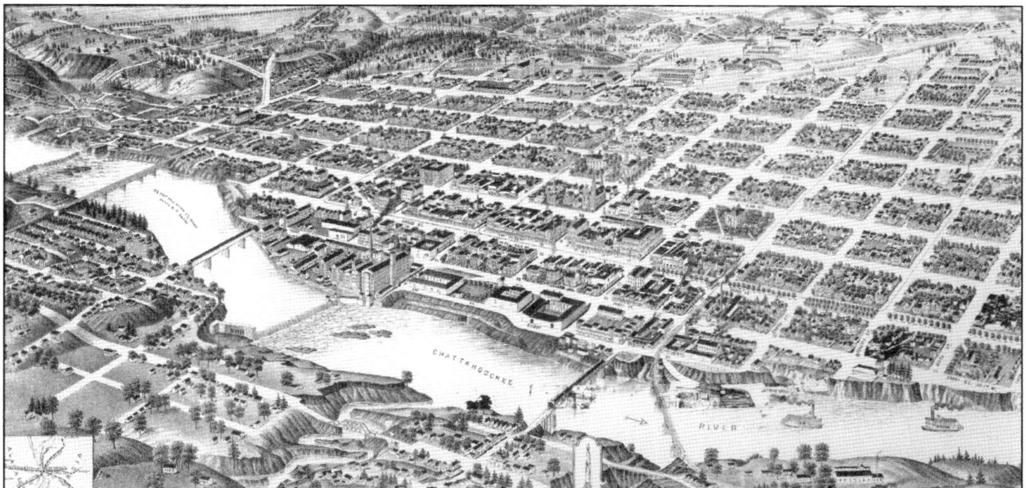

Perspective View of Columbus, Georgia, 1883. This bird's-eye view of Columbus illustrates the rapid expansion of the city in terms of suburban residential areas and industrial development along the Chattahoochee River. Columbus's Alabama suburbs are listed as Girard, Lively, and Eagle and Phenix Property. In February 1883, the Alabama legislature incorporated Lively and the Eagle property as Brownville. The name Lively was retained as the post office. Phenix City would not become the official name until February 19, 1889. (Courtesy of the Columbus Public Library.)

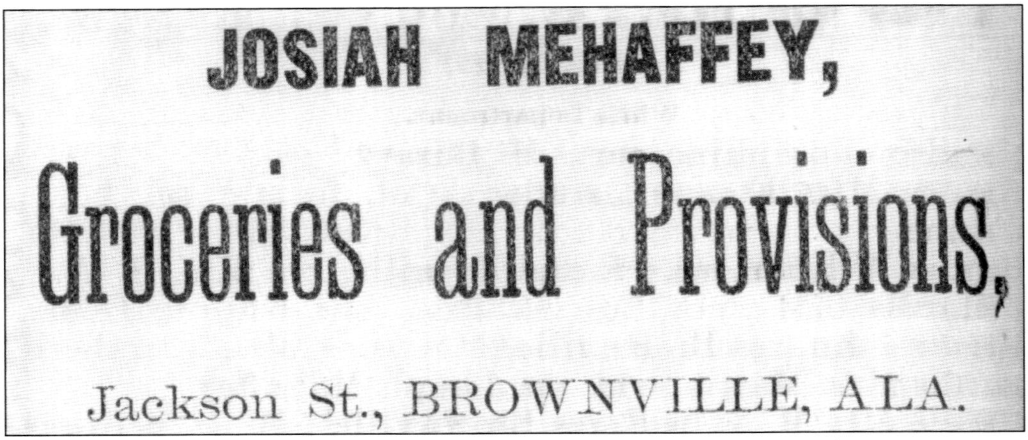

JOSIAH MENAFFEY ADVERTISEMENT. Small retail shops and groceries were the most common commercial enterprises in Girard and Brownville. In addition to catering to urban dwellers, they drew customers and suppliers from the nearby countryside. Several small shops were often located next to each other in a row or in one large building, forerunners of today's shopping centers. (Courtesy Columbus Public Library.)

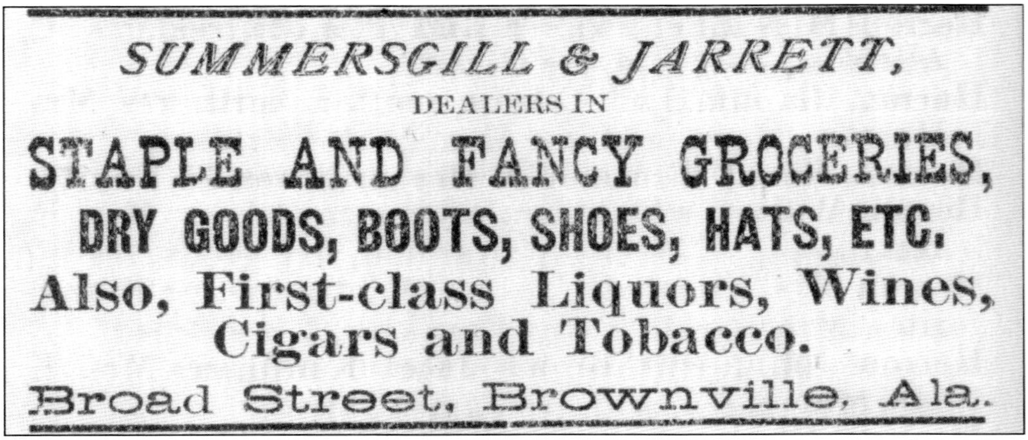

SUMMERSGILL AND GARRETT ADVERTISEMENT. While country storekeepers attempted to carry a complete range of products, their urban counterparts were becoming increasingly specialized. Dry goods shops, groceries, apothecaries, and hardware stores all competed for business. (Courtesy Columbus Public Library.)

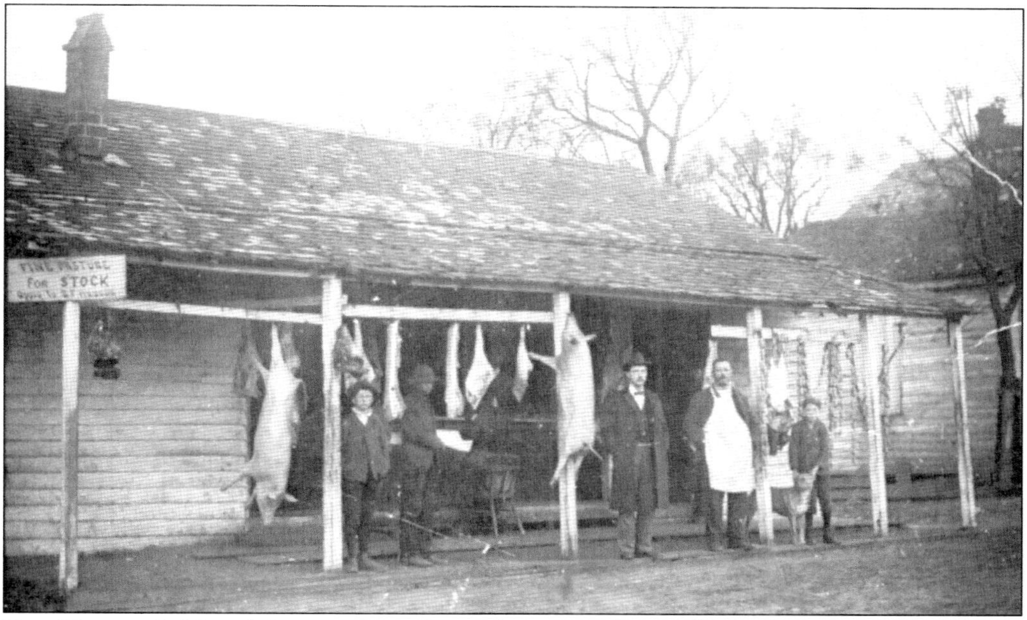

BILL HERRING'S MEAT MARKET. Specialty craftsmen, such as Bill Herring, found ready markets in Girard and Brownville for their products and services. The *Columbus Enquirer* reported that over 4,000 pounds of meat was sold every Saturday in Girard and Brownville. As society became more urban, specialty stores and craftsmen served a vital function in meeting the daily needs of town dwellers. (Courtesy Columbus Public Library.)

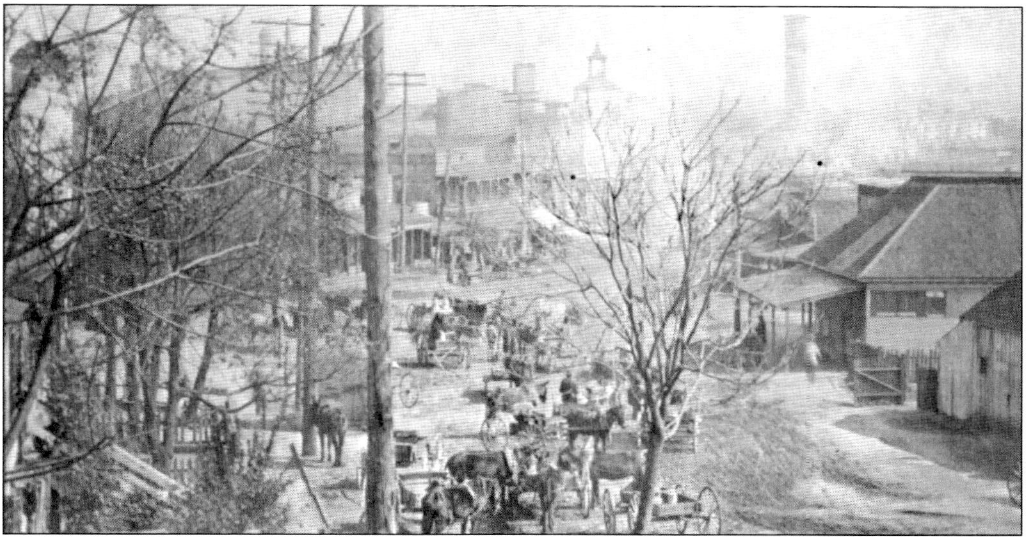

"VINEGAR HILL," AROUND 1900. Typically stores and shops lined the principal streets near a market hall or town square. Girard and Phenix City merchants, however, crowded the streets nearest the bridges to Columbus. Phenix City's commercial district ran east to west from the bridge along Fourteenth and Sixteenth Streets to Broad Street. Pictured is a view of Fourteenth Street, also known as Vinegar Hill, facing east towards Columbus. Girard's commercial district lined Dillingham Street and ran north towards Phenix City along Broad Street. The Muscogee Manufacturing Company can be seen on the horizon. (Courtesy Sean Driggers.)

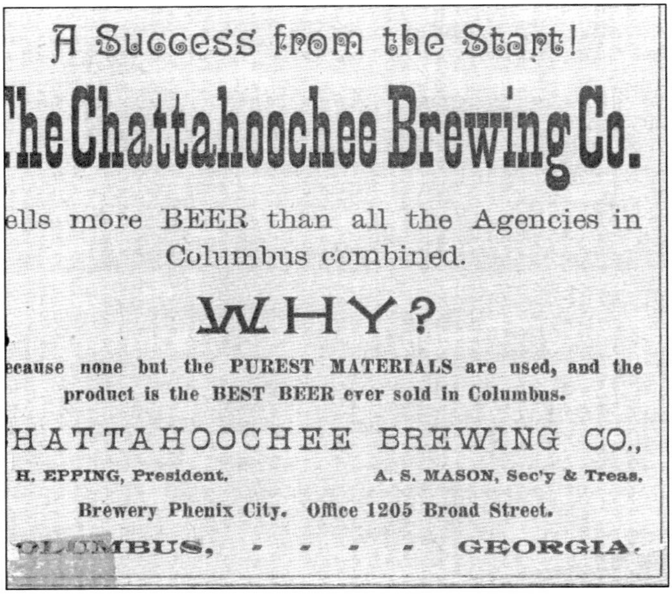

CHATTAHOOCHEE BREWING COMPANY ADVERTISEMENT, 1888. The brewery was built in 1888. Situated on Crawford Road, just beyond Brownville, it harnessed power from Holland Creek. German brewmasters Carl Willaeur and Earnest Koenueker were the proprietors. The two-story storage building of "German architecture" was described as six buildings in one. Initial production capacity of the brewery was estimated at 50 barrels per day. Like most local manufacturers, the brewery maintained its business office in Columbus. (Courtesy Columbus Public Library.)

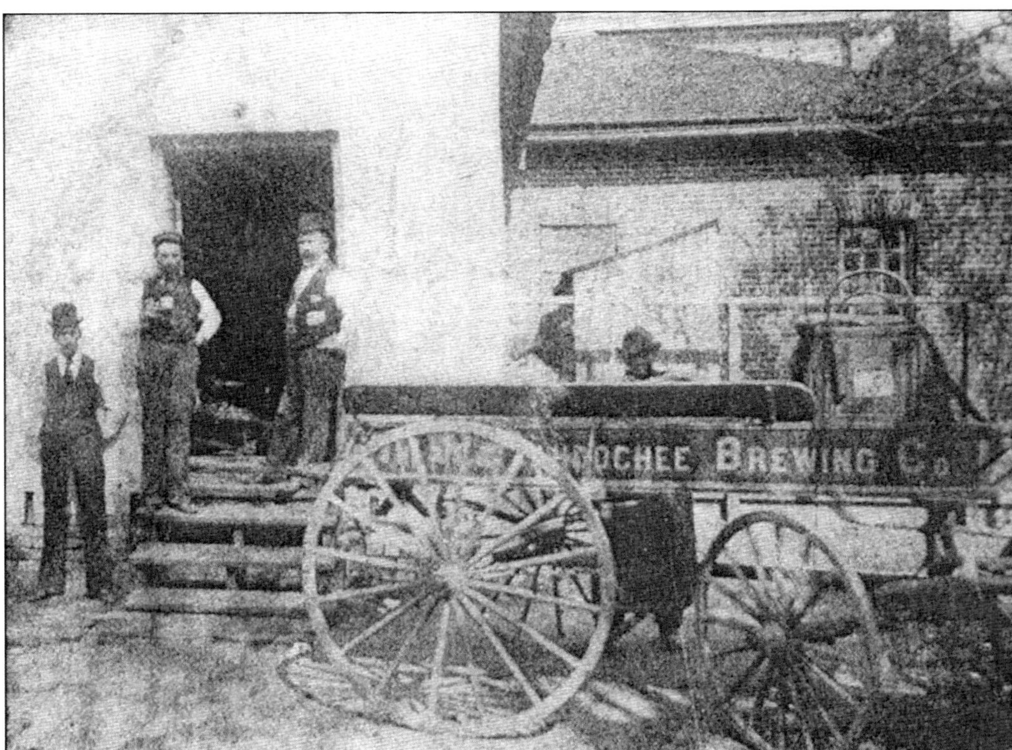

CHATTAHOOCHEE BREWING COMPANY. The brewery boasted of being a homegrown institution. Although the owners were of Germanic origins, the brewery made tanks from Chattahoochee River cypress, manufactured its kegs from Uchee Swamp white oak, and produced beer from southern corn. (Courtesy Columbus Public Library.)

Our Alabama Suburbs. "Our Alabama Suburbs" was a running column that appeared in the *Columbus Enquirer* in the late 1870s and contained historical notes and news of local happenings in Brownville and Girard. This 1879 column pays particular note to the numerous names applied to Brownville. Common names include Browneville, Lively, McAllisterville, Skipperville, Marshall, and Eagle City. The writer deems Eagle City the most appropriate name "by common consent," and in doing so hints at the domination of the mill over the Alabama suburbs. (Courtesy Columbus Public Library.)

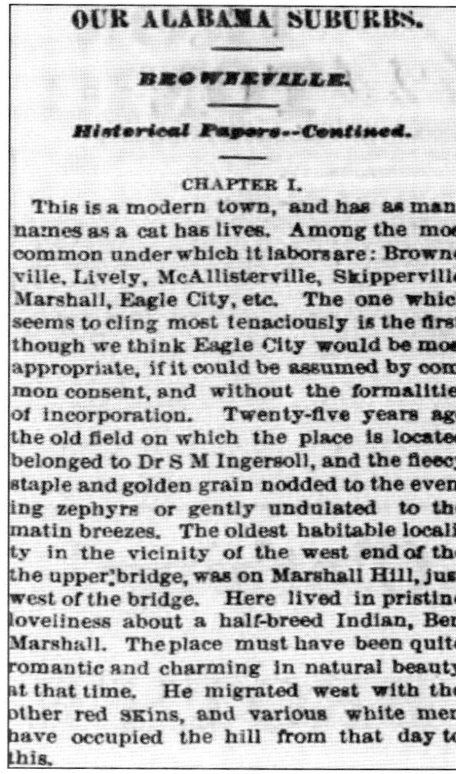

OUR ALABAMA SUBURBS.

BROWNEVILLE.

Historical Papers--Contined.

CHAPTER I.

This is a modern town, and has as many names as a cat has lives. Among the most common under which it labors are: Browneville, Lively, McAllisterville, Skipperville, Marshall, Eagle City, etc. The one which seems to cling most tenaciously is the first, though we think Eagle City would be most appropriate, if it could be assumed by common consent, and without the formalities of incorporation. Twenty-five years ago the old field on which the place is located belonged to Dr S M Ingersoll, and the fleecy staple and golden grain nodded to the evening zephyrs or gently undulated to the matin breezes. The oldest habitable locality in the vicinity of the west end of the the upper bridge, was on Marshall Hill, just west of the bridge. Here lived in pristine loveliness about a half-breed Indian, Ben Marshall. The place must have been quite romantic and charming in natural beauty at that time. He migrated west with the other red skins, and various white men have occupied the hill from that day to this.

River and Railroad Traffic. The sternwheeler *J. W. Hires* was built in Columbus, Georgia. Through the port at Apalachicola, the *J. W. Hires* connected the lower Chattahoochee Valley with foreign markets. The primary commodity transported was cotton. The Mobile and Girard Railroad and the Dillingham Bridge can be seen in the distance. (Courtesy Columbus State University Archives.)

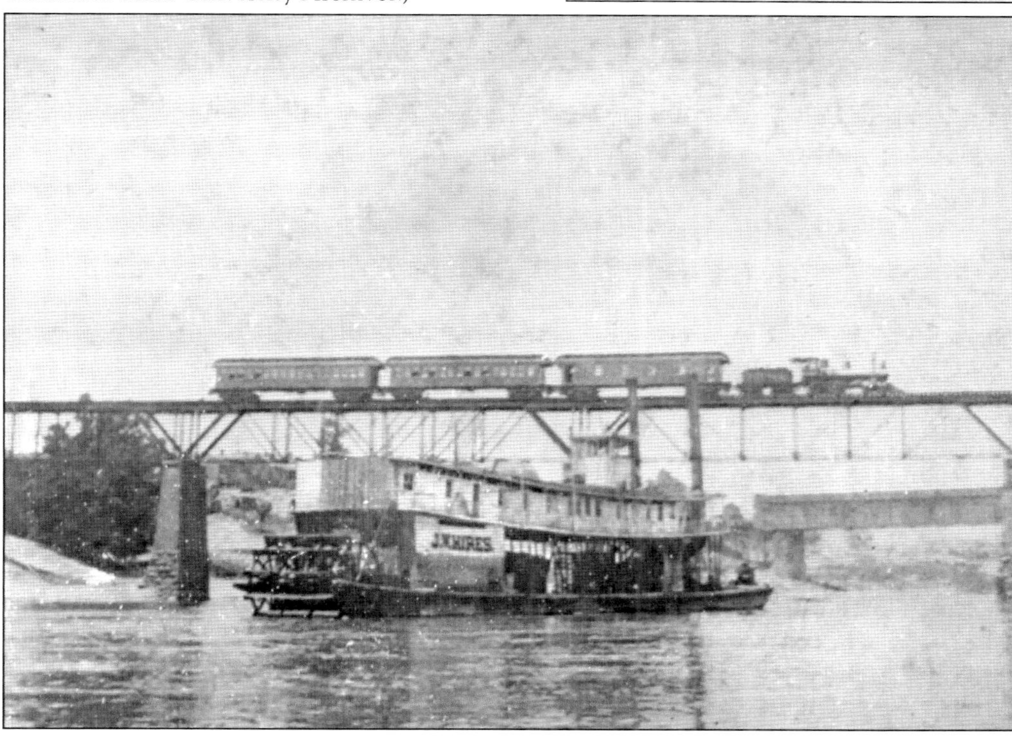

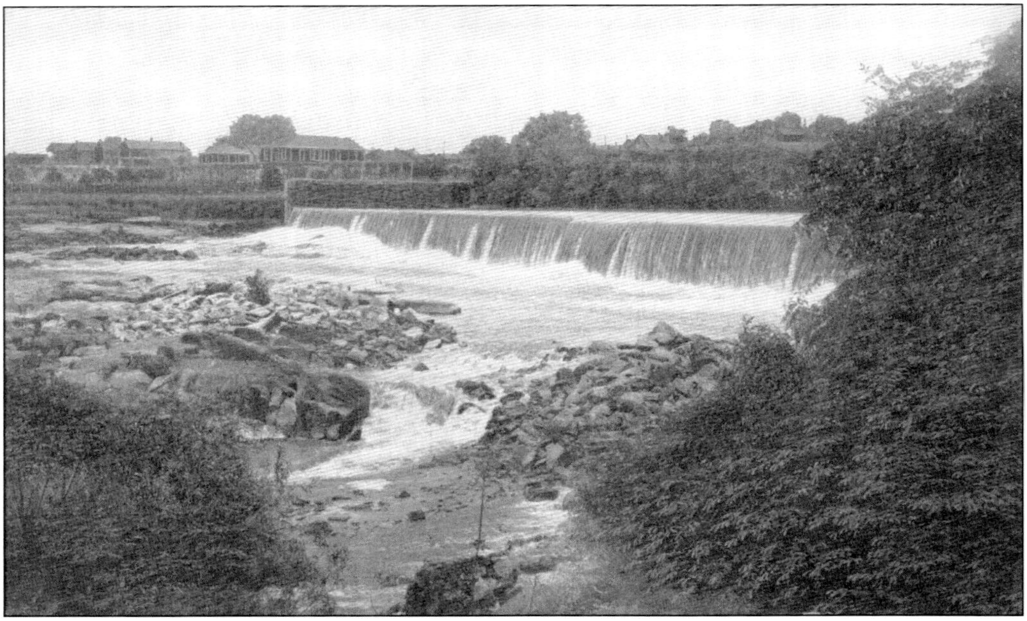

CHATTAHOOCHEE FALLS. The textile industry attracted hundreds of white workers from rural farms, who traded the life of a sharecropper for life in the mill village. There, workers lived in homes owned by the mill, shopped in the mill store, deposited savings in the mill saving department, and in the case of the Eagle and Phenix were briefly paid in mill currency. Brownville is pictured on the opposite bank. (Courtesy Dennis Jones.)

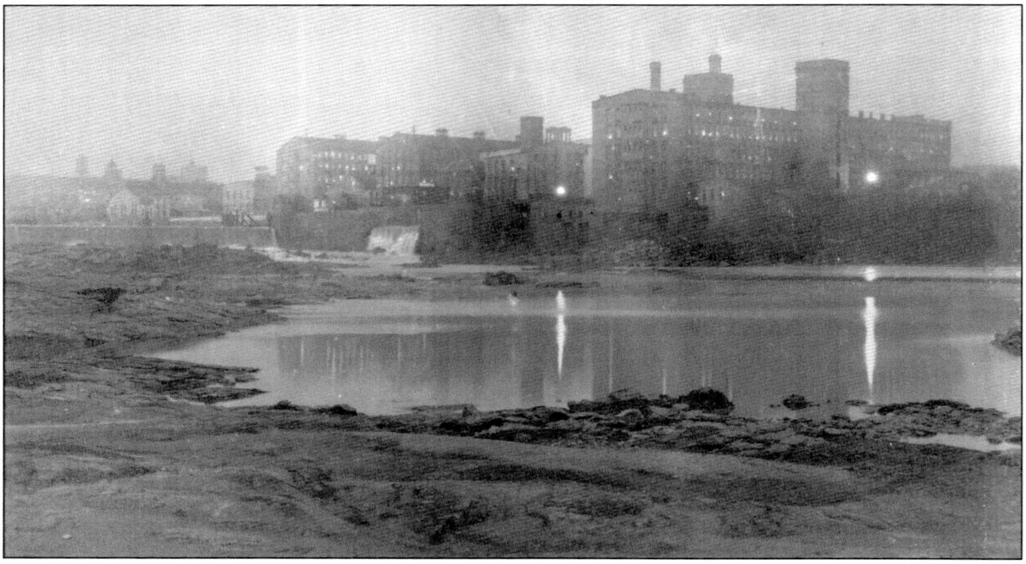

EAGLE AND PHENIX MILL AT NIGHT. Eagle and Phenix's labor practices were both progressive and paternalistic. The mill paid its operatives a high wage, provided housing, created recreational and educational facilities, developed savings departments, and provided employees with other non-cash amenities. The chief aim was to produce a tractable labor force. The mill sought to attract the best available operatives, reduce labor turnover, and develop a permanent workforce. (Courtesy Library of Congress.)

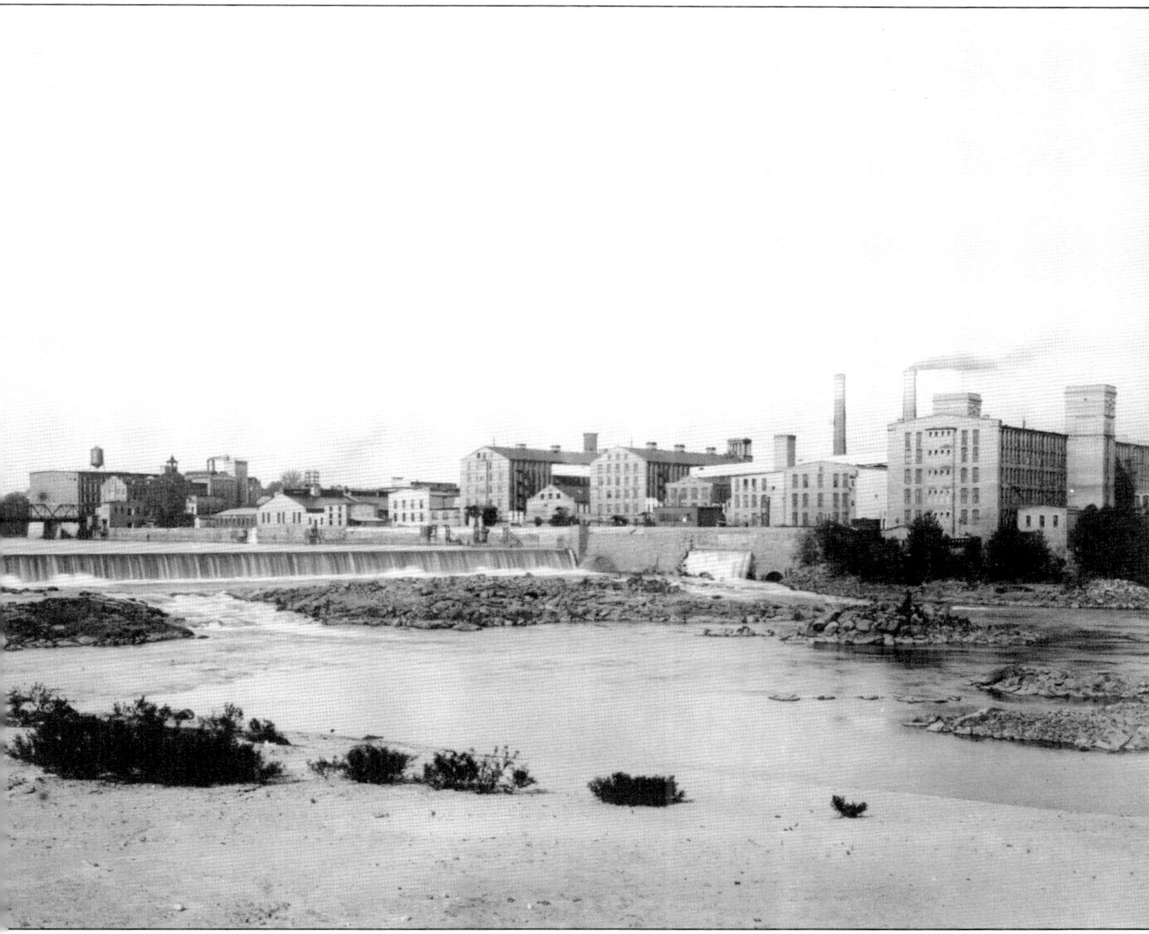

Eagle and Phenix Mill. The Muscogee Mills and the Eagle and Phenix were the two largest employers in the region. The Eagle's Mill No. 3 is estimated to have contributed $600,000 to the local economy per year. (Courtesy Library of Congress.)

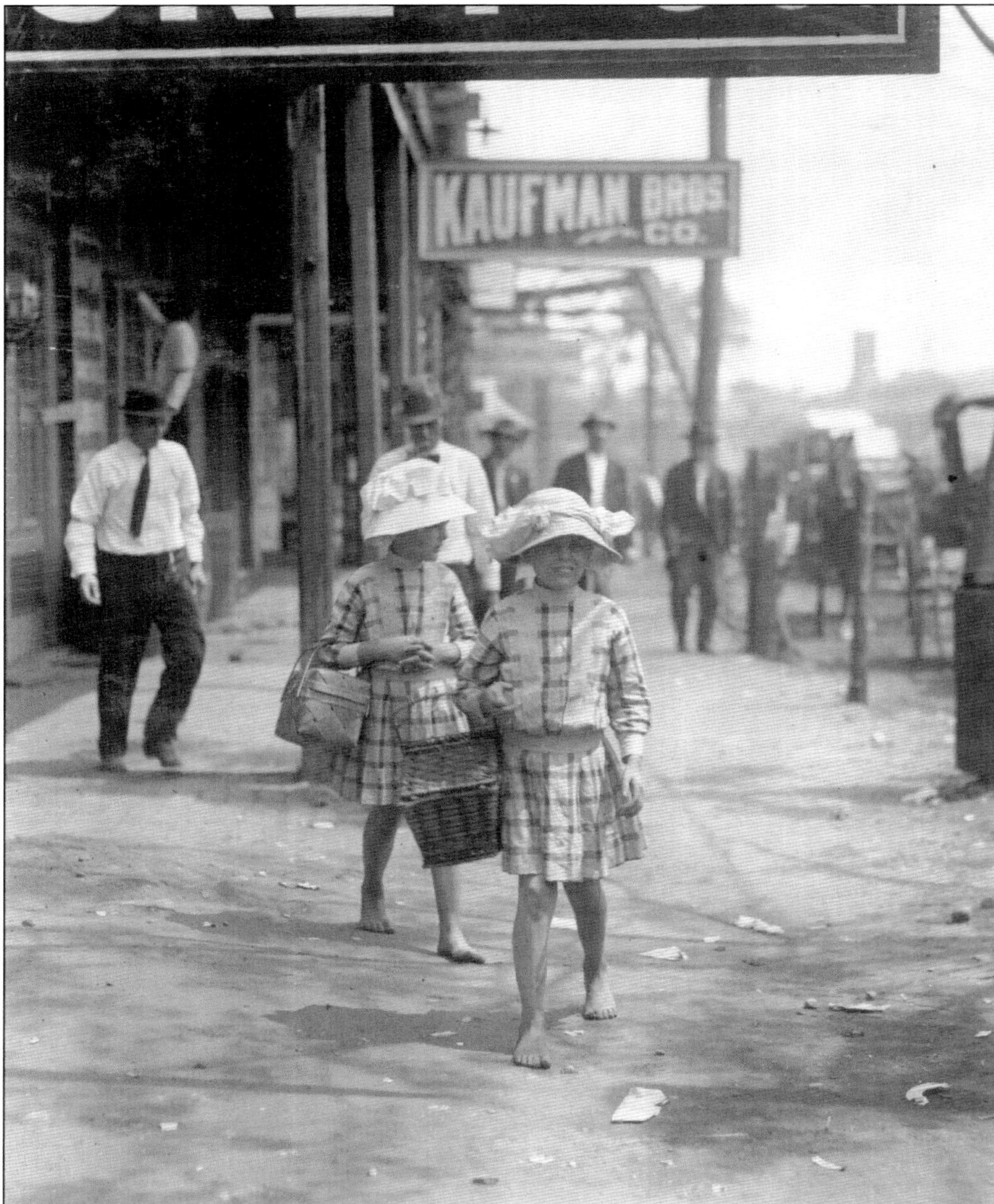

Dinner-Toters. The cotton mills of the South were at once a blessing and a curse. The mills in Columbus provided jobs and sustained the economies on both sides of the river. The welfare capitalism of mill villages also created a family labor system where mothers, fathers, and children worked in the factories. This image depicts two young "dinner-toters" in Girard. (Courtesy Library of Congress.)

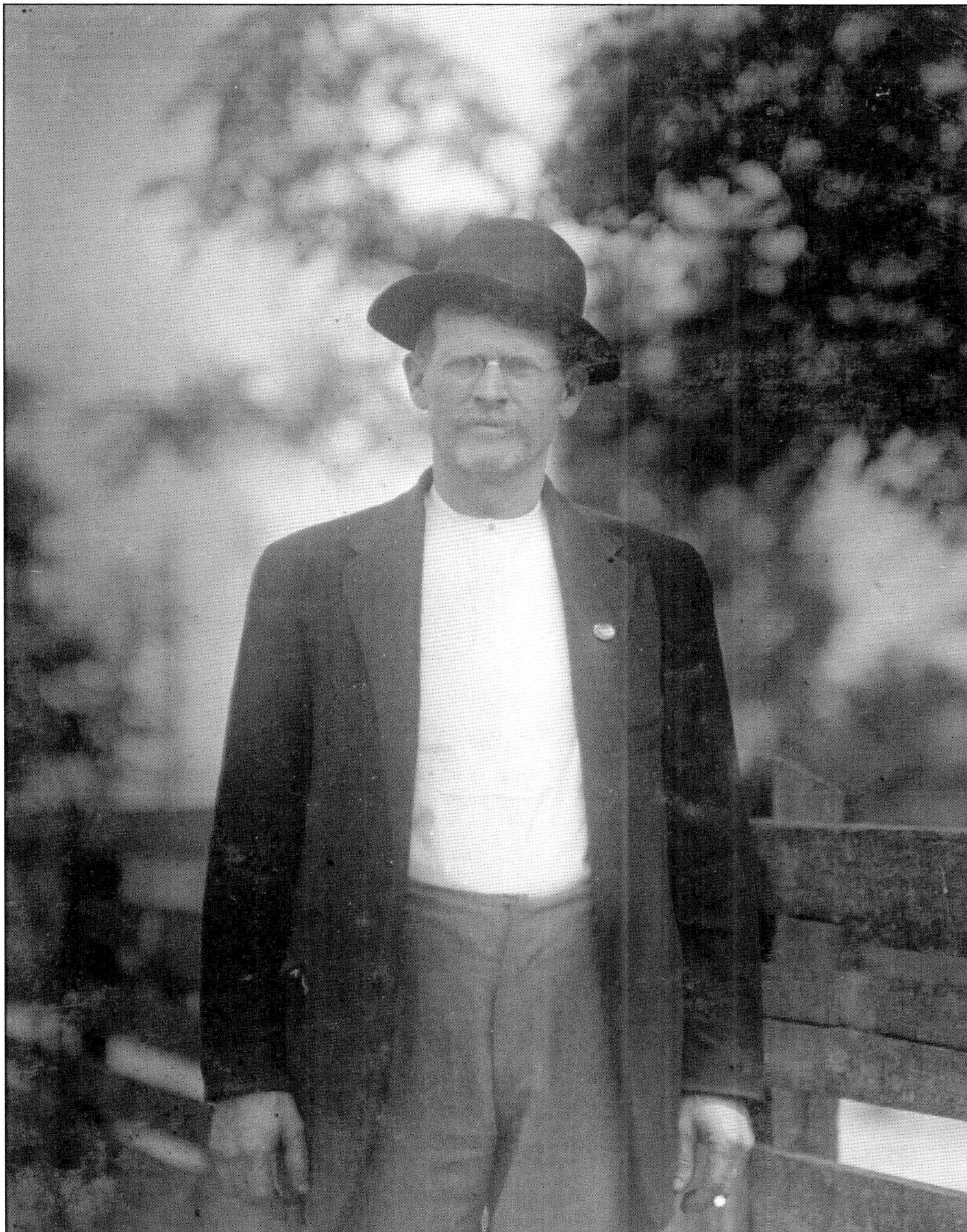

FRANK BARNES. A product of the cotton mills, Frank Barnes, of Phenix City, Alabama, worked over 40 years in the cotton mills. Barnes, an ardent socialist, claimed to have started work at age four for 20¢ a day. (Courtesy Library of Congress.)

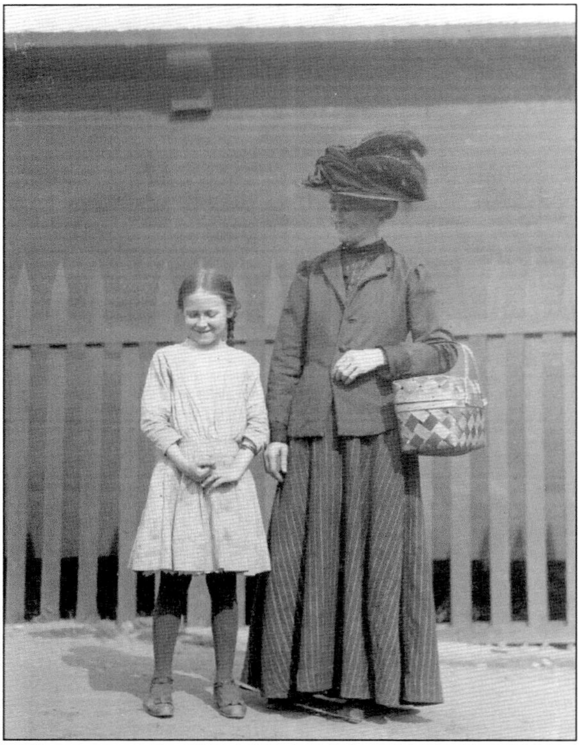

Willie McPherson, a 10-Year-Old Helper. Willie McPherson carried dinners and helped her mother in Muscogee Mill. "She helps me a good deal." (Courtesy Library of Congress.)

Helper Crossing the Bridge. This is another view of Willie McPherson and her mother. (Courtesy Library of Congress.)

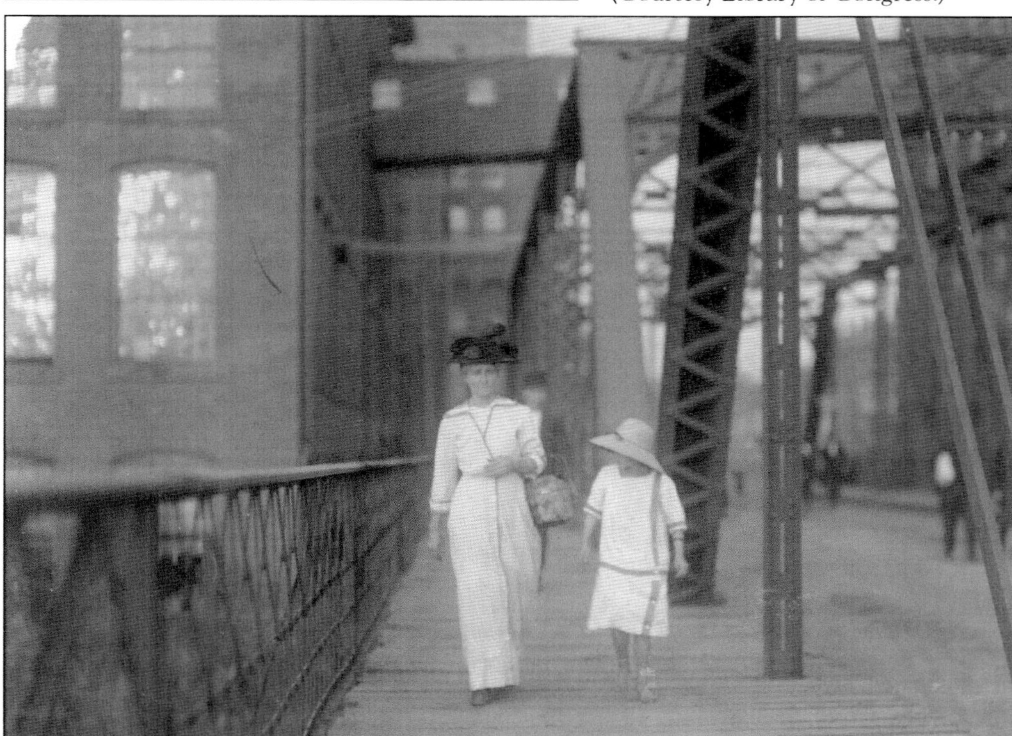

Charley Herring, 1913. Charley Herring was a "helper" in Georgia Hosiery Mill at nine years of age. Charley lived at 219 Broad Street, Girard, Alabama. The term "helper" was a way the mill owners skirted child labor laws. (Courtesy Library of Congress.)

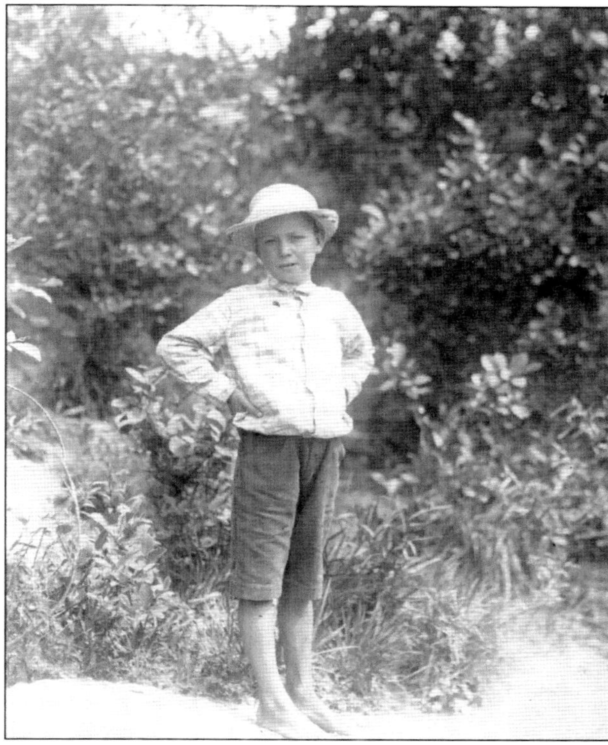

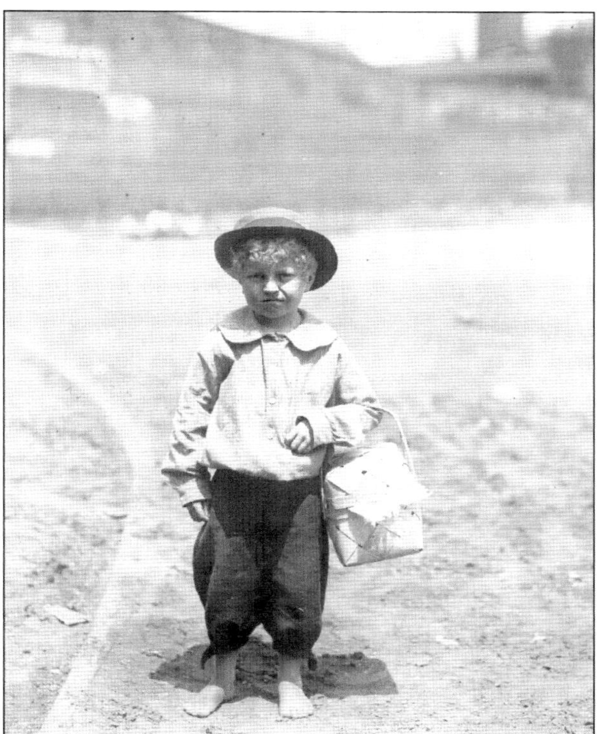

Dinner-Toters at the Eagle and Phoenix Mill. Pictured in this 1913 photograph is one the little dinner-toter waiting for the gate to open. (Courtesy Library of Congress.)

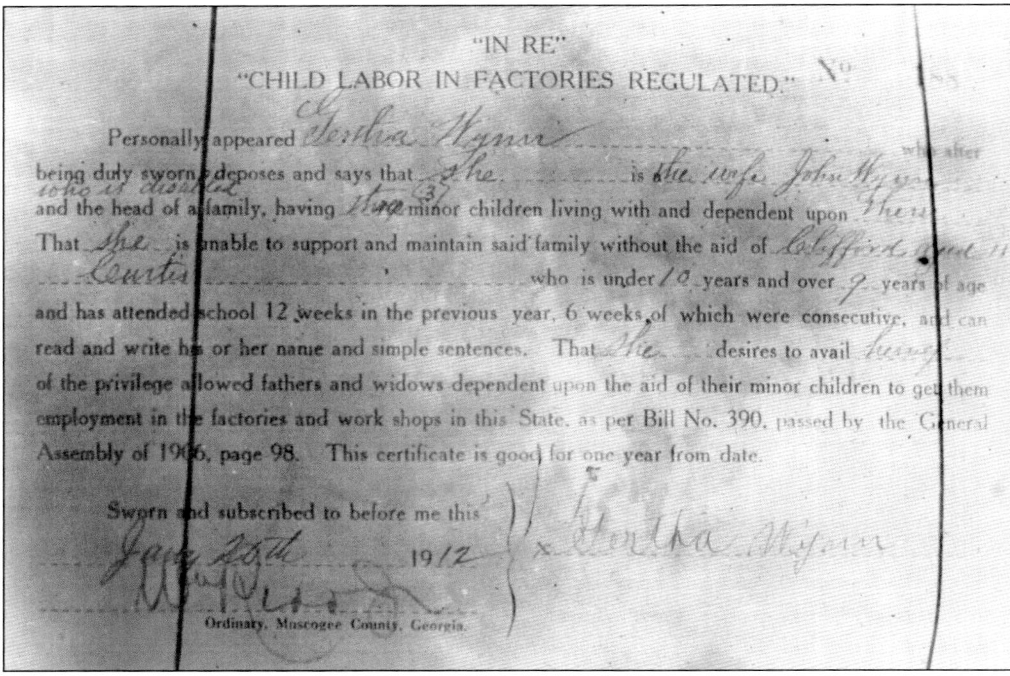

"IN RE"

"CHILD LABOR IN FACTORIES REGULATED." No.

Personally appeared Gertha Wynn who after being duly sworn deposes and says that she is the wife John Wynn who is disabled and the head of a family, having three (3) minor children living with and dependent upon them. That she is unable to support and maintain said family without the aid of Clifford [illegible] Curtis who is under 10 years and over 9 years of age and has attended school 12 weeks in the previous year, 6 weeks of which were consecutive, and can read and write his or her name and simple sentences. That she desires to avail herself of the privilege allowed fathers and widows dependent upon the aid of their minor children to get them employment in the factories and work shops in this State, as per Bill No. 390, passed by the General Assembly of 1906, page 98. This certificate is good for one year from date.

Sworn and subscribed to before me this Jan 25th 1912 x Gertha Wynn

Ordinary, Muscogee County, Georgia.

CURTIS WYNN'S LABOR CERTIFICATE. Gertha Wynn signed this child labor certificate insisting that nine-year-old Curtis Wynn be allowed to work in the mills to support his family. Gertha certified that her husband, John Wynn, was disabled and that she had three minor children. (Courtesy Library of Congress.)

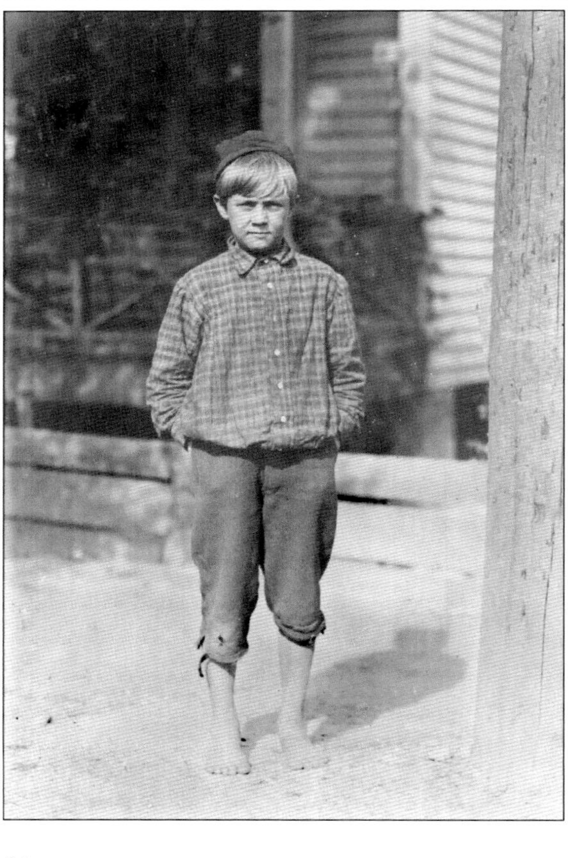

BRUCE TILLERY, A DINNER-TOTER. Bruce Tillery, 10-year-old Girard resident, claimed, when interviewed by National Child Labor Committee photograph Lewis Hine, to have been employed by the Eagle and Phenix Mills. He previously swept in the Eagle Mill and claimed to be going to work again. Tillery had been toting 13 dinners a day, for which his mother received most of the money. Child labor was not always seen as an evil. Many families could not survive without financial contributions from working children. (Courtesy Library of Congress.)

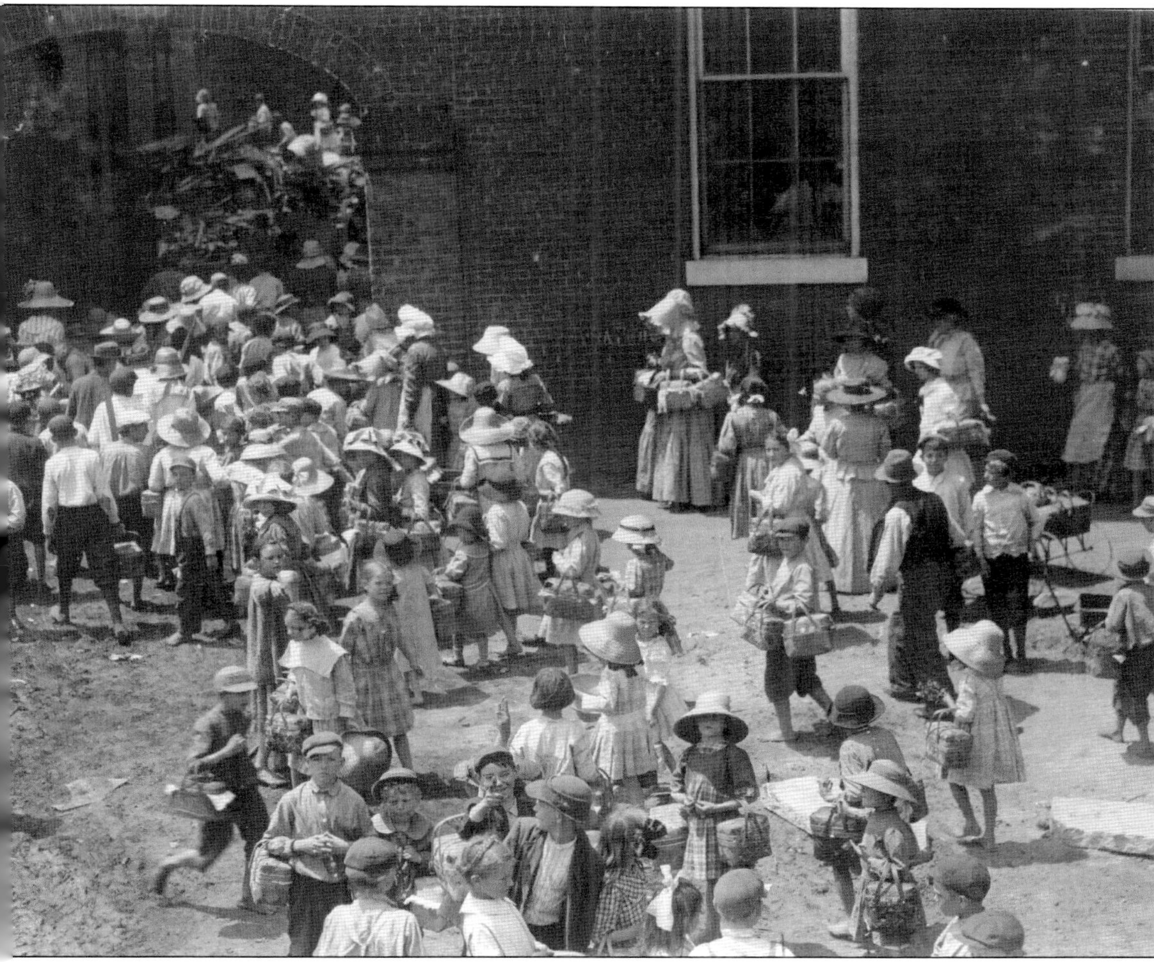

DINNER-TOTERS AT THE GATES, 1913. After the dinners are delivered, toters help tend the machines. Toting dinners allowed families to earn additional income and served as a form of on-the-job training. (Courtesy Library of Congress.)

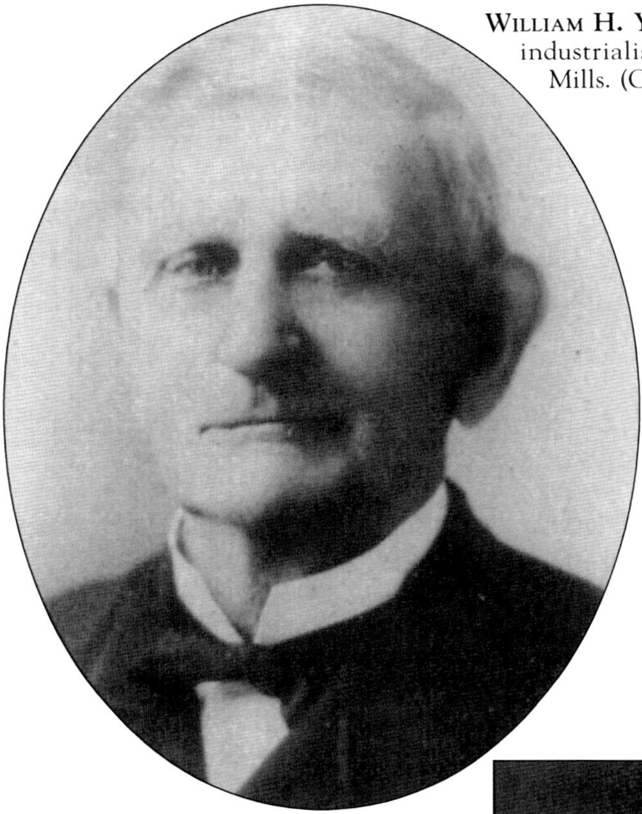

William H. Young. William H. Young was an industrialist. In 1851, he established Eagle Mills. (Courtesy Columbus Public Library.)

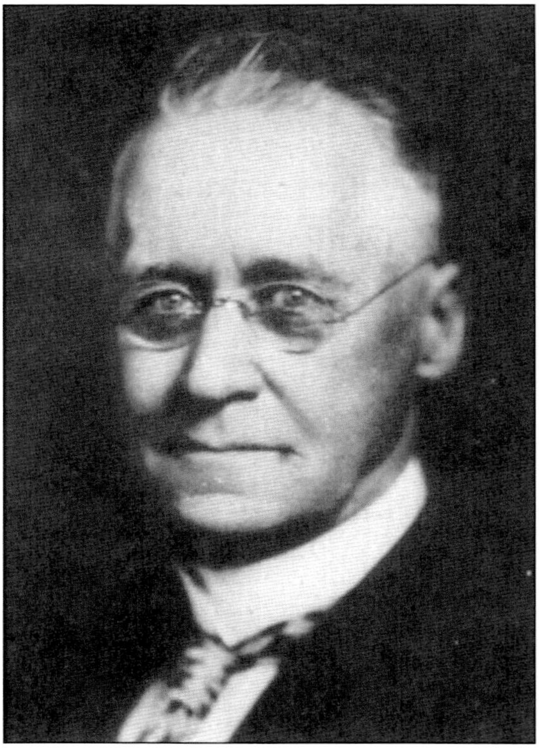

Dr. Franklin Ashby Floyd. Dr. Ashby Floyd (1866–1947) was a prominent physician and civic leader. In addition to practicing medicine, Floyd served as mayor and city court judge in Phenix City. (Courtesy Columbus Public Library.)

Rev. Henry Nasby Newsome. Henry Newsome was born in Russell County, Alabama. He attended the common schools of Crawford and Girard, Alabama, and Columbus, Georgia. Afterward, he studied Hebrew, Greek, and Latin under private instructors and took a course in theology at Morris Brown College. (Courtesy Columbus Public Library.)

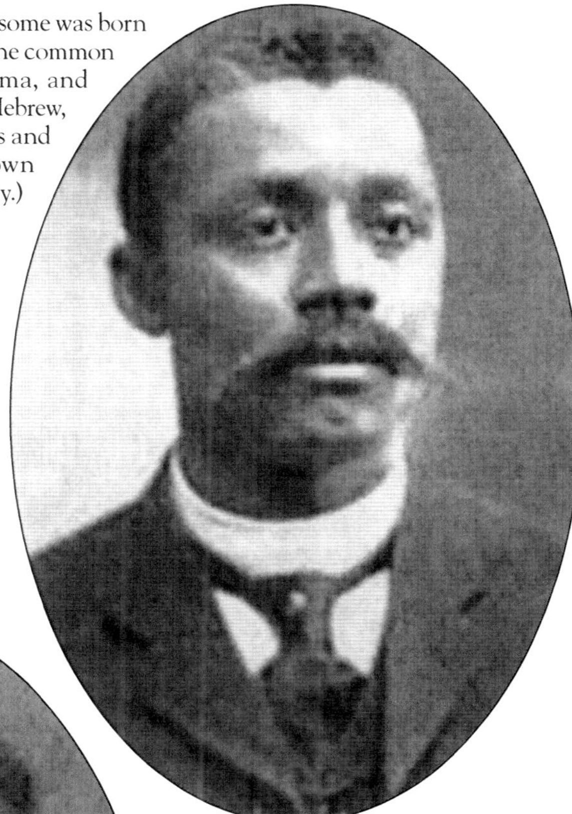

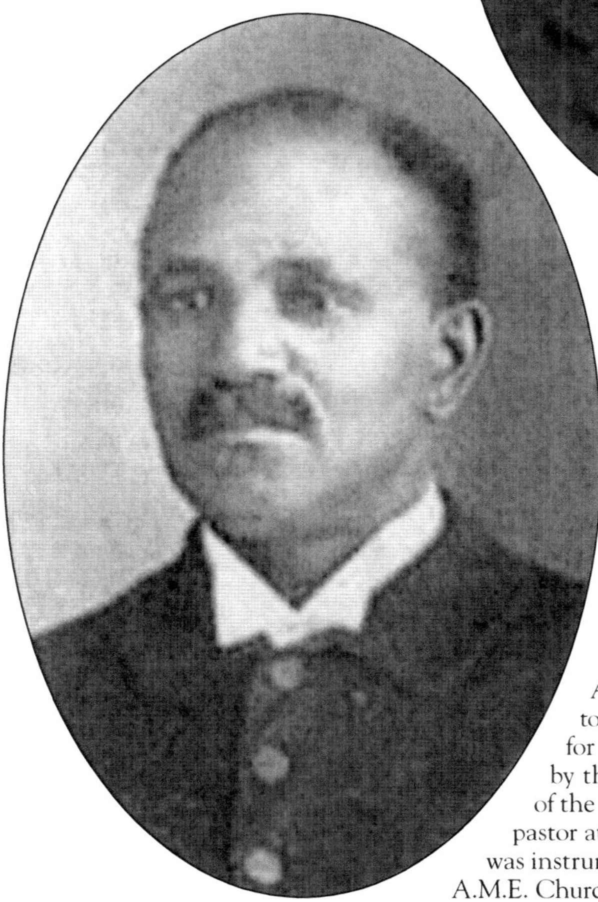

Rev. G. W. Allen, D.D. Born near Smith Station, Alabama, on August 10, 1850, Allen advocated equal rights for African Americans. In 1874, he was elected to the Alabama legislature and was reelected for a second term in 1878 but counted out by the opposition. Allen served as principal of the public schools in Girard City and also as pastor at several mission points near Girard. He was instrumental in the building of Gaines Chapel A.M.E. Church. (Courtesy Columbus Public Library.)

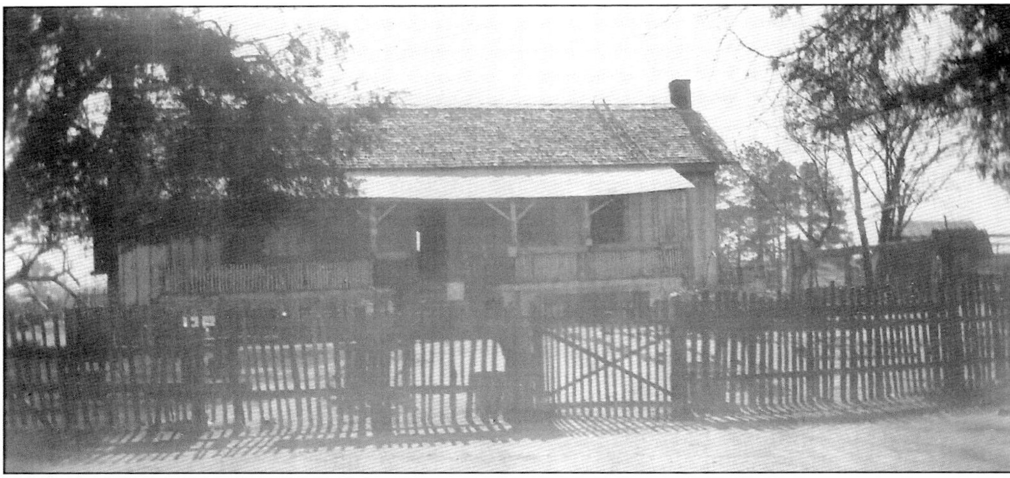

RUSSELL COUNTY FARMHOUSE. By 1900, the rural landscape of Russell County resembled antebellum days. Slave cabins had been replaced by tenant houses, but African Americans were still bound to the land. African American sharecroppers operated 73 percent of Russell County's total farms from 1900 to 1920. During this same period, white tenancy accounted for nine percent of total farmers. One reason for the black majority of sharecroppers was the exodus of white farmers to the mills. (Courtesy Library of Congress.)

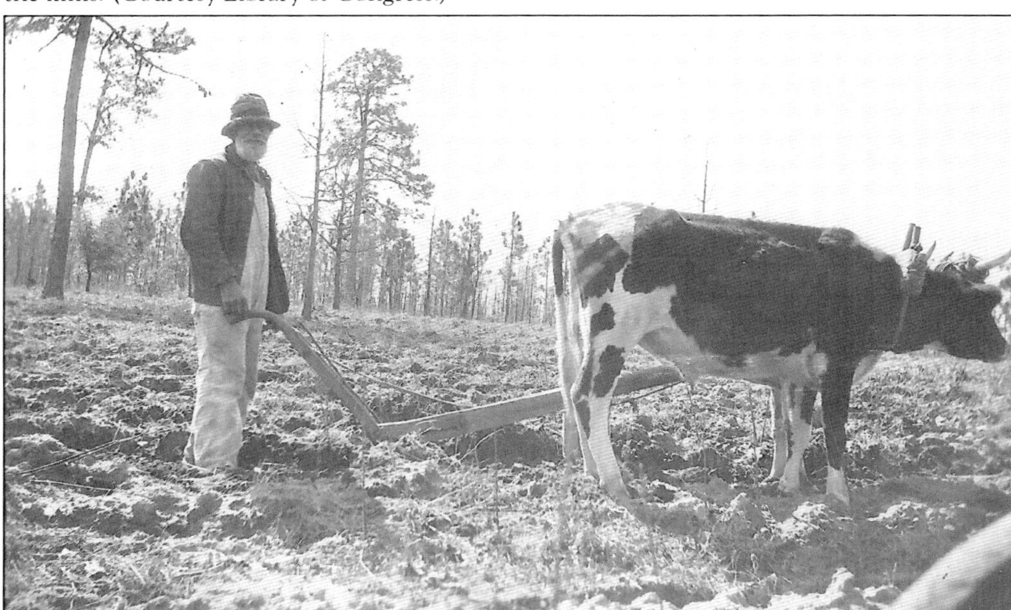

SHARECROPPER. As tenant farmers struggled to produce a crop and settle their debts, landowners benefited from the formation of co-ops. Farmer owners organized co-ops to address problems of expensive and scarce credit. The Longview Agricultural Club of Russell County was established around 1890. It drew upon family networks and friends as the foundation for membership. The Longview club had no clear relationship with the larger movements of the Patrons of Husbandry, Agricultural Wheel, or the Farmers' Alliance. Its goals were to increase production and acreage yields, reduce costs, and improve farm prices. The club participated in cooperative buying campaigns to reduce costs. (Courtesy Library of Congress.)

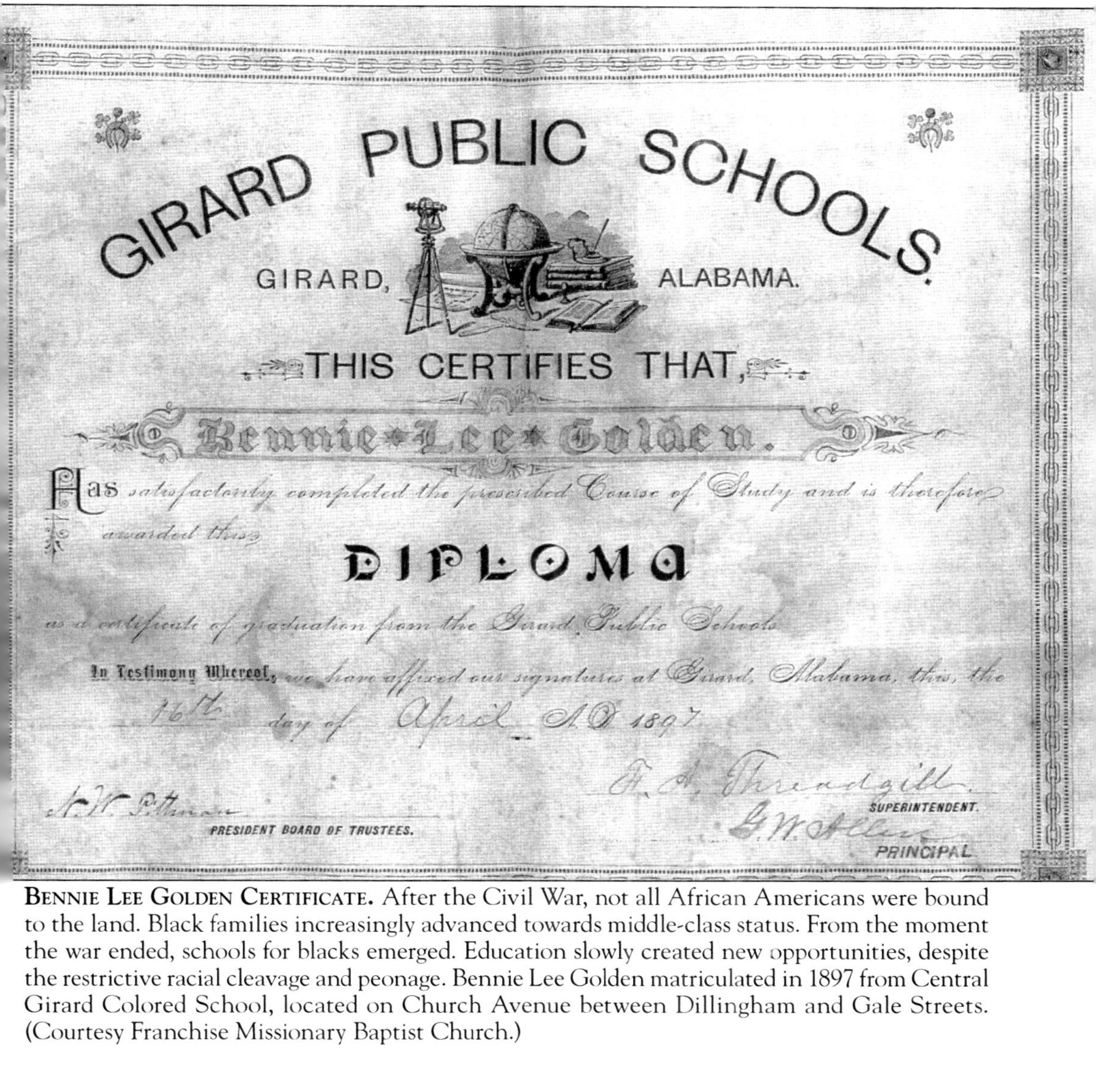

GIRARD PUBLIC SCHOOLS.

GIRARD, ALABAMA.

THIS CERTIFIES THAT,

Bennie Lee Golden.

Has satisfactorily completed the prescribed Course of Study and is therefore awarded this

DIPLOMA

as a certificate of graduation from the Girard Public Schools.

In Testimony Whereof, we have affixed our signatures at Girard, Alabama, this, the 16th day of April A.D. 1897.

F. A. Threadgill
SUPERINTENDENT.

N. W. Pittman
PRESIDENT BOARD OF TRUSTEES.

G. W. Allen
PRINCIPAL

BENNIE LEE GOLDEN CERTIFICATE. After the Civil War, not all African Americans were bound to the land. Black families increasingly advanced towards middle-class status. From the moment the war ended, schools for blacks emerged. Education slowly created new opportunities, despite the restrictive racial cleavage and peonage. Bennie Lee Golden matriculated in 1897 from Central Girard Colored School, located on Church Avenue between Dillingham and Gale Streets. (Courtesy Franchise Missionary Baptist Church.)

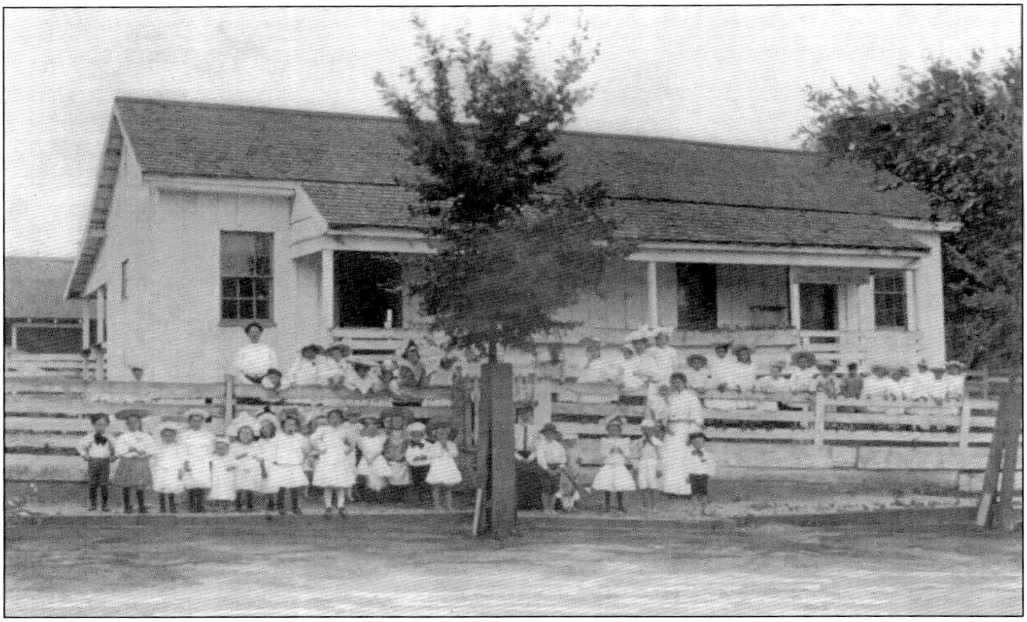

Eagle and Phenix Free Kindergarten, Phenix City Branch, Around 1903. Few mill children attended schools. In response, the Eagle and Phenix Mills opened a kindergarten in the fall 1903. The kindergarten operated under the auspices of the Columbus Free Kindergarten Association. Pictured is the original Phenix City branch, constructed at a cost of $400. In 1904, a kindergarten gymnasium was added at a cost of $188. (Courtesy Phenix City Public Library.)

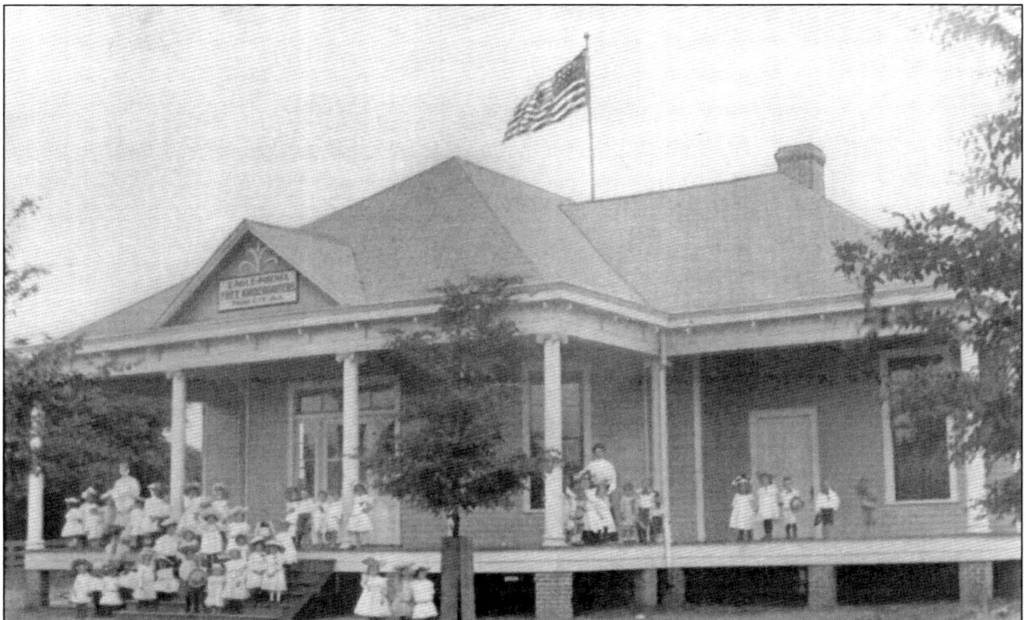

Eagle and Phenix Free Kindergarten, Phenix City Branch. The kindergarten was expanded to meet the growing enrollment. The exact construction date of this more modern Phenix City branch is unknown. (Courtesy Phenix City Public Library.)

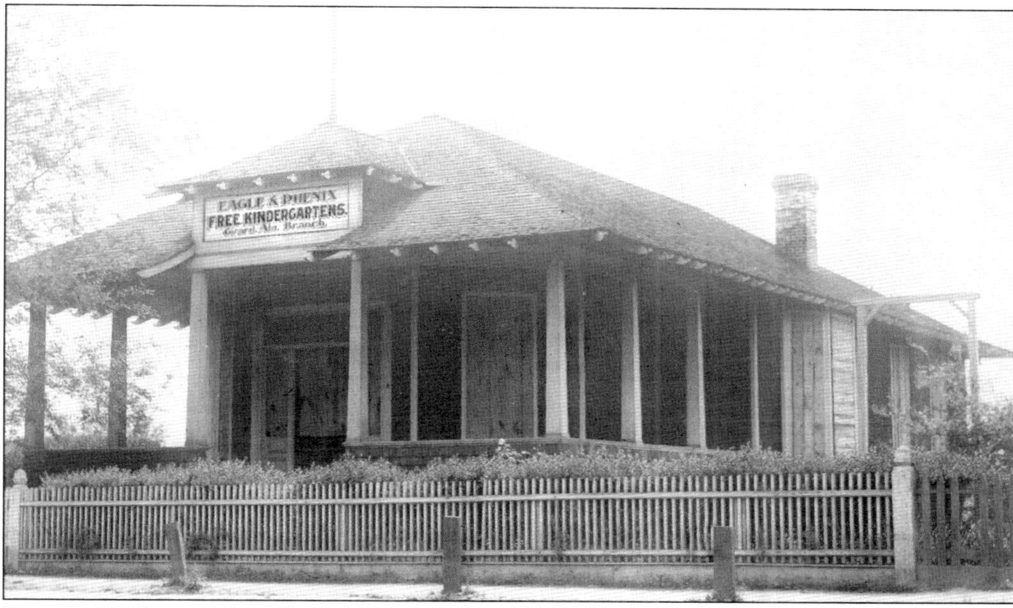

EAGLE AND PHENIX FREE KINDERGARTEN, GIRARD BRANCH. Capitalizing on the success of the Phenix City branch, Eagle and Phenix Mills opened a second branch in Girard. The Girard building accommodated 75 children and contained a large hall, piano alcove, cloakroom, bathroom, and platform with chairs for parents and visitors. (Courtesy Phenix City Public Library.)

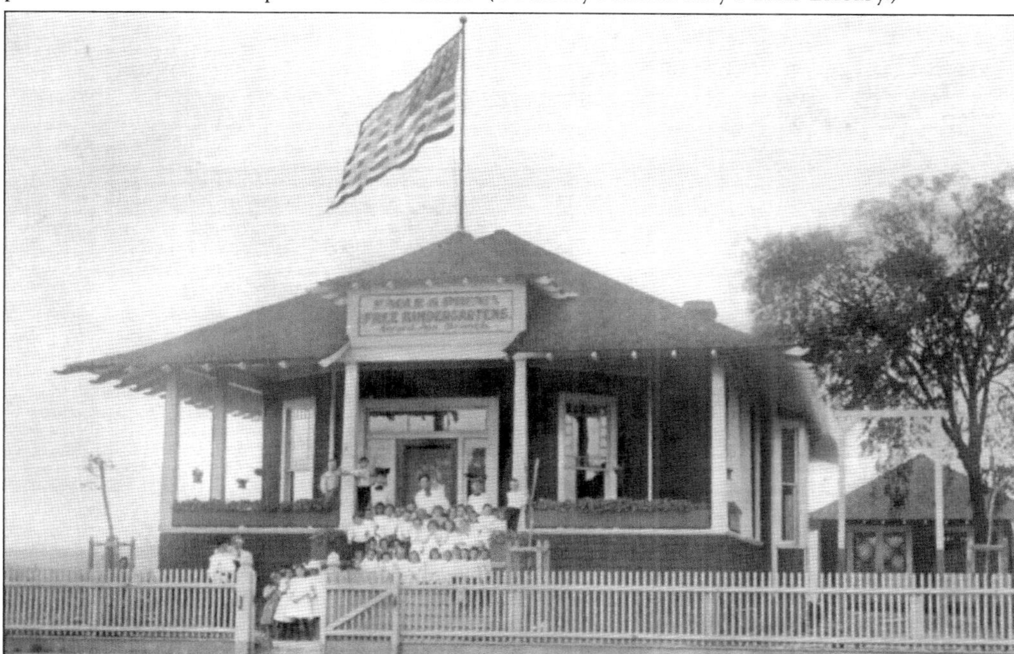

EAGLE AND PHENIX FREE KINDERGARTEN, GIRARD BRANCH. The total expense of the Girard building, including equipment, amounted to over $2,500. Eagle and Phenix Mills operated the Phenix City and Girard branches for $888 per term. Each term lasted eight months. (Courtesy Phenix City Public Library.)

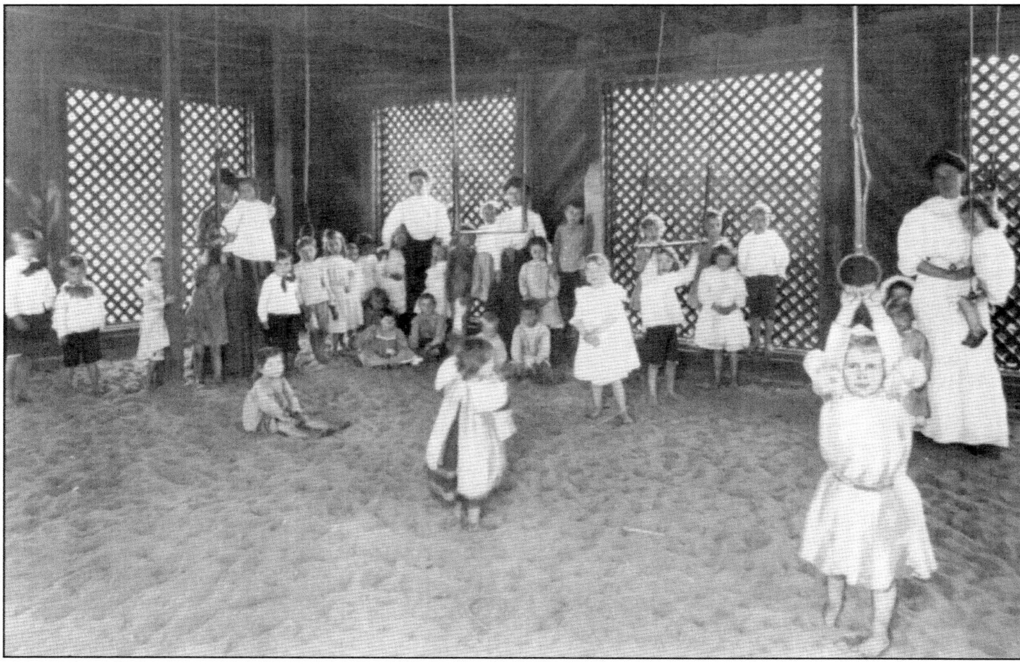

Eagle and Phenix Free Kindergarten Gymnasium. A gymnasium was provided in the yard of the kindergarten for the amusement and physical development of the children. The floor is covered with 8 inches of sand. (Courtesy Phenix City Public Library.)

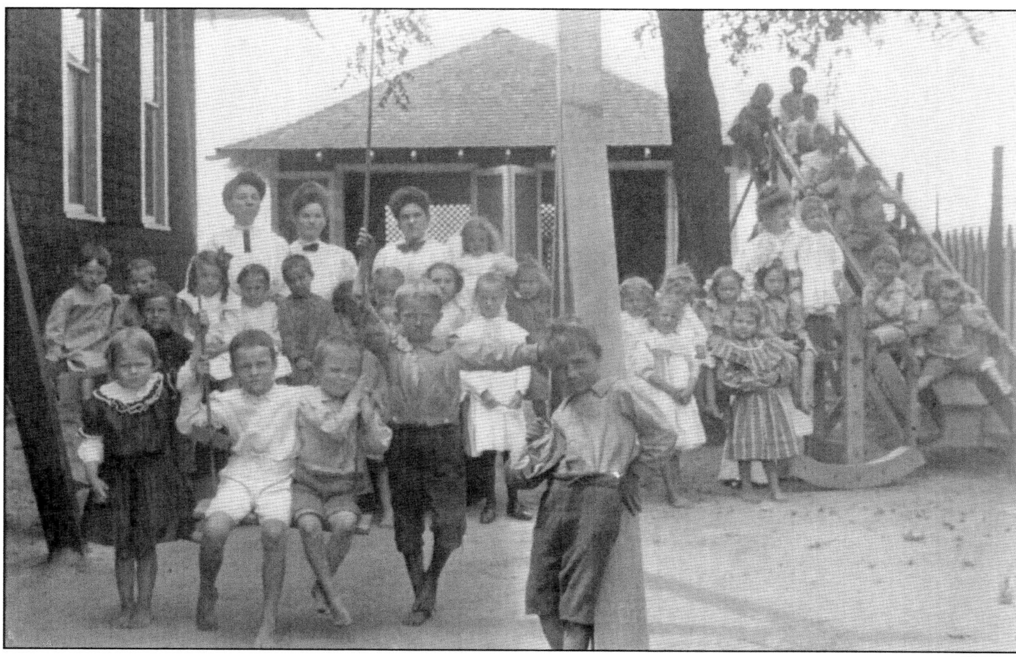

Eagle and Phenix Free Kindergarten Yard. The kindergarten children play on a swing and toboggan behind the gymnasium. (Courtesy Phenix City Public Library.)

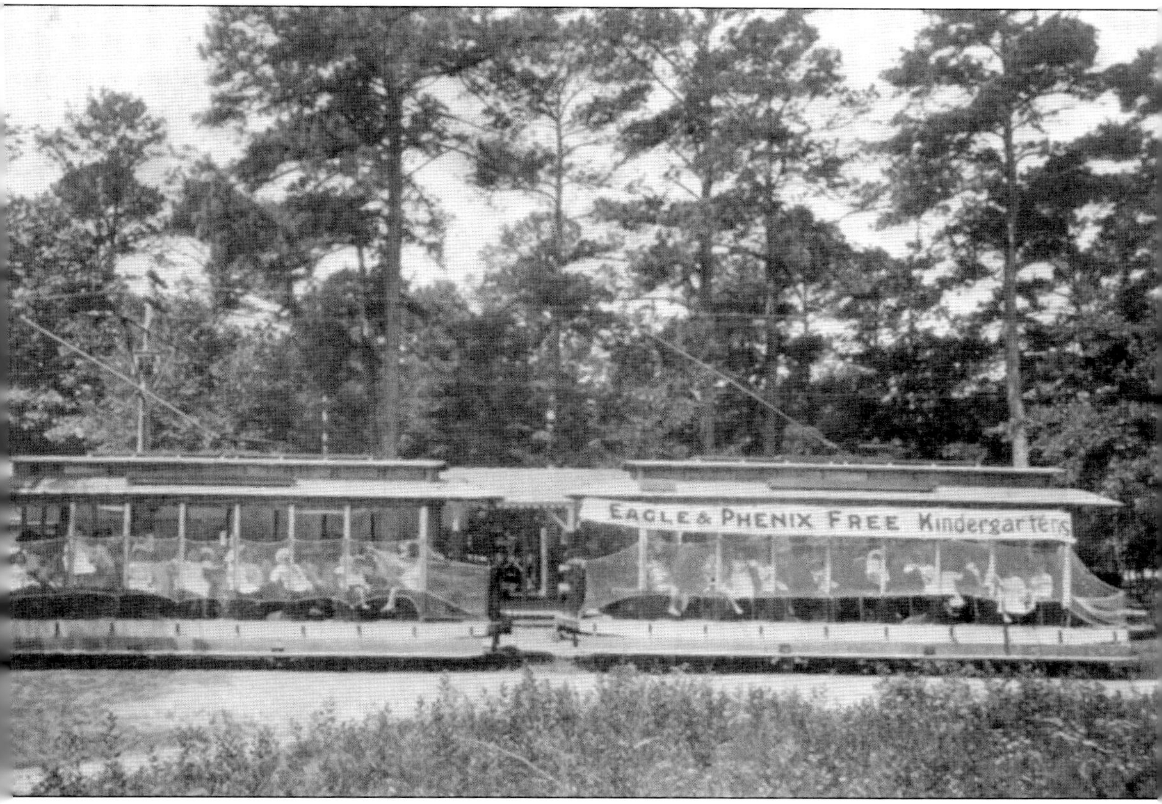

EAGLE AND PHENIX FREE KINDERGARTEN OUTING. This photograph was probably taken at Wildwood Park in Columbus, Georgia. (Courtesy Phenix City Public Library.)

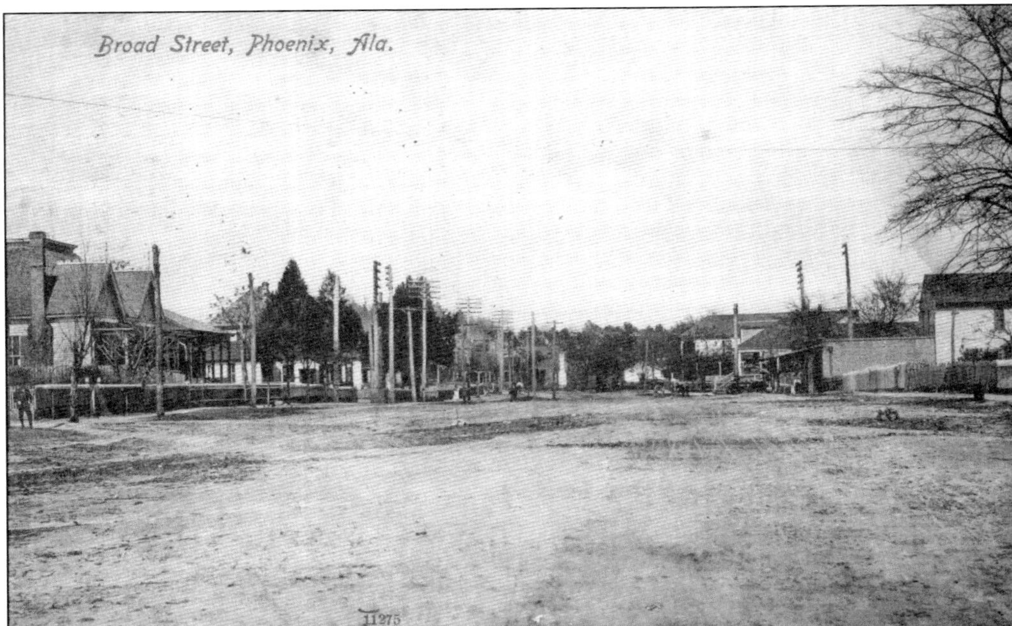

BROAD STREET, PHENIX CITY, ALABAMA, AROUND 1900. Pictured is Flat Crossing at Broad Street, south of Summerville. In 1923, the boundary of Phenix City was extended to include Girard, and the total population was 10,374. (Courtesy Dennis Jones.)

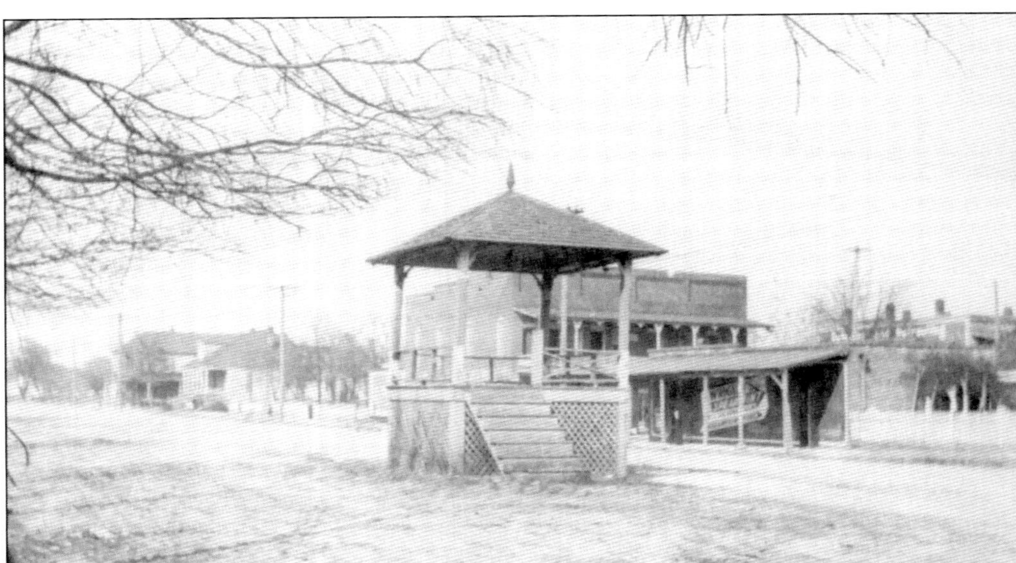

BROAD STREET BANDSTAND. The bandstand on Broad Street was located just south of the Sixteenth Street intersection, almost directly across from St. Patrick's Church. The bandstand on Broad functioned as the town commons and played host to many community celebrations and oratory events. (Courtesy St. Patrick's Church.)

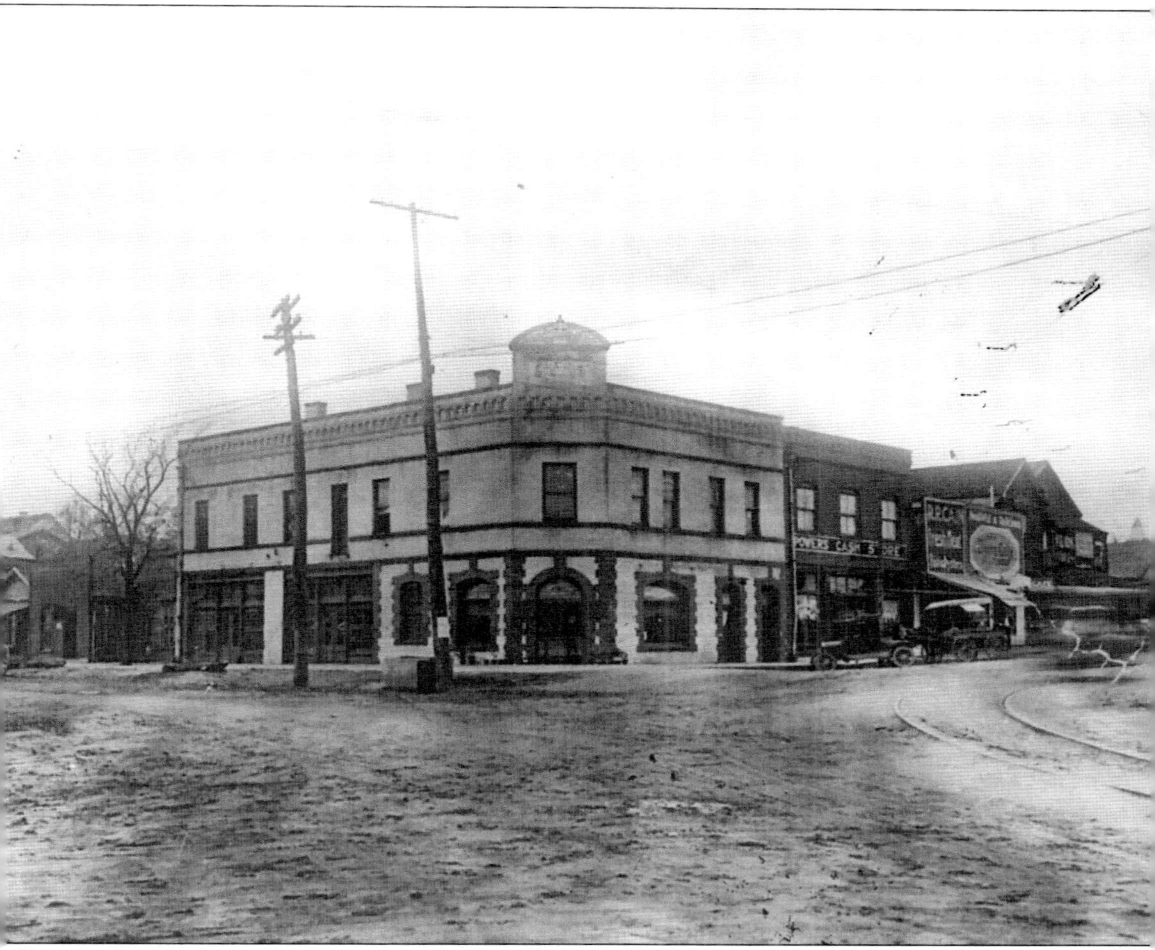

PHENIX-GIRARD BANK, AROUND 1905. Established in 1904, Phenix-Girard Bank served Phenix City and Girard merchants and their banking needs. Until sentiments arose that Columbus banks did not understand their needs, these merchants had conducted banking business in the Georgia city. (Courtesy Columbus Public Library.)

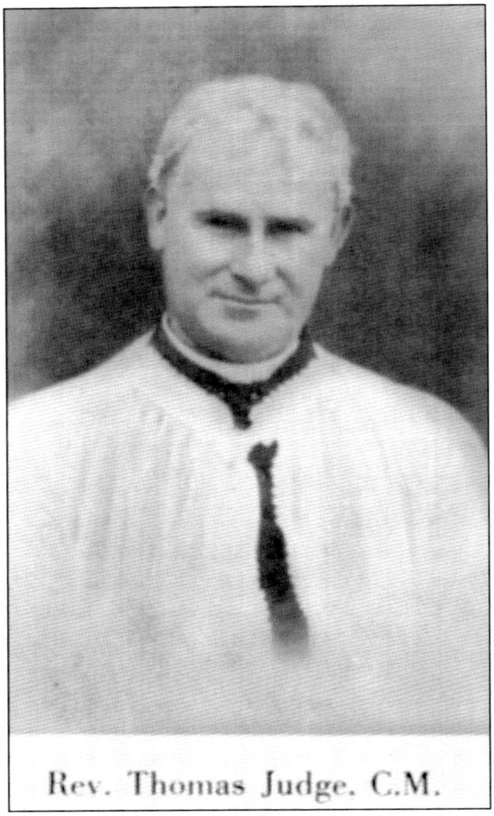

Fr. Thomas A. Judge, C.M. Father Judge (1868–1933) was ordained a priest in 1899. He was sent in 1915 as pastor to the Vincentian mission in Opelika, Alabama, where he attempted to found a school. The openly anti-Catholic hatred proved intractable; in 1916, Judge moved the school to Phenix City, at Flat Crossing on Broad Street. Judge sought the help of the missionary cenacle to operate the school, and six volunteers arrived in January 1916. By 1919, some of the early women volunteers banded together under Father Judge's direction to form a religious community dedicated to the work of the missionary cenacle. They took the title Missionary Servants of the Most Blessed Trinity. (Courtesy St. Patrick's Church.)

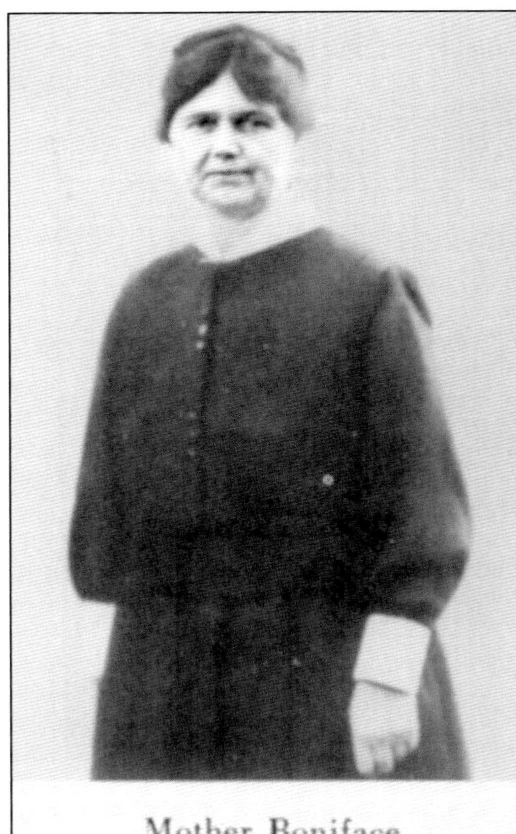

Mother Mary Boniface. Within the cenacle was a young schoolteacher from Butler, Pennsylvania. Louise Margaret Keasey had come south in 1916 to render service to the struggling cenacle and to teach in the mission school in Phenix City. By 1919, she was appointed by Father Judge to be the first general custodian of the new sisters' community and received the name Mother Mary Boniface. (Courtesy St. Patrick's Church.)

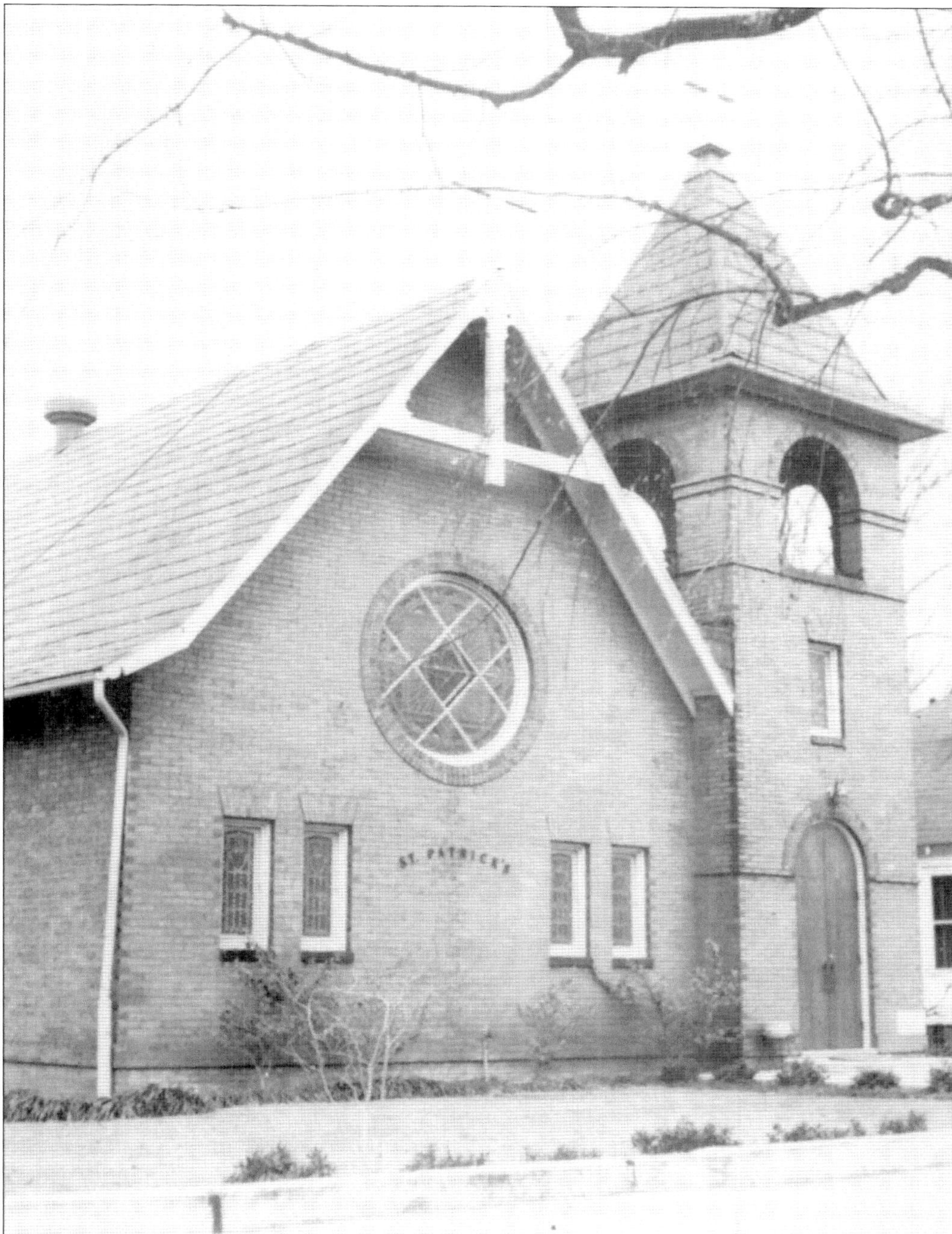

ST. PATRICK'S CHURCH. St. Patrick's Church was established in Phenix City at the urging of Fr. Thomas McDonald, C.M. The Vincentian fathers purchased a lot on Broad Street in early 1911, and construction began July 24. The cornerstone was laid on October 22 and the sanctuary dedicated on November 5, 1911. St. Patrick's was served by priests residing in Opelika, Alabama. They traveled by rail to conduct Sunday services and the administration of the sacraments. (Courtesy Freda Page.)

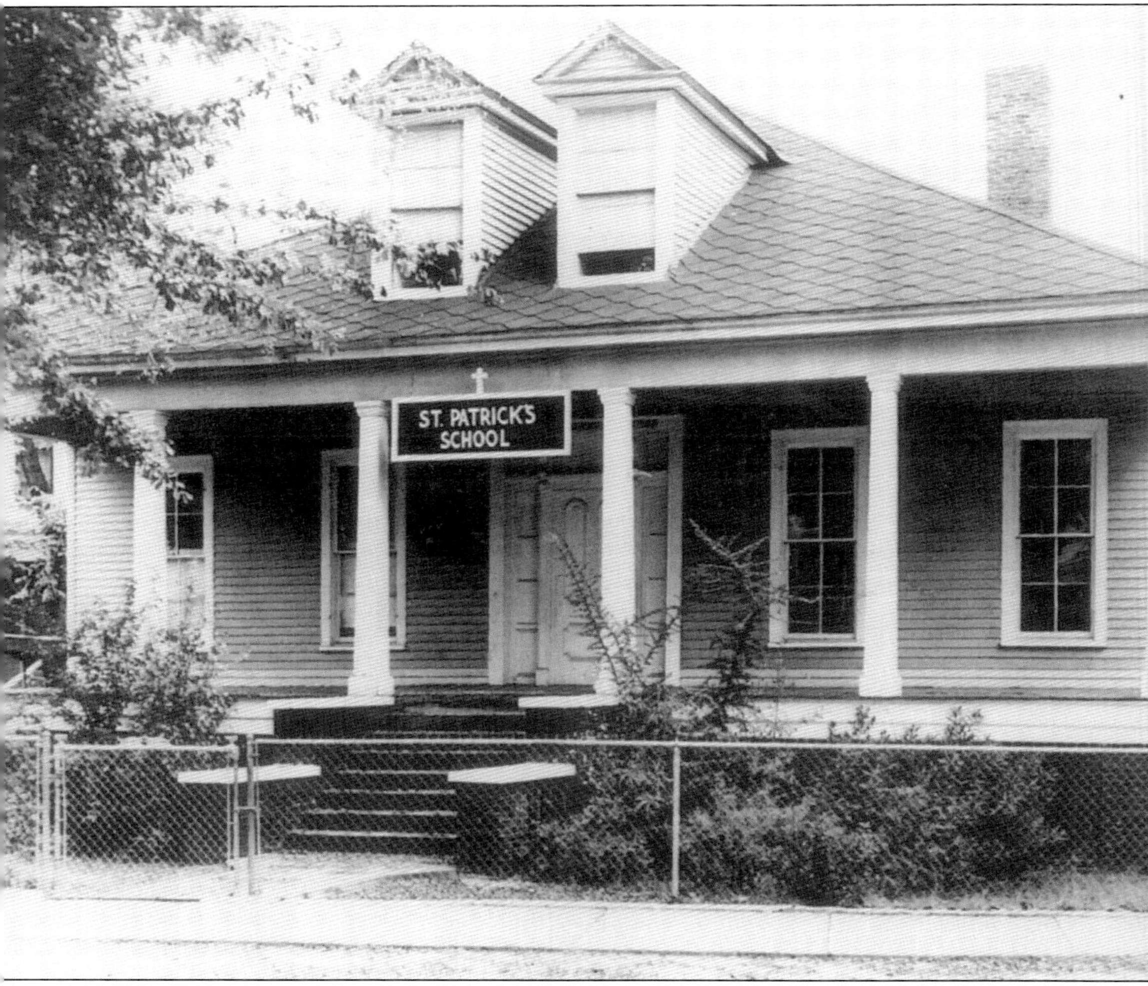

St. Patrick's School. In 1916, St. Patrick's School opened as an extension of the missionary work of Father Judge. Two houses on Broad Street were purchased in 1917 and 1920 and served as the school and a home for the sisters. (Courtesy Freda Page.)

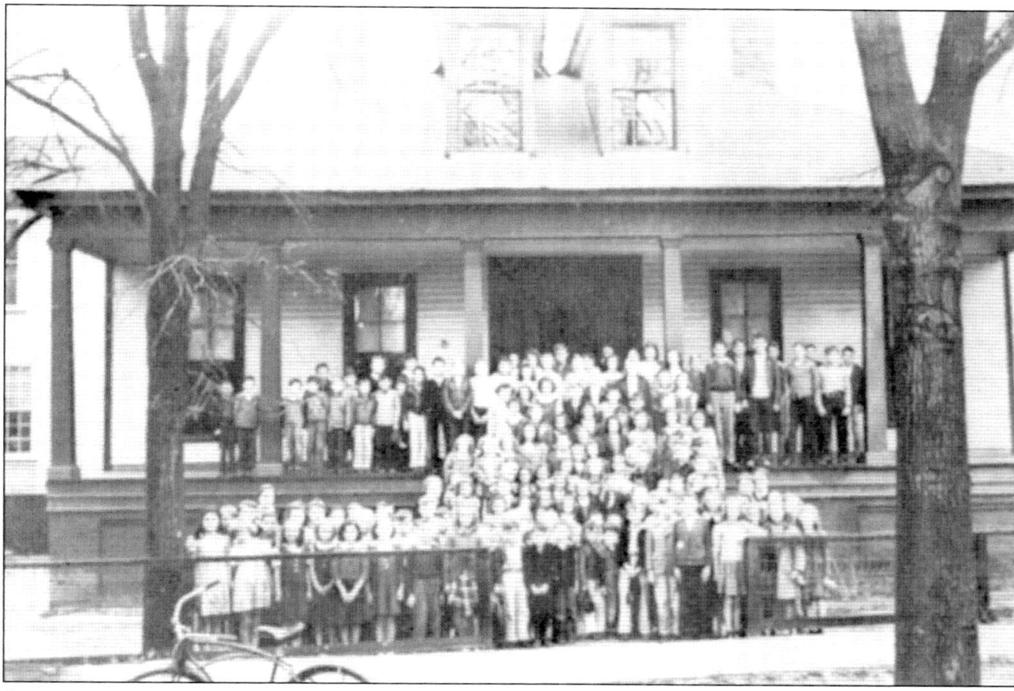

Students at St. Patrick's Academy School. Students were initially the dinner-toters who carried meals to the mill workers. These children missed a considerable amount of school, and most did not attend at all. St. Patrick's School understood the mill families' dependence on the dinner-toters and accommodated their schedules. The children were dismissed at 11:30 a.m. and returned to complete their studies as their schedule permitted; most were back by late afternoon. (Courtesy Freda Page.)

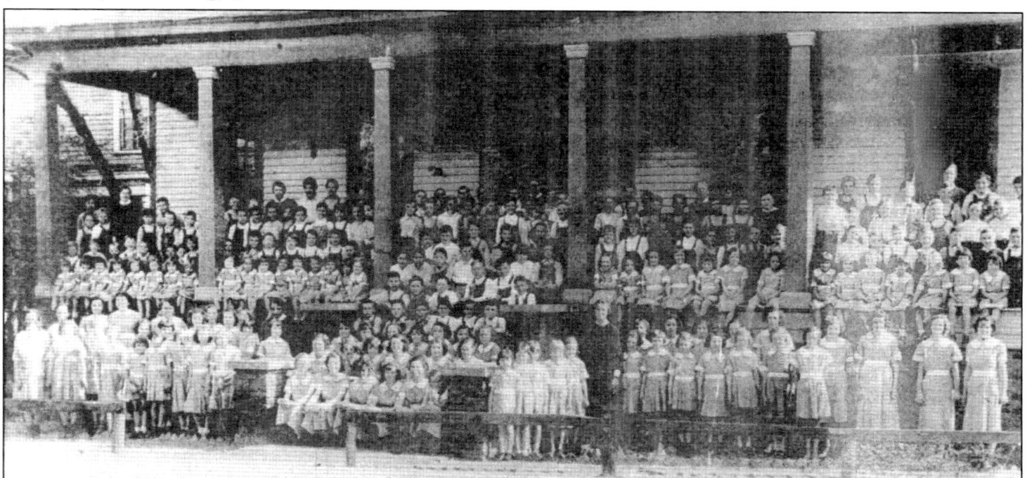

St. Patrick's Academy School Annex, Around 1925. St. Patrick's School opened with three students. As prejudice and suspicion of the Catholics waned, the school's total enrollment increased each year. By 1922, it reported an average attendance of 300 students. It was estimated that over 90 percent of St. Patrick's students were non-Catholic. The school was eventually moved to Lakewood Drive in 1942. (Courtesy Freda Page.)

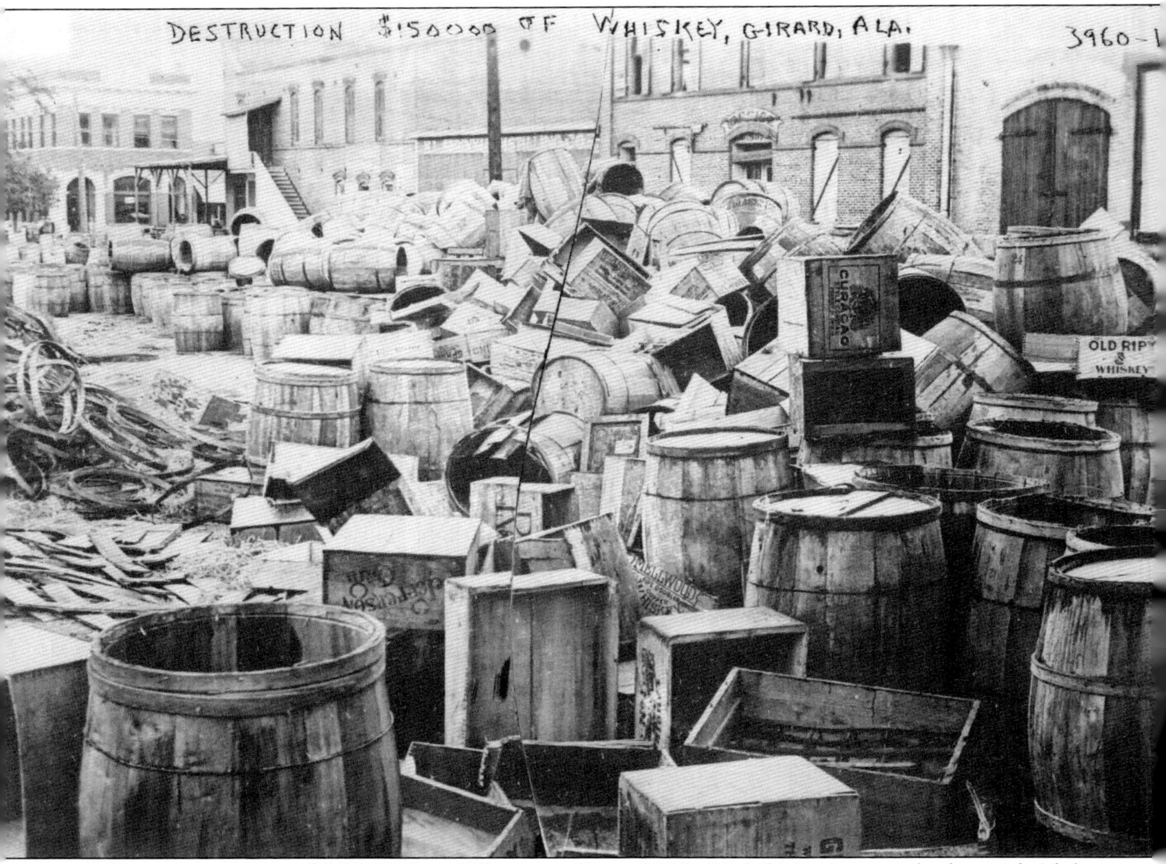

Destruction of $150,000 of Whiskey. From 1909, Prohibitionists worked to rid Alabama and Russell County of whiskey. In 1914, the faction gained control of the Alabama legislature. The following year, Alabama passed a law that outlawed the manufacture and sale of alcoholic beverages. Within Girard, one legal distillery and two whiskey warehouses operated. Girard's whiskey trade supported two financial institutions and countless farmers in Russell County. The economic impact proved too great for city officials to enforce the law. Girard ignored Prohibition and remained wet by local option. The Citizen's Bank, established to service the whiskey district, can be seen in the upper left corner. (Courtesy Library of Congress.)

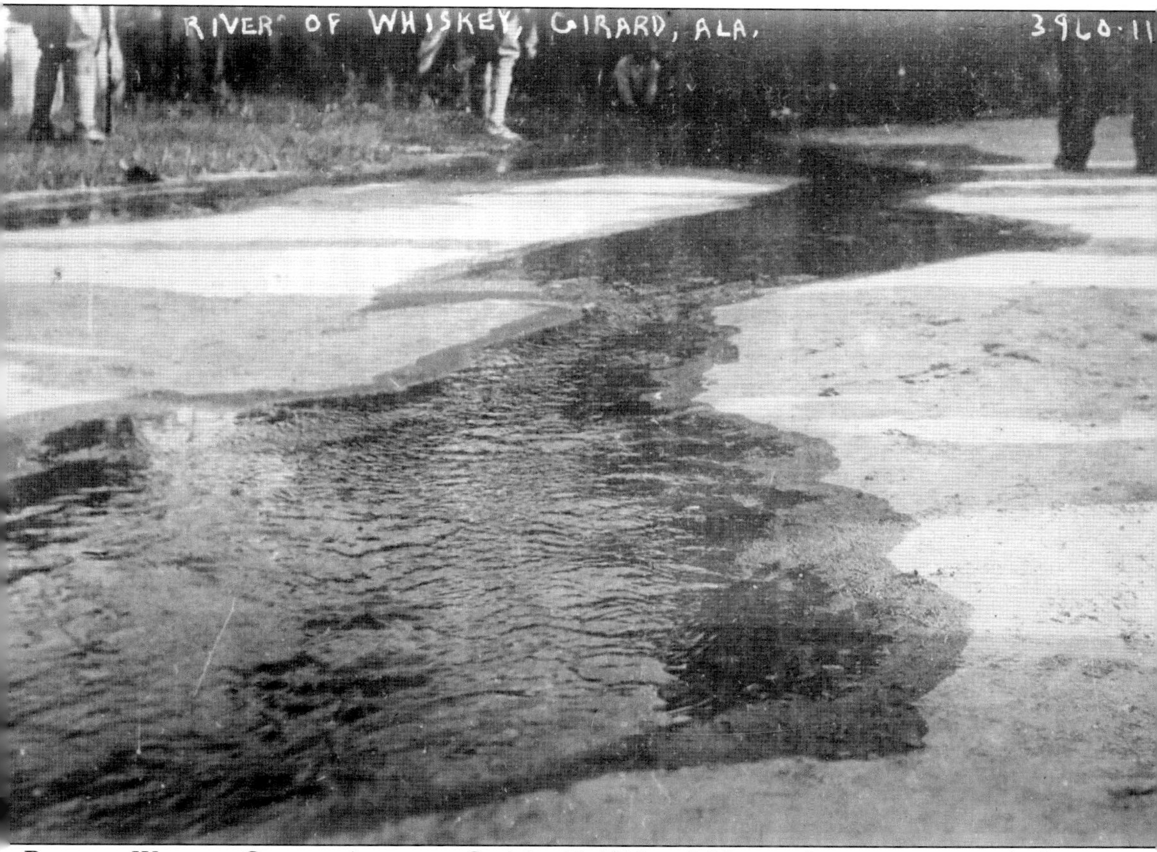

River of Whiskey, Girard, Alabama. On May 17, 1916, at 8:00 a.m., the attorney general of Alabama, William Logan Martin, sent deputies on a special train to enforce Alabama's prohibition laws in Girard. The deputies executed 12 search warrants and found huge quantities of liquor in eight. Following weeks of grand jury testimony, the destruction of the liquor seizure was ordered on August 10. An estimated 4,000 people viewed the destruction. The cleanup ended with compliance to Prohibition, the impeachment of Russell County sheriff Pat M. Danzel, and the resignation of Girard's mayor and all five aldermen. (Courtesy Library of Congress.)

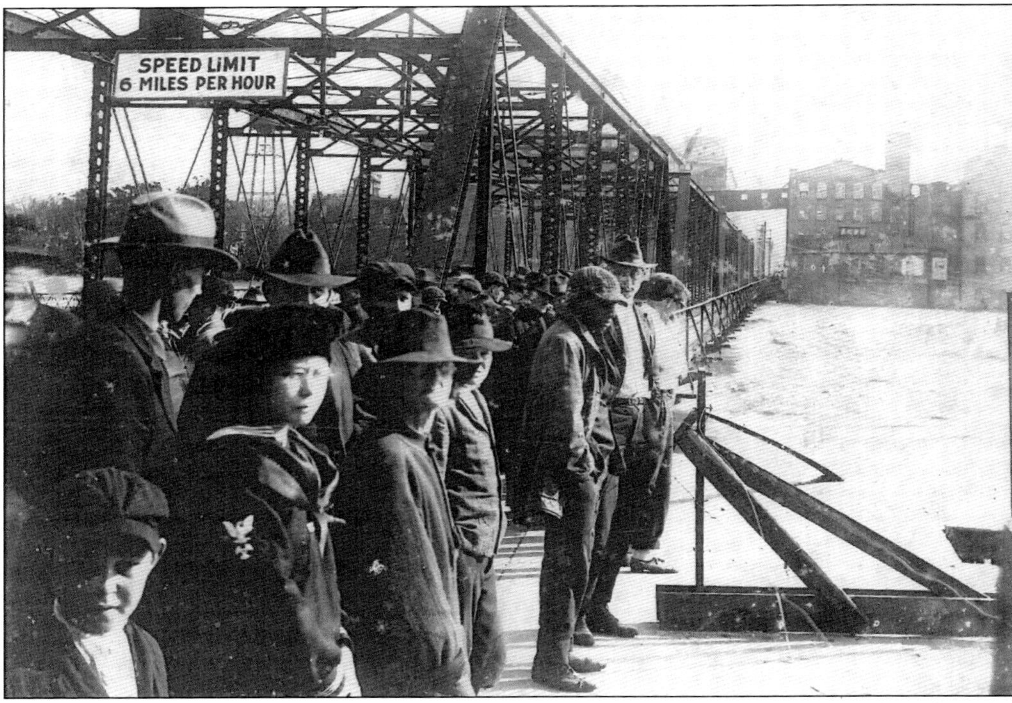

FOURTEENTH STREET BRIDGE FLOOD, 1919. Spectators watch in amazement as the Chattahoochee River rushes under the Fourteenth Street Bridge in Phenix City. The December 1919 flood caused considerably more damage in the Girard section. Phenix City is situated on much higher ground. However, the Fourteenth Street Bridge was destroyed by floods on two separate occasions—in 1841 and 1902. (Courtesy Sean Driggers.)

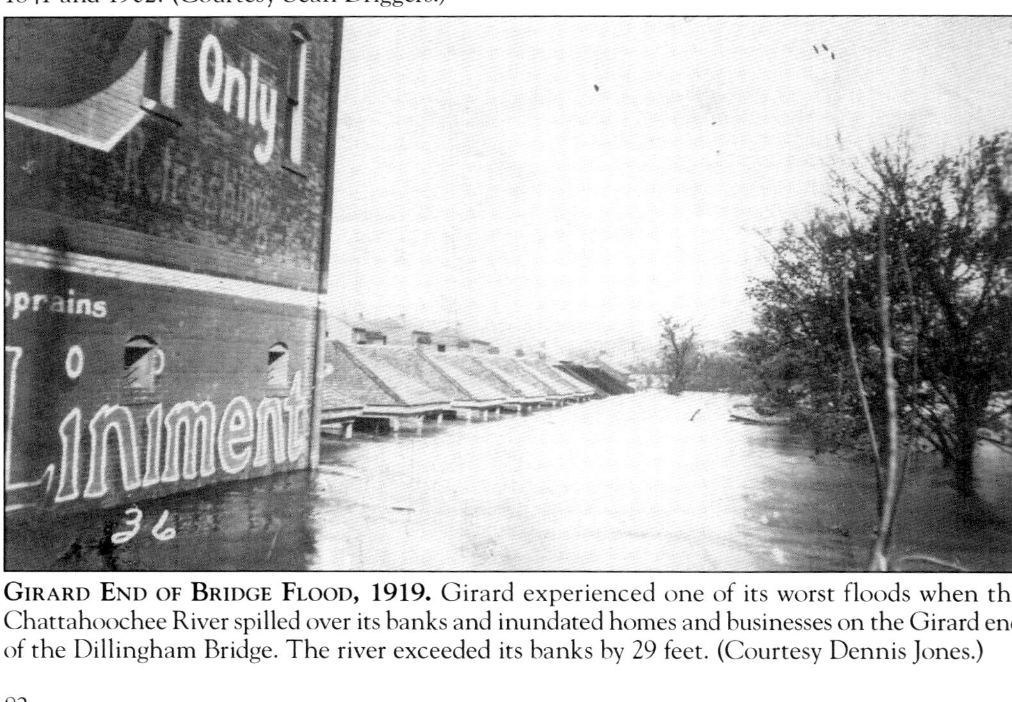

GIRARD END OF BRIDGE FLOOD, 1919. Girard experienced one of its worst floods when the Chattahoochee River spilled over its banks and inundated homes and businesses on the Girard end of the Dillingham Bridge. The river exceeded its banks by 29 feet. (Courtesy Dennis Jones.)

Five

THE NEW SOUTH 1920–1953

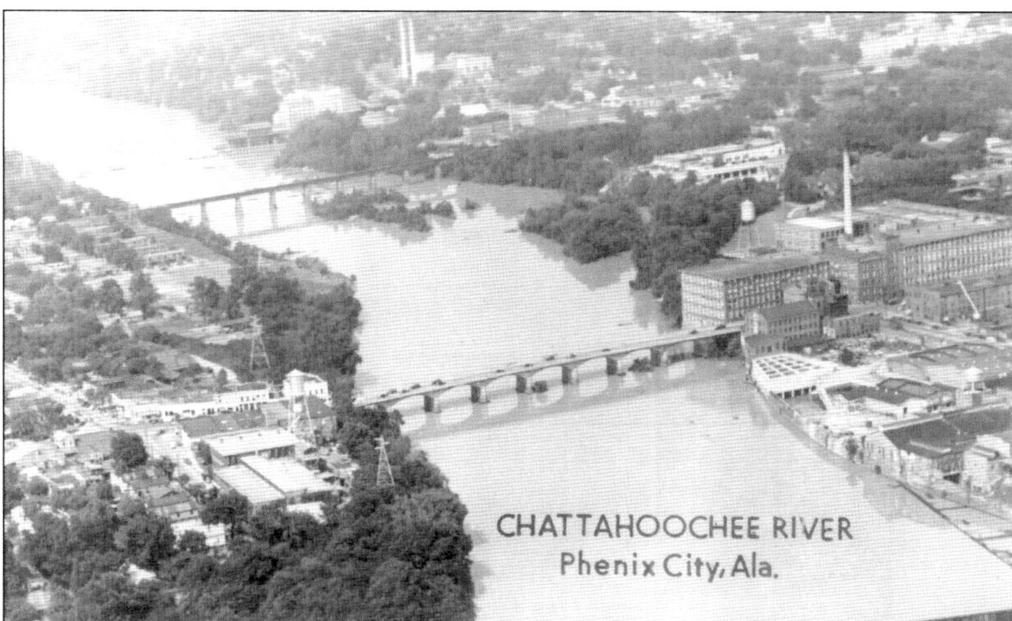

CHATTAHOOCHEE RIVER, PHENIX CITY, ALABAMA. Phenix City entered the 1920s as a rural, agrarian suburb of Columbus, Georgia, but the next three decades brought change. Urbanization, the Depression, World War II, and organized crime changed Phenix City for both better and worse. (Courtesy Dennis Jones.)

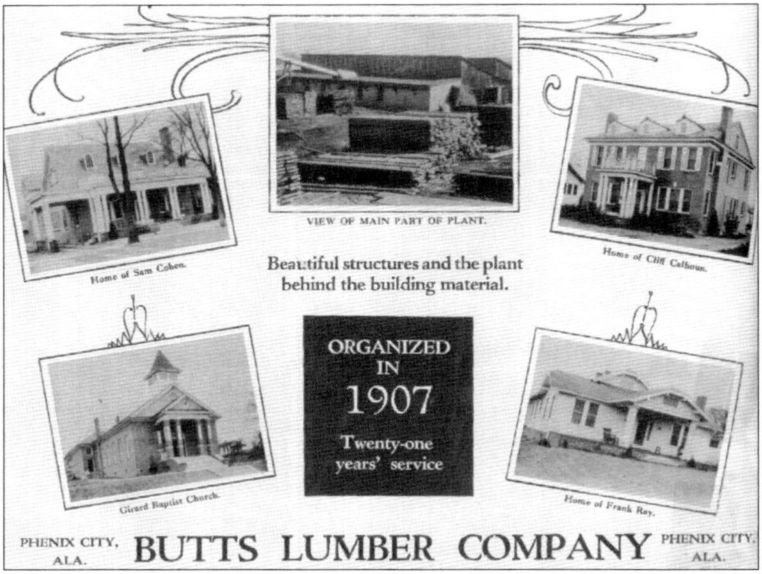

BUTTS LUMBER MILL. The Butts Lumber Mill, founded in 1907, played a role in the construction boom of the 1920s. Pictured in this advertisement is a view of the main part of the plant, Girard Baptist Church, and recent residential constructions. (Courtesy Columbus Public Library.)

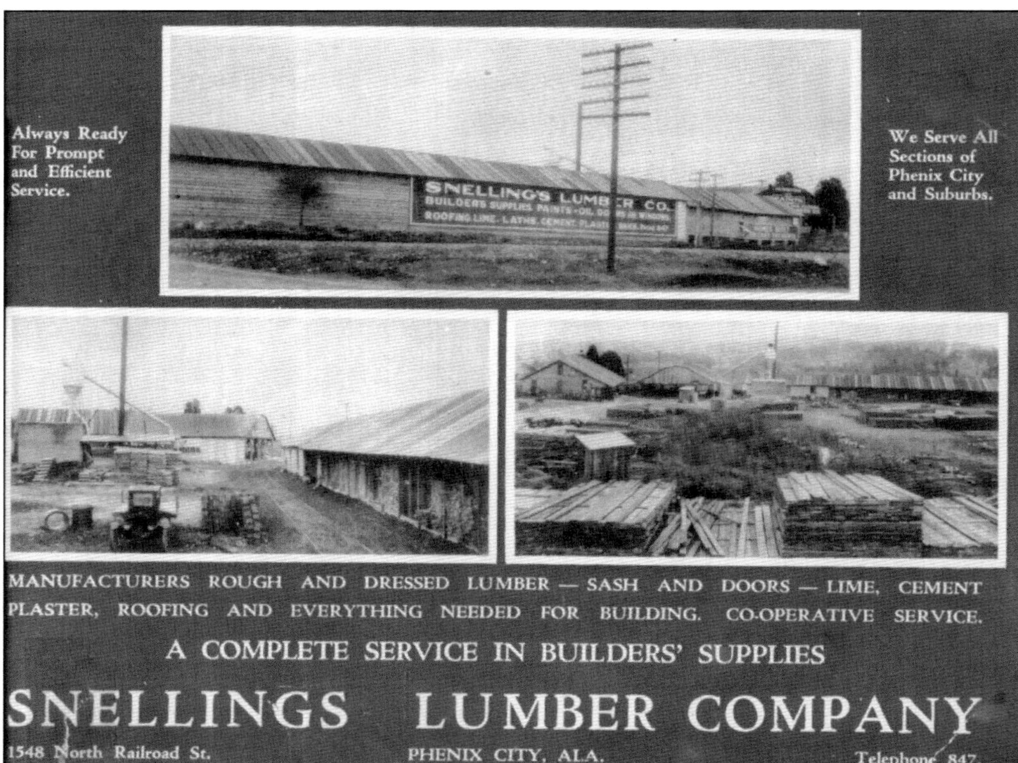

SNELLINGS LUMBER COMPANY. Like Butts Lumber Mill, Snellings was instrumental in Phenix City's construction boom. In addition to providing building supplies, Snellings developed residential neighborhoods off Summerville Road. Pictured in the advertisement are views of the lumberyard and warehouse. (Courtesy Columbus Public Library.)

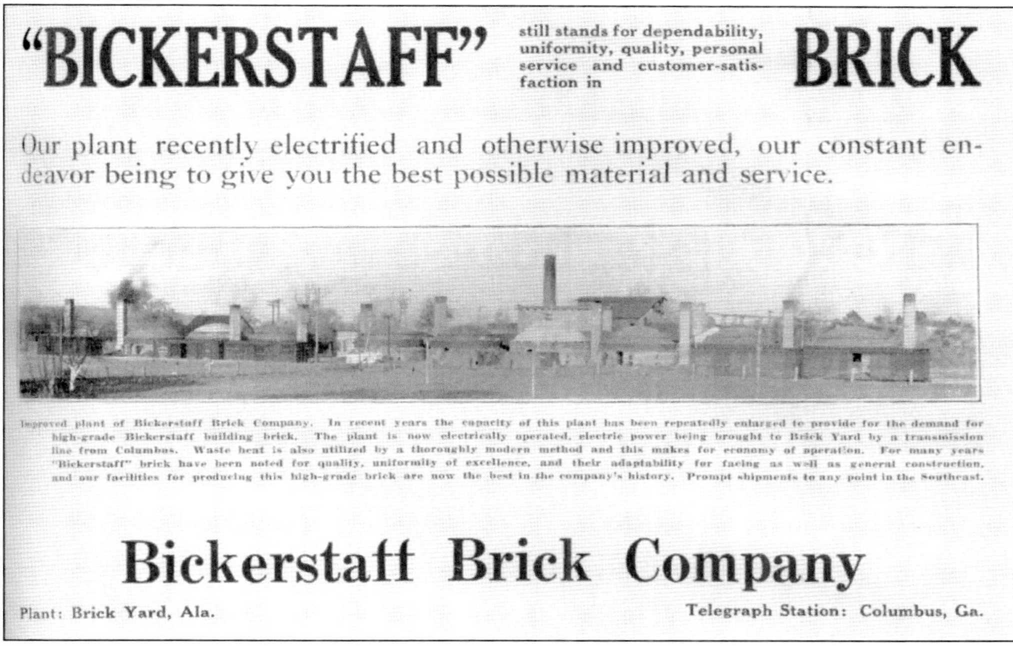

BICKERSTAFF BRICK COMPANY. The Bickerstaff Brick Company was founded in 1879 by August Howard Bickerstaff and William Jefferson Bickerstaff. The brothers rented the Abercrombie Brickyard just south of Girard. Pictured are the kilns and boxcars. Many of the company's operatives lived in the communities of Bryke and Brickyard. Both were stations of the Central of Georgia Railroad and located just below Girard. (Courtesy Columbus Public Library.)

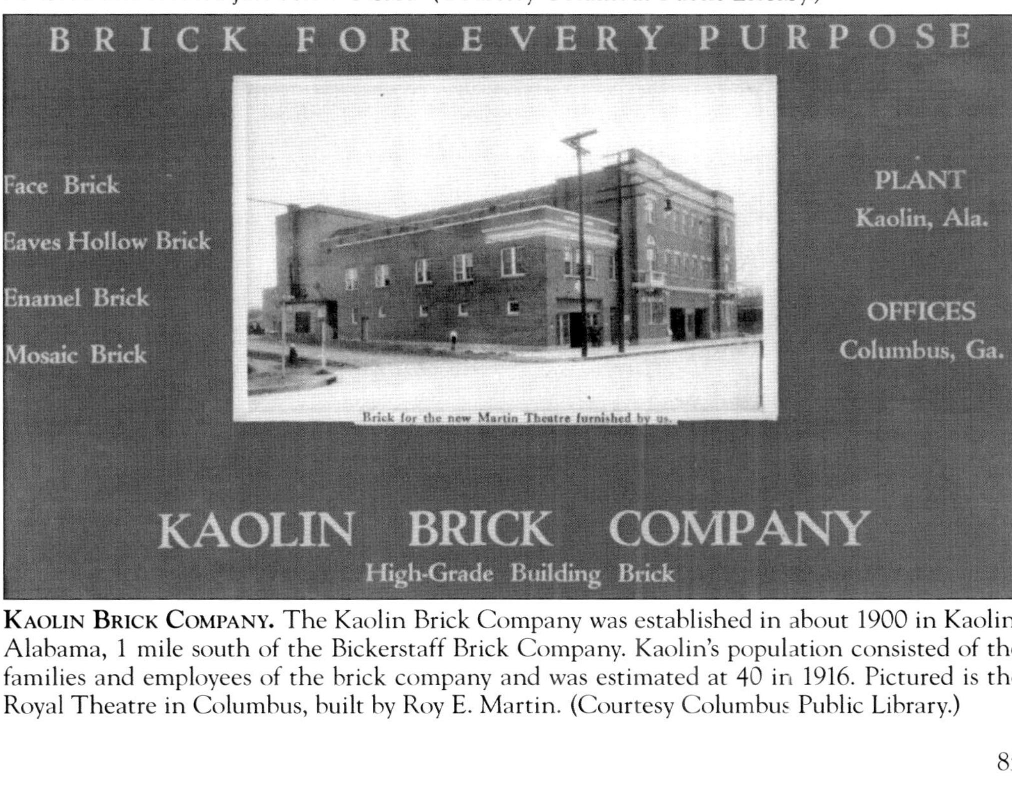

KAOLIN BRICK COMPANY. The Kaolin Brick Company was established in about 1900 in Kaolin, Alabama, 1 mile south of the Bickerstaff Brick Company. Kaolin's population consisted of the families and employees of the brick company and was estimated at 40 in 1916. Pictured is the Royal Theatre in Columbus, built by Roy E. Martin. (Courtesy Columbus Public Library.)

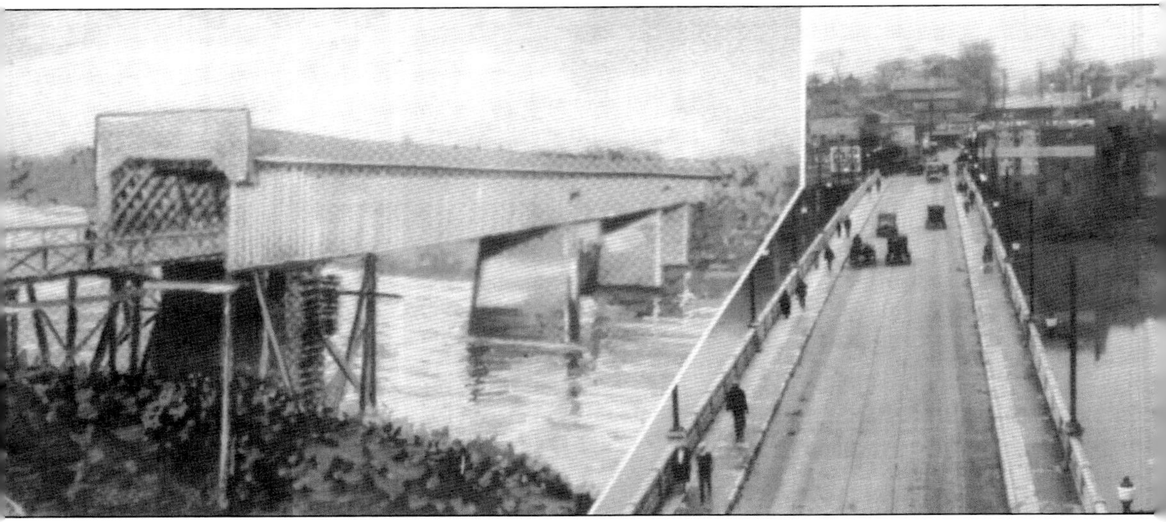

SPLIT VIEW, FOURTEENTH STREET BRIDGE. The Fourteenth Street Bridge is one of the most iconic images of both Phenix City and Columbus. Presented in a split view, the 1858 Horace King construction is compared to the 1902 concrete bridge erected by the Hardaway Company. (Courtesy Columbus Public Library.)

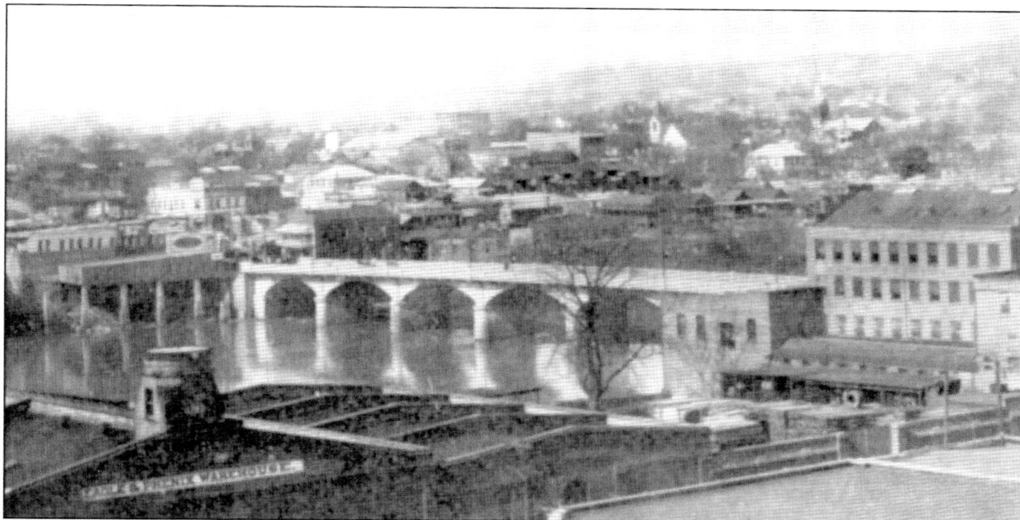

Glimpse of Phenix City, Around 1915. Pictured is a bird's-eye view from the Swift Kyle building of Phenix City. The Eagle and Phenix warehouses are in the foreground. At right is the original Muscogee Manufacturing Company. In the center is the Fourteenth Street Bridge. The steeples of Trinity United Methodist Church and First Baptist Church are in the distance to the right. (Courtesy Columbus Public Library.)

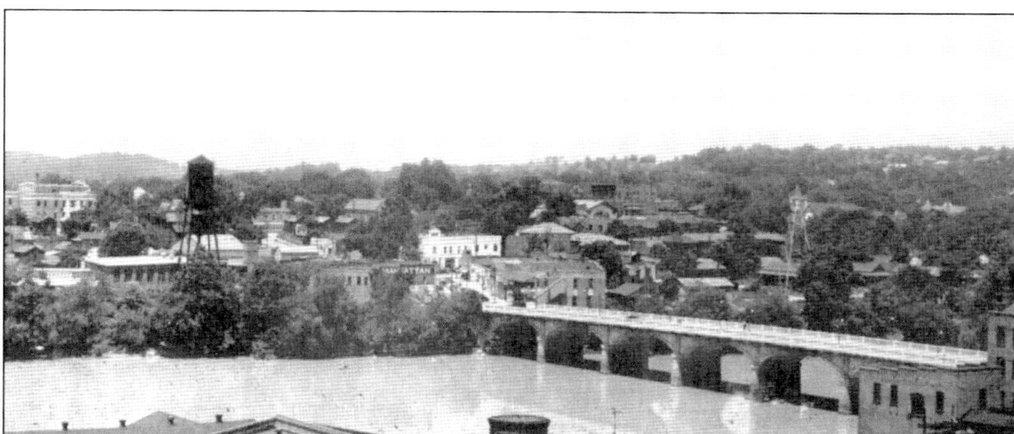

Glimpse of Phenix City, Around 1940. Pictured is another bird's-eye view of Phenix City from the Swift Kyle building. At left in the distance is the Russell County Courthouse. In the center is the Fourteenth Street Bridge. Signs of vice have emerged. The Manhattan's billboard can be seen at the foot of the bridge. The Manhattan was Phenix City's largest lottery. (Courtesy Columbus Public Library.)

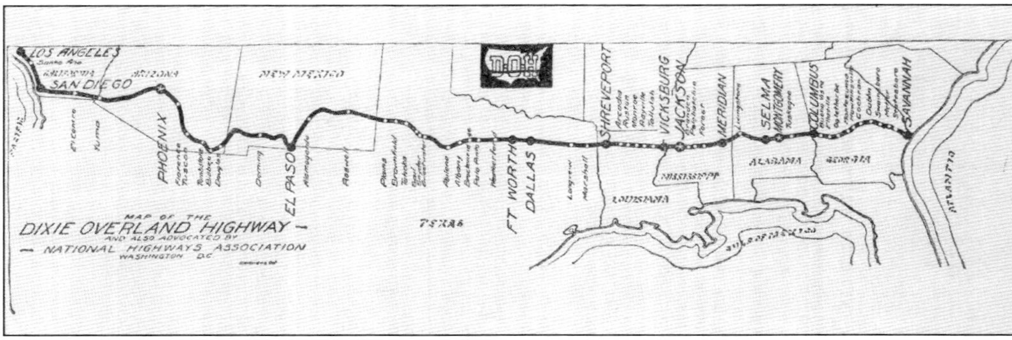

DIXIE OVERLAND HIGHWAY. Formed after a path-finding trip from Savannah to Columbus by the Automobile Club of Savannah, the Dixie Overland Highway Association campaigned for good roads. The Good Road Movement was organized to improve economic development by expanding and upgrading highways. The Dixie Overland Highway traversed a total of 2,726 miles from Savannah, Georgia, to San Diego, California. In 1927, the route was renamed U.S. Highway 80. (Courtesy Columbus State University Archives.)

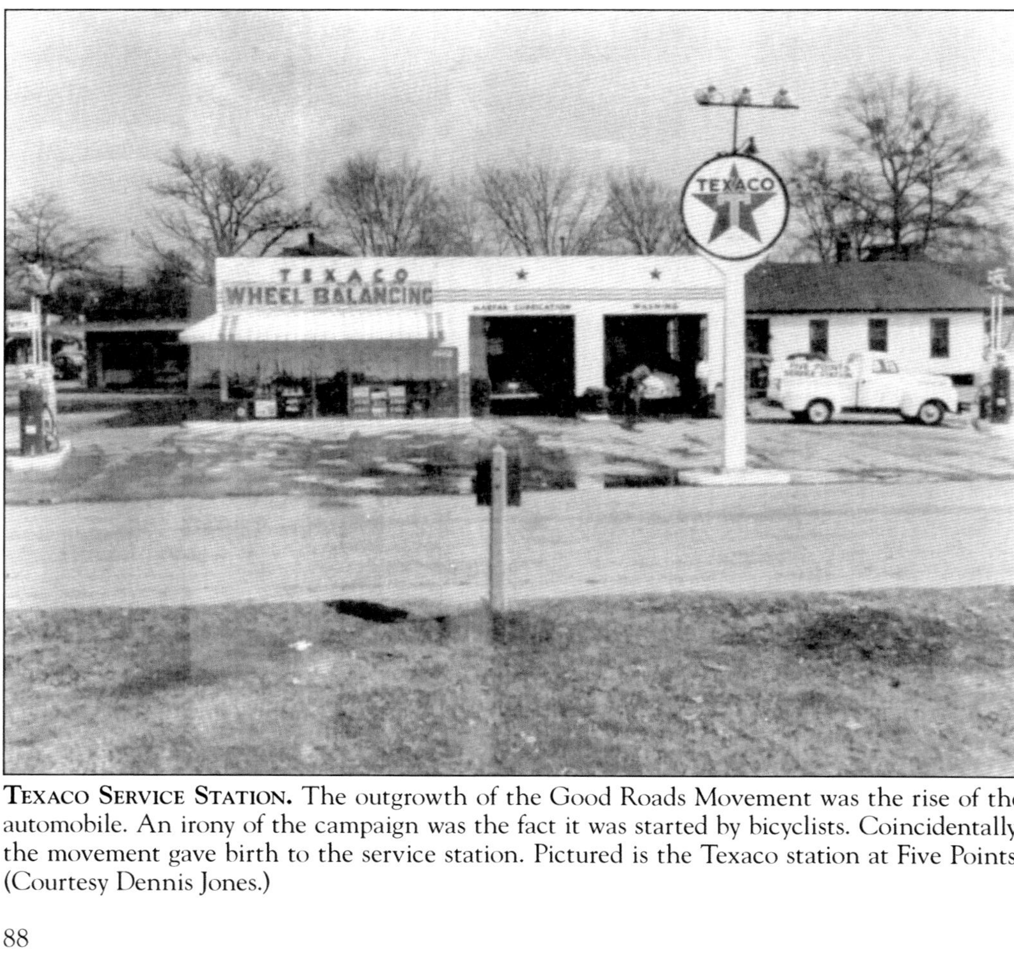

TEXACO SERVICE STATION. The outgrowth of the Good Roads Movement was the rise of the automobile. An irony of the campaign was the fact it was started by bicyclists. Coincidentally, the movement gave birth to the service station. Pictured is the Texaco station at Five Points. (Courtesy Dennis Jones.)

Brown's Service Station Advertisement. Brown's Service Station styled itself as a full-service auto laundry. (Courtesy Columbus Public Library.)

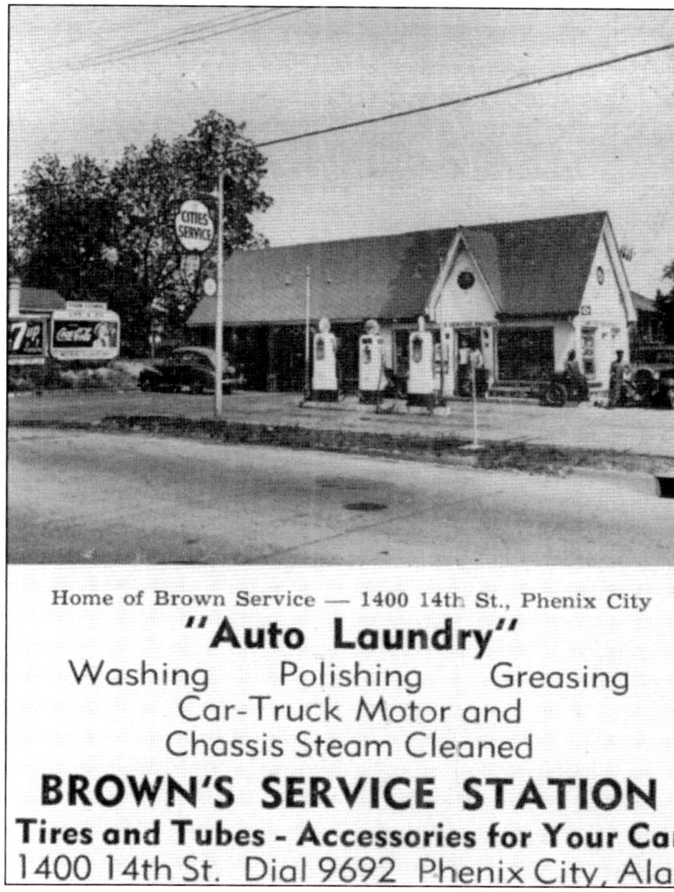

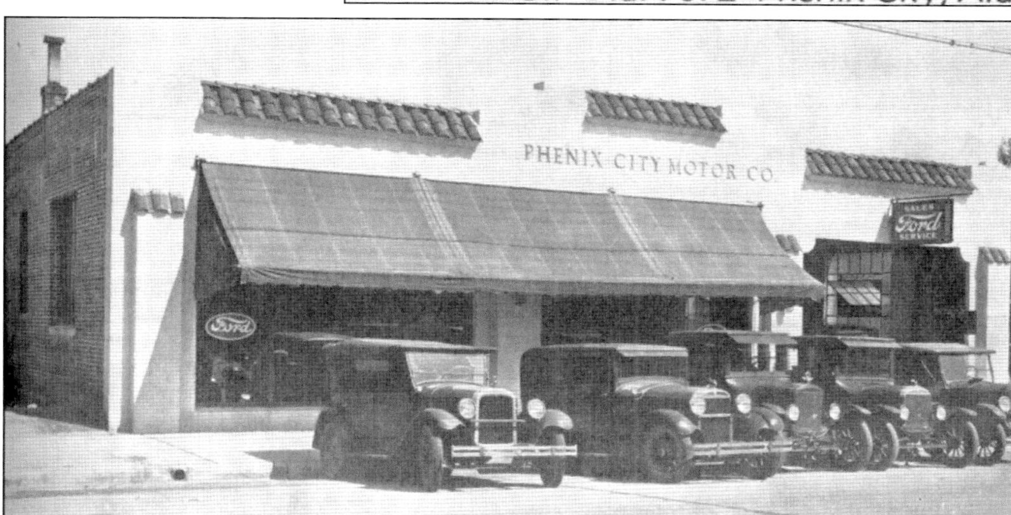

Phenix City Motor Company. The Phenix City Motor Company was one of the town's first auto dealers. Established in 1929, the Ford dealership signaled the dawn of the automobile age. (Courtesy Columbus Public Library.)

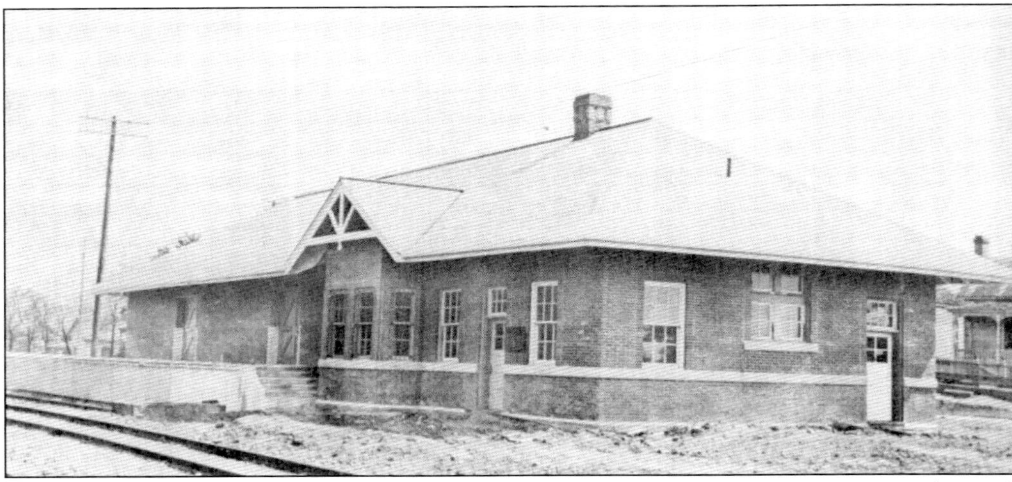

PHENIX CITY RAILWAY DEPOT. The Phenix City Depot, formally Knights Station, was located on South Railroad Street. A stop on the Central of Georgia Railway, the station was rebuilt in 1925 by Williams Lumber Company at a cost of $15,000. (Courtesy Columbus Public Library.)

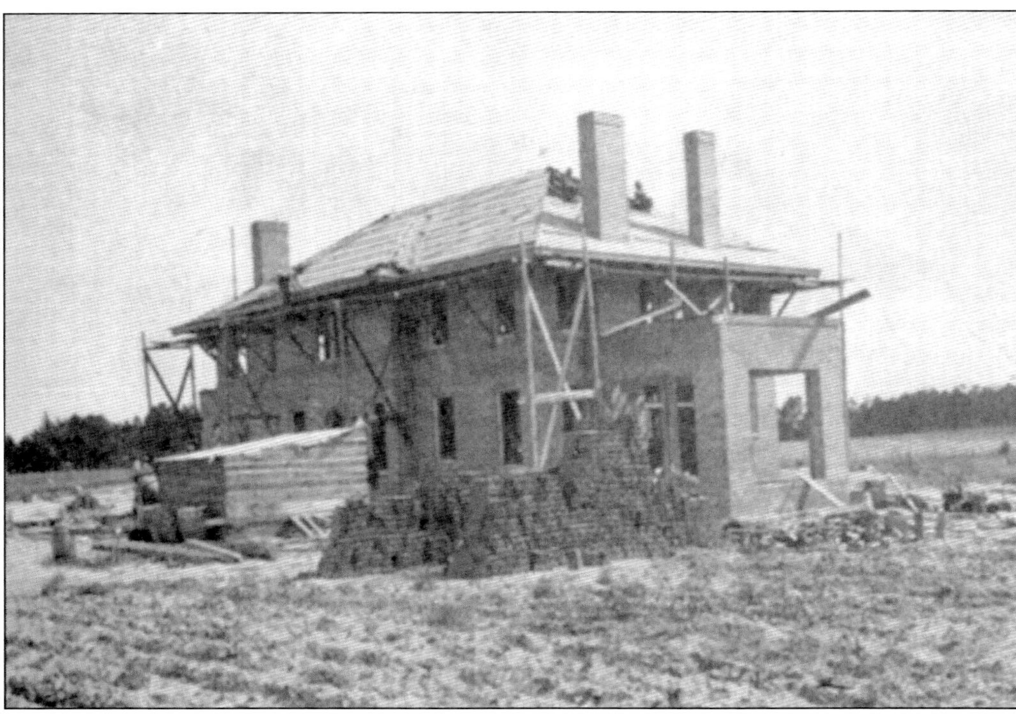

SNELLINGS HOME. The home of Frank J. Snellings is shown during construction in 1927. The Snellings home is one example of the construction boom that occurred in Phenix City prior to the Depression. The Summerville district of the city developed at a rapid pace. (Courtesy Columbus Public Library.)

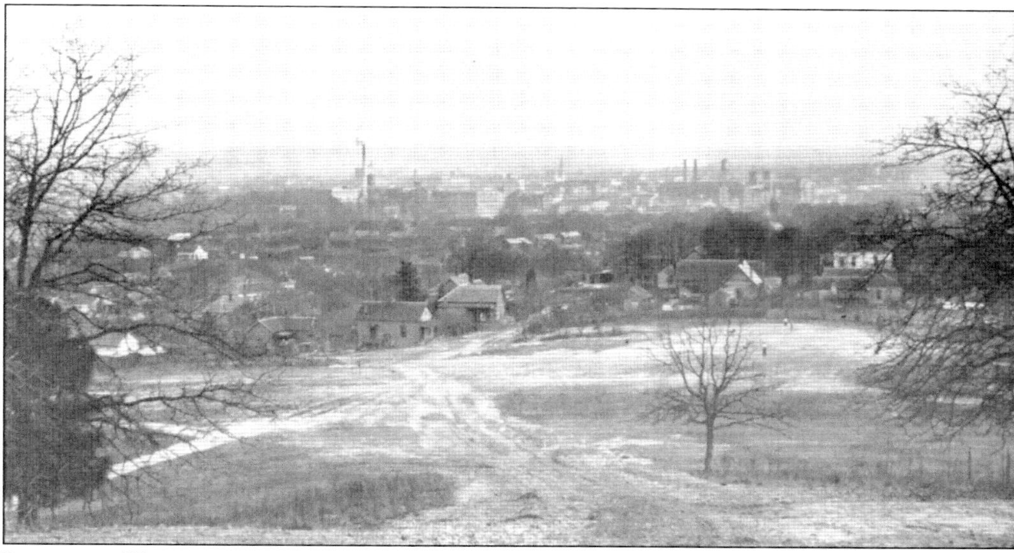

Ingersoll Hill. The industrial might of Columbus is seen from this commanding view on Ingersoll's Hill. (Courtesy Columbus Public Library.)

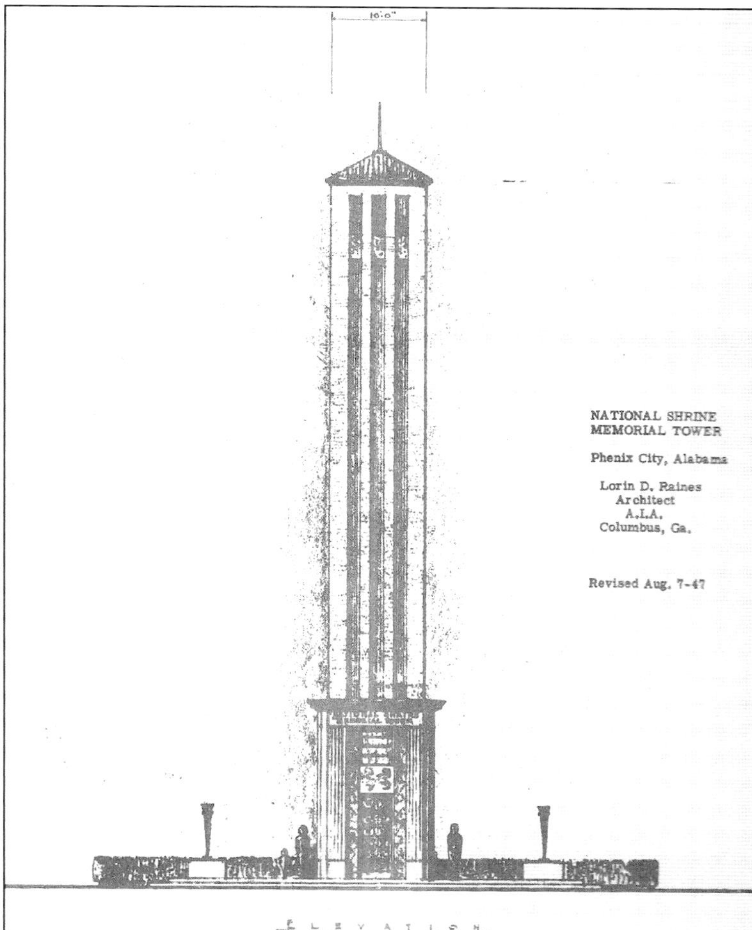

Confederate Memorial Tower. Ingersoll Hill is often commemorated as the scene of the last major battle of the Civil War. Plans were made to establish a Confederate memorial tower. Although Roy Martin deeded the land to the United Daughters of the Confederacy, the plans were never realized. The monument was to be a 100-foot bell tower. (Courtesy Columbus Public Library.)

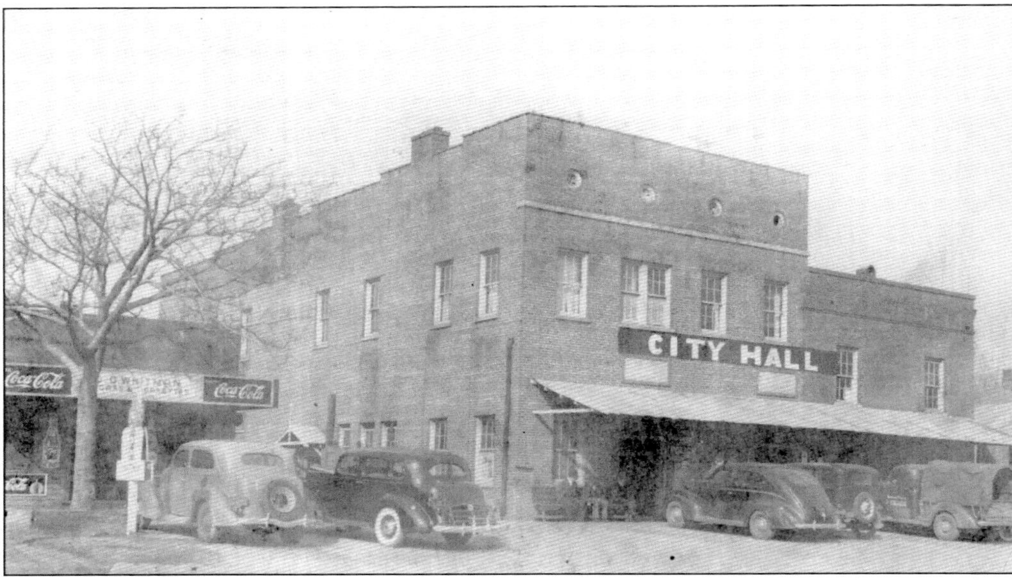

City Hall. In 1927, a two-story brick addition was completed to the original structure built in 1910. The expansion provided offices for city commissioners and a headquarters for the fire department. (Courtesy Dennis Jones.)

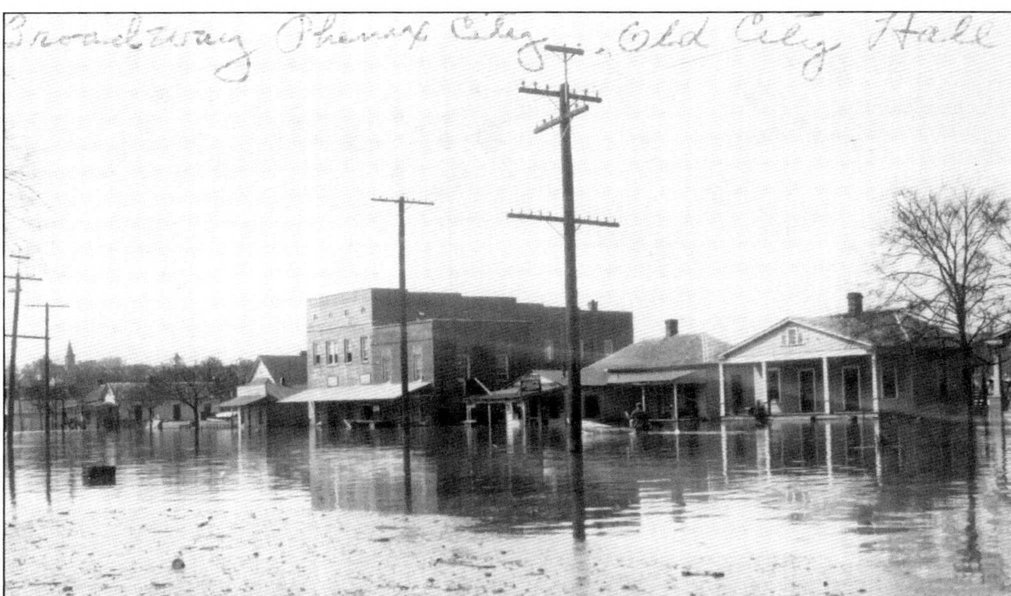

Broadway, Phenix City Hall. In 1929, the Chattahoochee River crested its banks. A man navigates the swollen river in his canoe. (Courtesy Dennis Jones.)

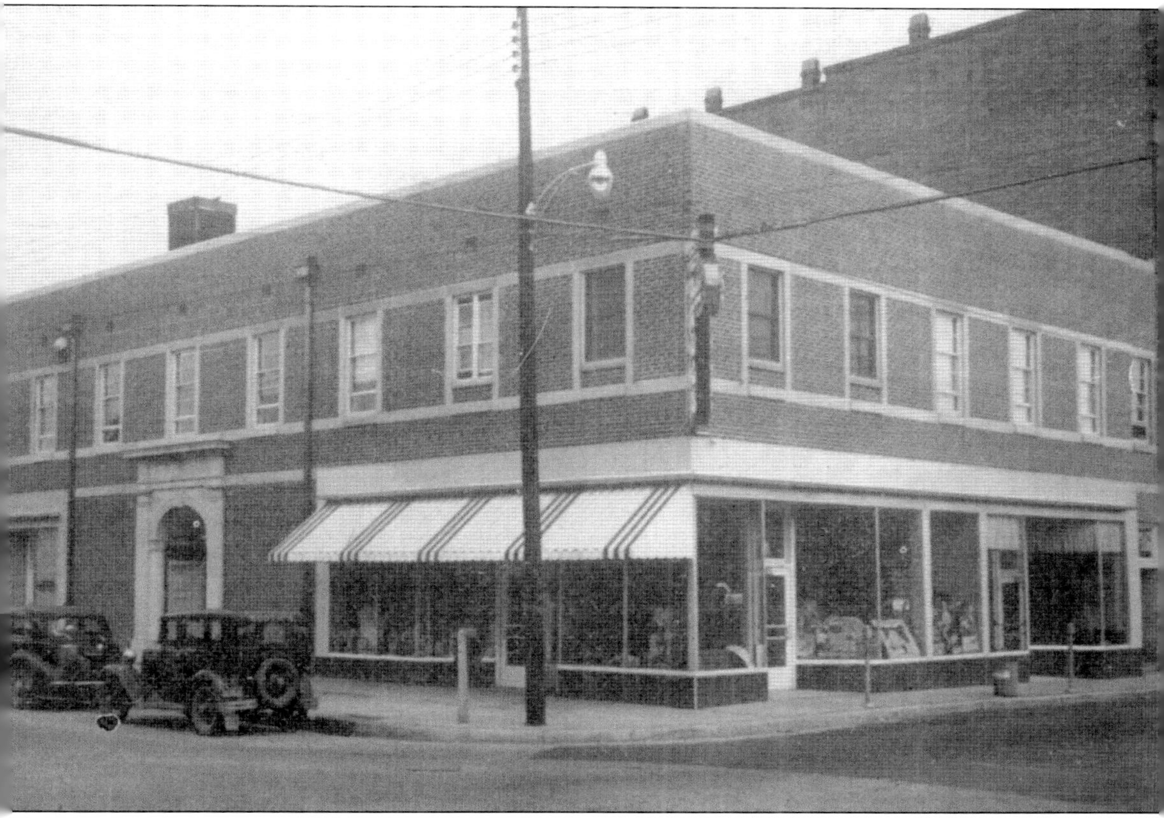

Masonic Building, 1949. Wilson Williams Lodge No. 351, Ancient Free and Accepted Masons, was chartered in 1869. The lodge featured three floors. (Courtesy Columbus Public Library.)

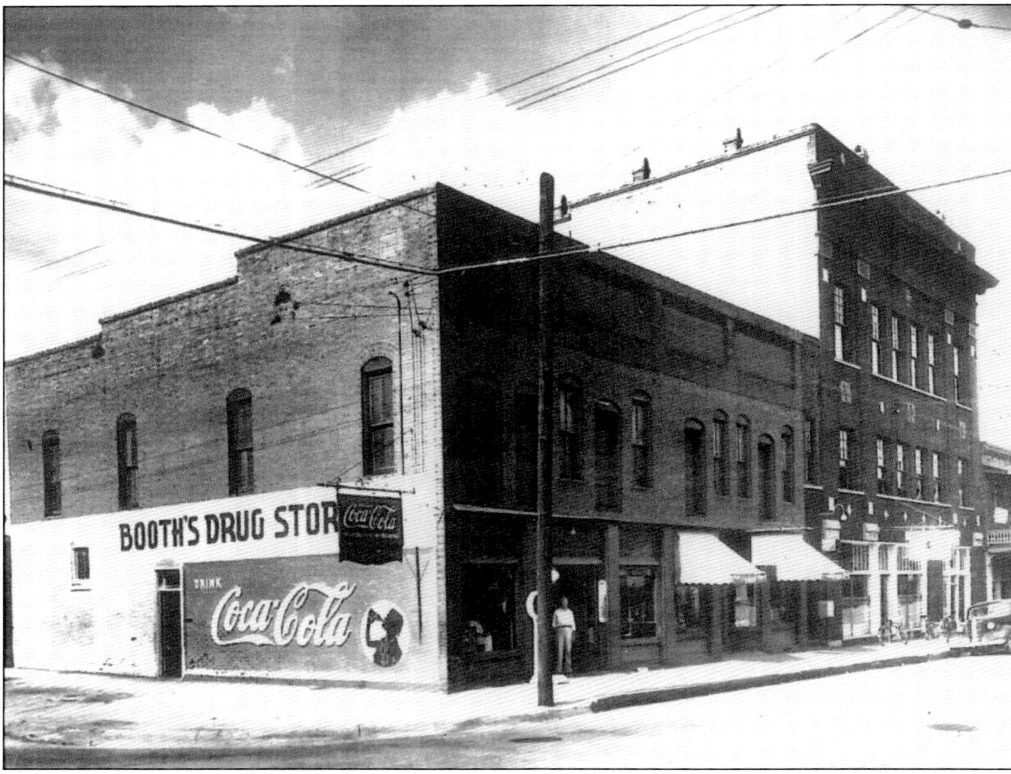

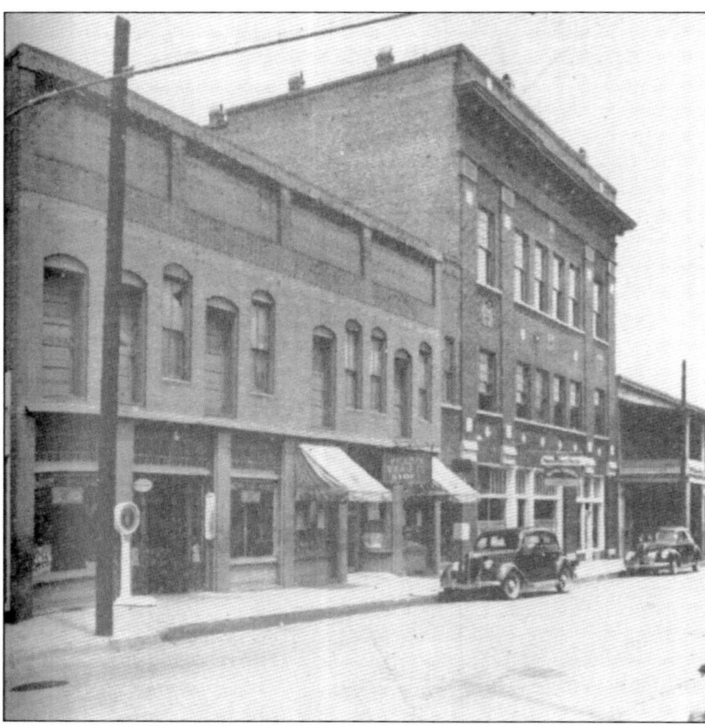

Booth's Drug Store. One of Phenix City's early commercial thoroughfares, Sixteenth Avenue featured a variety of retail establishments. Booth's Drug Store is in the foreground. Beyond Booth's is the Masonic building. (Courtesy Sean Driggers.)

Sixteenth Street at Broad. Pictured in another view of the intersection of Sixteenth and Broad Streets are Booth's Drug Store, Phenix Variety Store, and the Masonic building. (Courtesy Sean Driggers.)

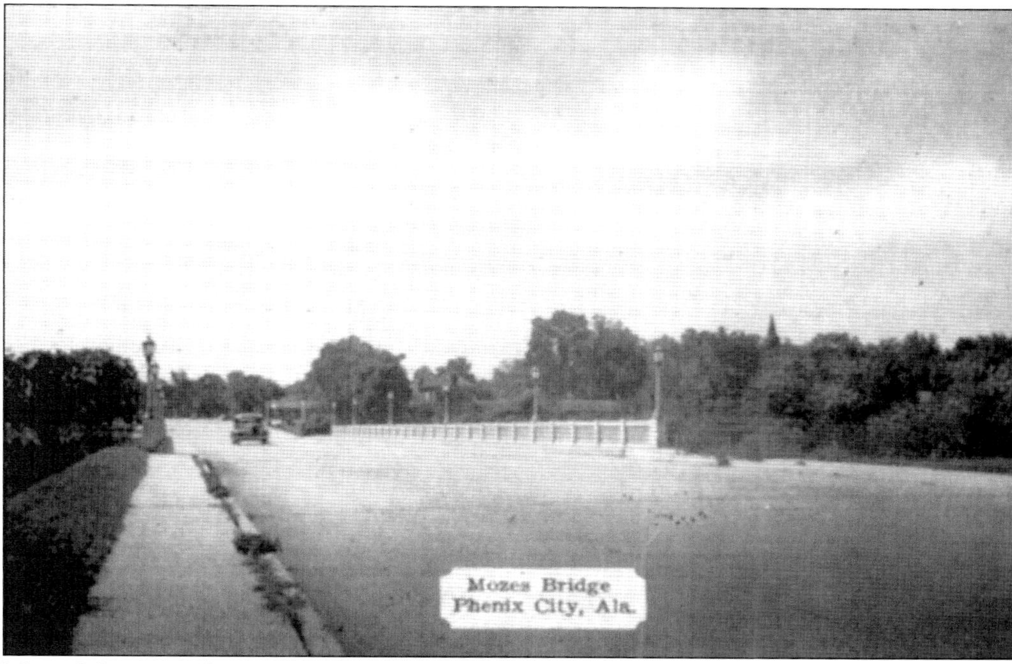

Moses Memorial Bridge. In 1933, Phenix City's financial situation was dire, and the city went into receivership. But Phenix City continued to upgrade its infrastructure and city services. Spanning Holland Creek on Broad Street, the Moses Memorial Bridge was completed in 1935 at a cost of $100,000. (Courtesy Dennis Jones.)

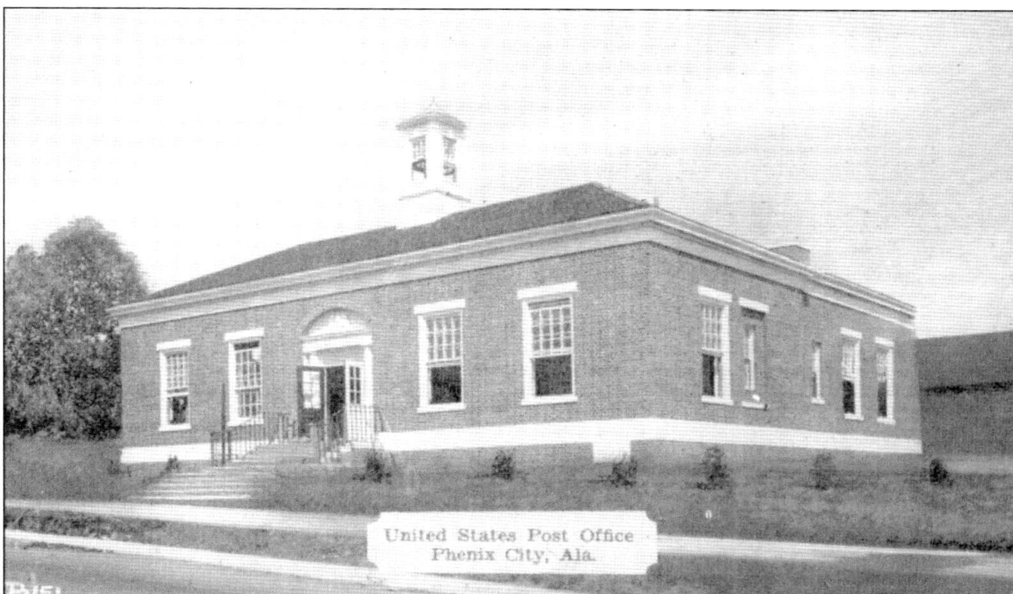

Phenix City Post Office. Phenix City became the county seat in 1932. Despite going into receivership in 1933, city officials worked to improve access to city and county services. In 1939, a post office was completed across the street from the courthouse, which was completed the previous year. (Courtesy Kenneth Thomas.)

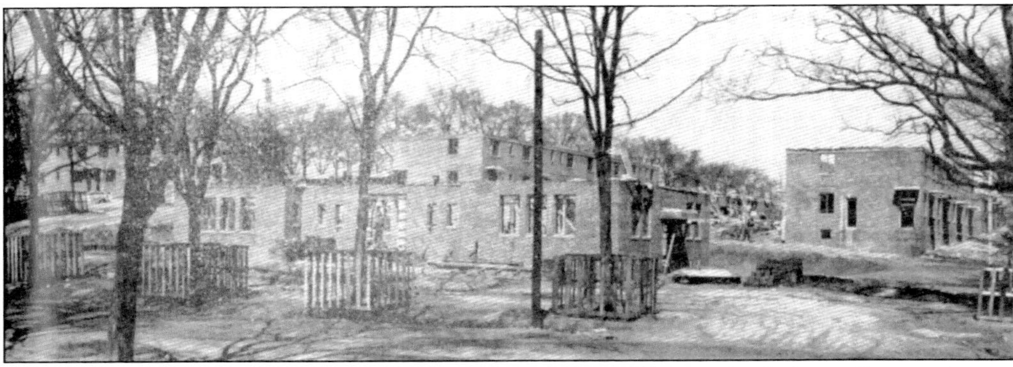

Riverview Apartments. As part of the Housing Authority of Phenix City's slum village eradication project, federal funding was obtained for two housing projects to be constructed. The Riverview Court Apartments for whites opened in 1940, and Frederick Douglass Homes for blacks opened in 1941. (Courtesy Columbus Public Library.)

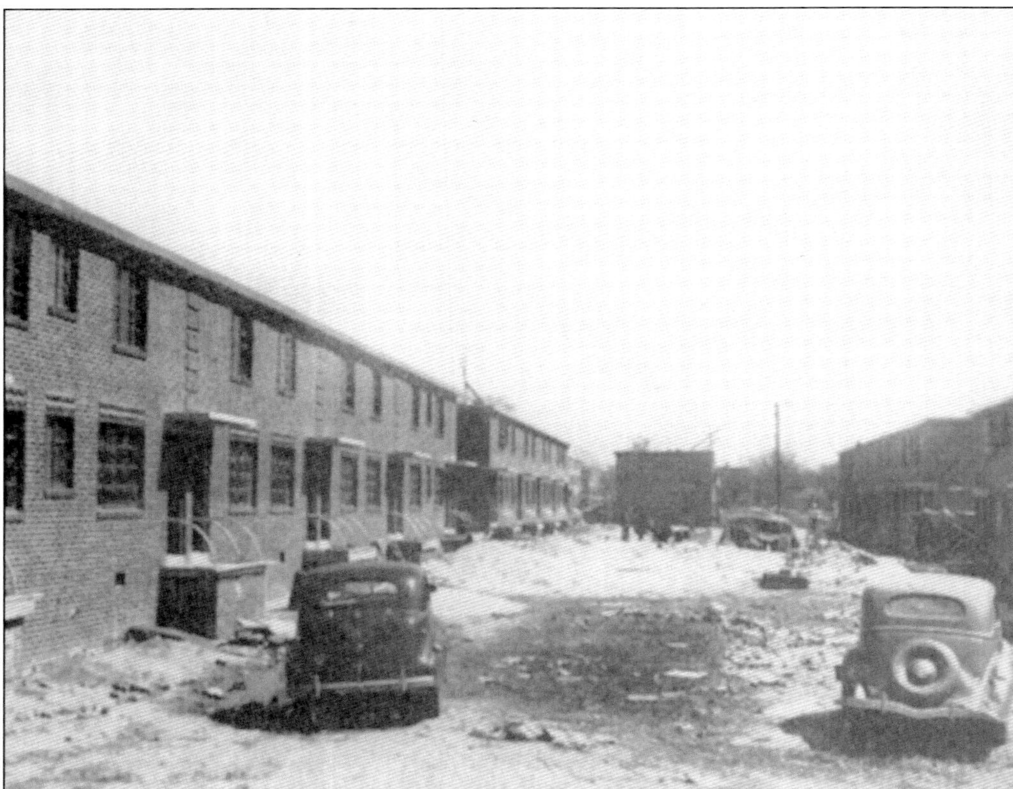

Frederick Douglass Homes. Riverview occupied the land formerly occupied by the Eagle and Phenix village. Frederick Douglass was situated between Fourteenth and Fifteenth Streets. Both Riverview Court and Frederick Douglass Homes were brick and concrete structures. Phenix City was the only city with a population of 15,000 to have two federal housing projects. (Courtesy Columbus Public Library.)

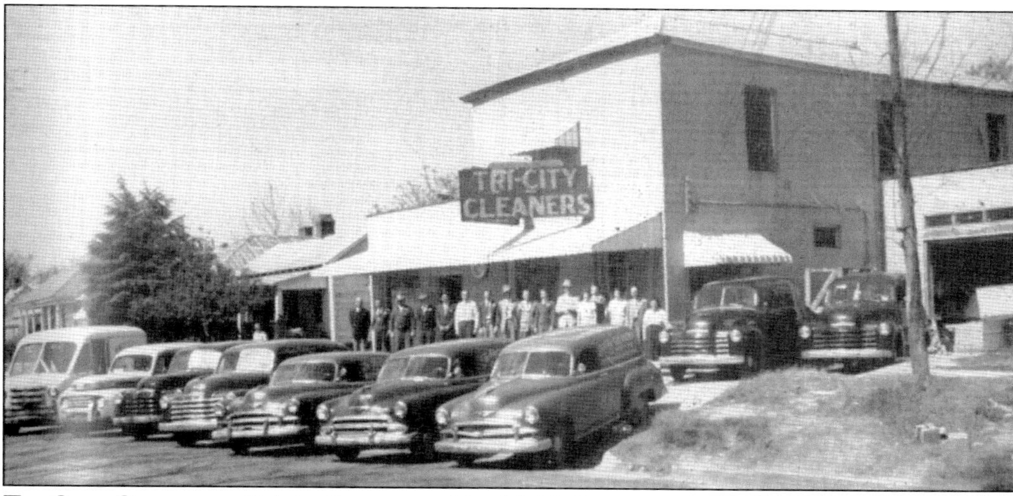

TRI-CITY CLEANERS. Originally operated by M. T. Scroggins in 1947, Tri-City Cleaners was counted as one of Phenix City's largest employers, especially of African American women. (Courtesy Columbus Public Library.)

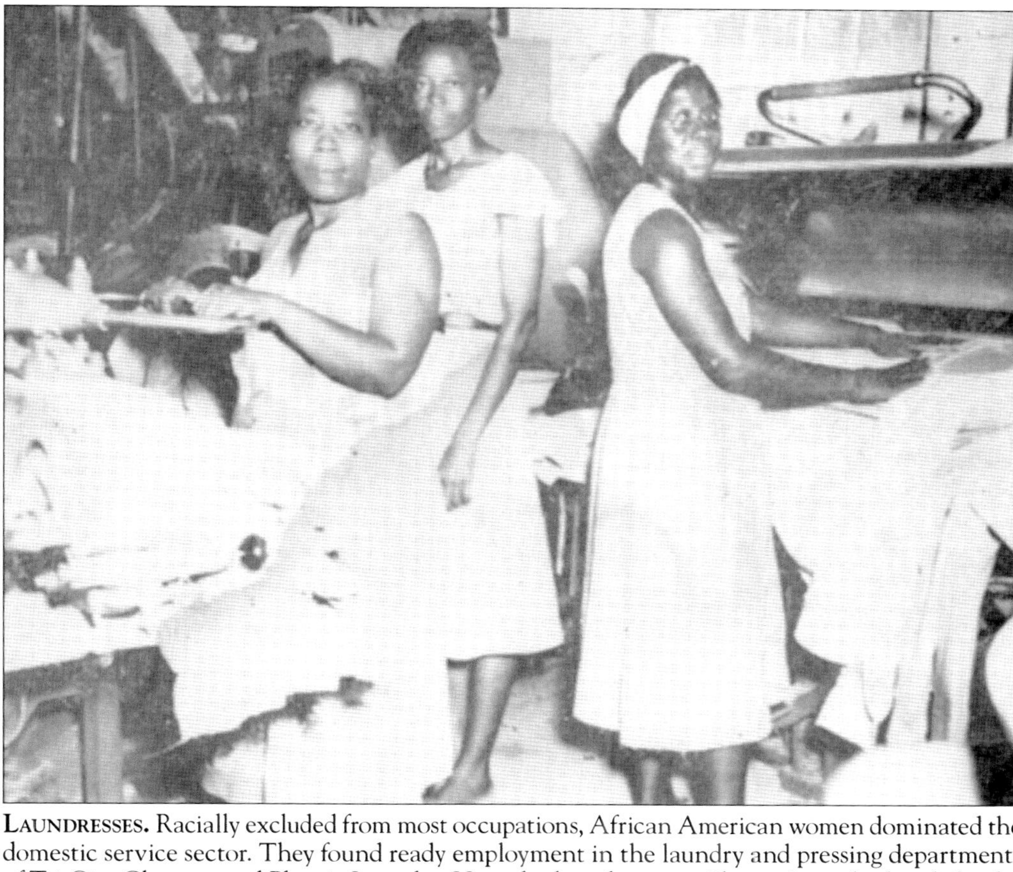

LAUNDRESSES. Racially excluded from most occupations, African American women dominated the domestic service sector. They found ready employment in the laundry and pressing departments of Tri-City Cleaners and Phenix Laundry. Here the laundresses at Phenix Laundry break for the camera. (Courtesy Columbus Public Library.)

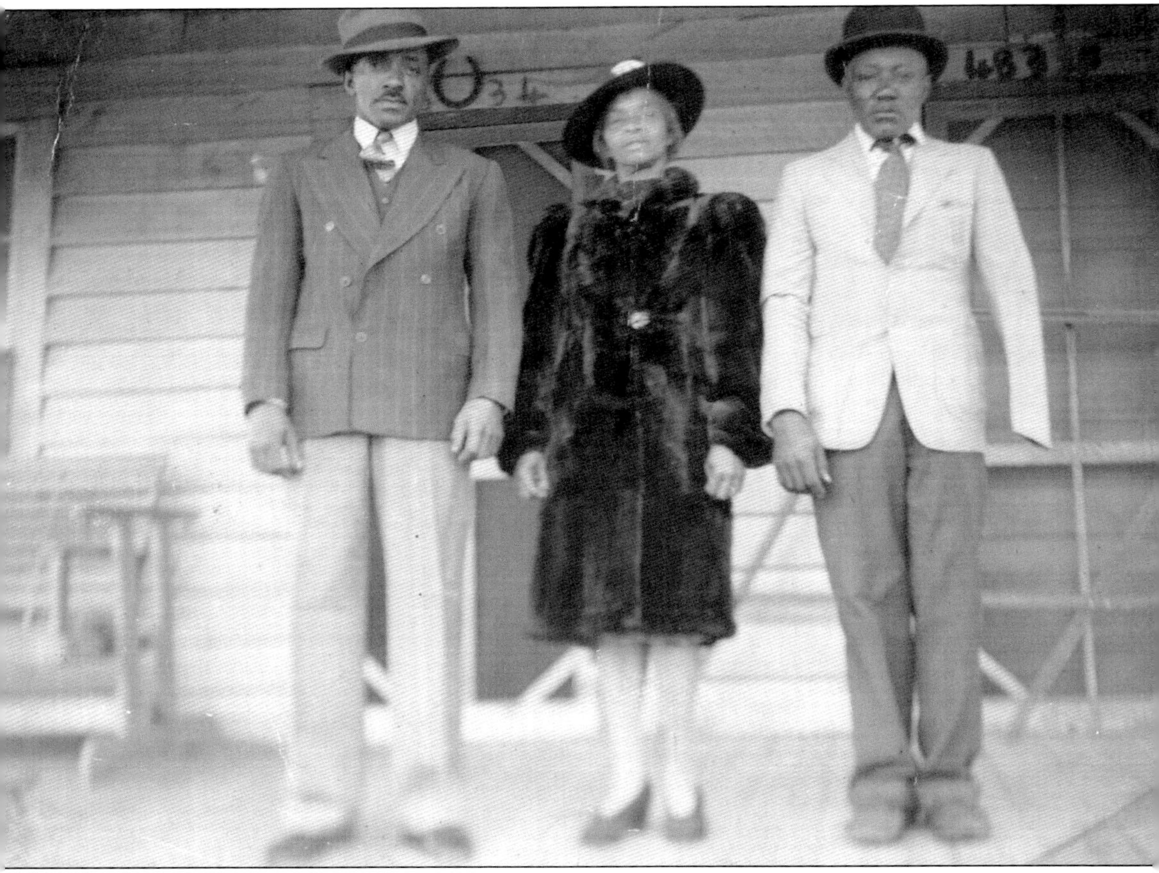

AFRICAN AMERICAN URBANIZATION. A black bourgeoisie composed of morticians, business owners, teachers, and ministers emerged in Phenix City between 1920 and 1953. While moving to the city improved their condition and opportunities, members of this African American middle class constituted a very small minority of the population and lived in substandard conditions relative to their white neighbors. In 1928, Austin Sumbry Jr. organized the Cooperative and Union Aid Society, which assisted families with funeral expenses. Within eight years, he entered the mortuary business. (Courtesy Columbus Black History Museum.)

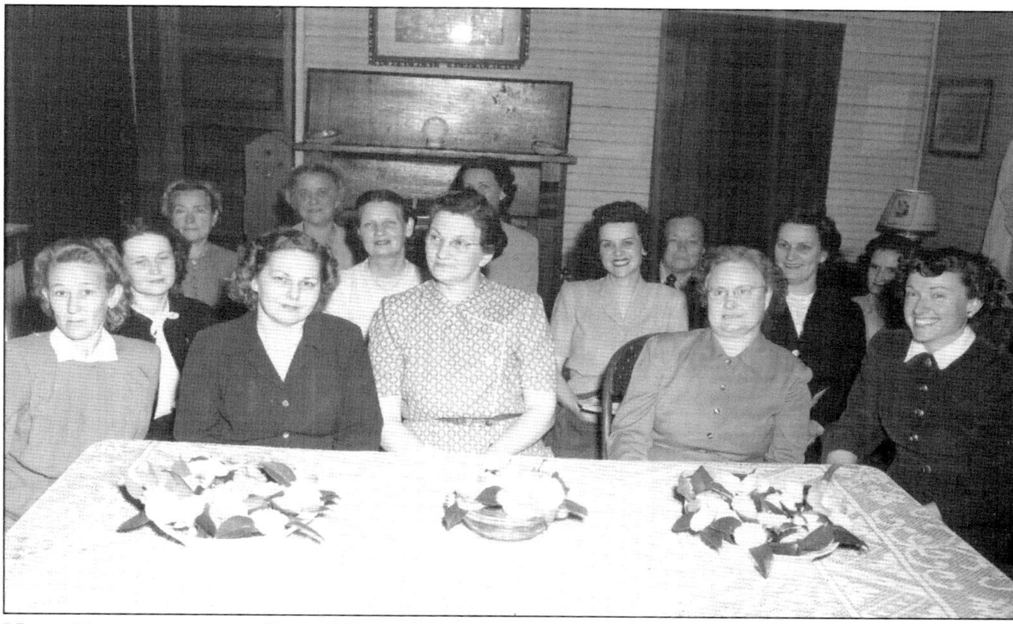

HOME DEMONSTRATION CLUB. Home demonstration clubs grew out of the agricultural extension programs that sought to improve the lives of rural women and their families. Alabama funded one white and one black agent to serve each county by offering training in the latest in advances in home economics, gardening, nutrition, and health. (Courtesy Auburn University Library.)

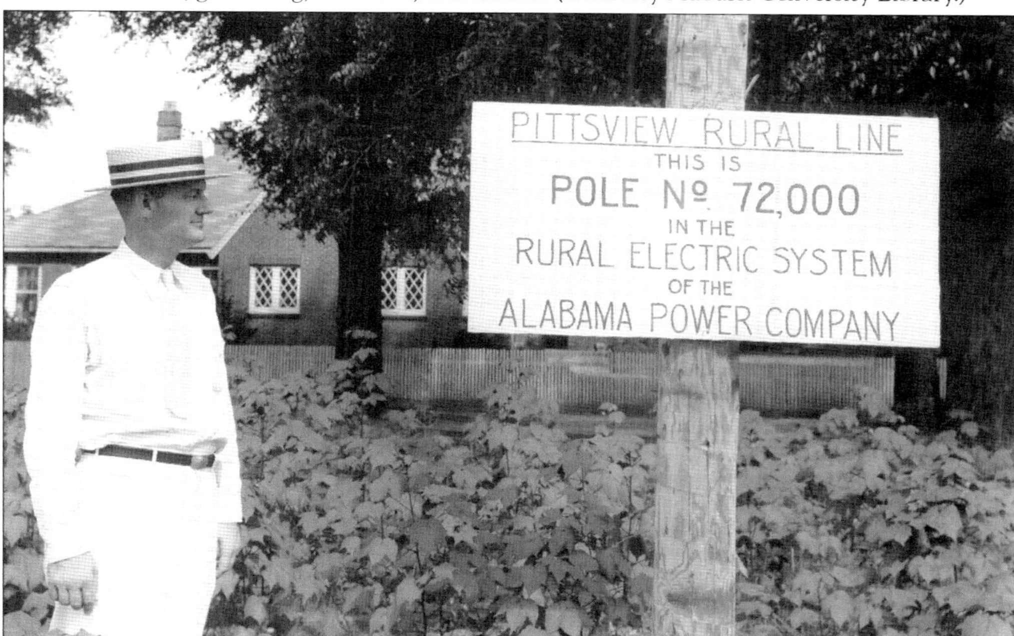

RURAL ELECTRIFICATION. Pictured is an administrator of the Alabama Power Company. The Columbus Electric and Power Company provided Phenix City's gas and electric services until 1935. By 1936, the Alabama Power Company provided Phenix City with electricity, and all of Russell County had access to electricity. (Courtesy Alabama Power Company.)

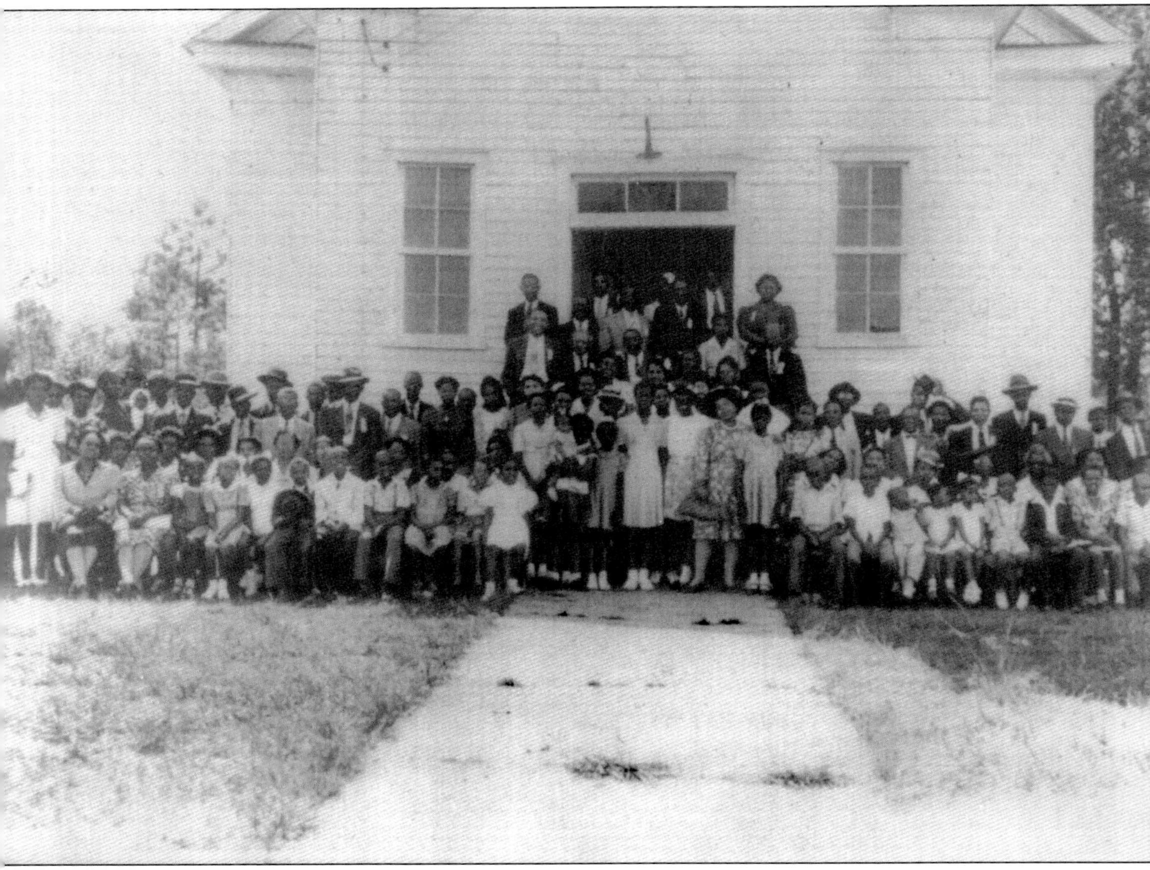

FRANCHISE MISSIONARY BAPTIST CHURCH. Since its inception, the black church functioned as the primary institution for social and political activities within the African American community. The church served not only a spiritual role but, in a segregated society, was necessary as a source of community support. Members pose in front of Franchise Missionary Church, founded in 1852. (Courtesy Franchise Missionary Baptist Church.)

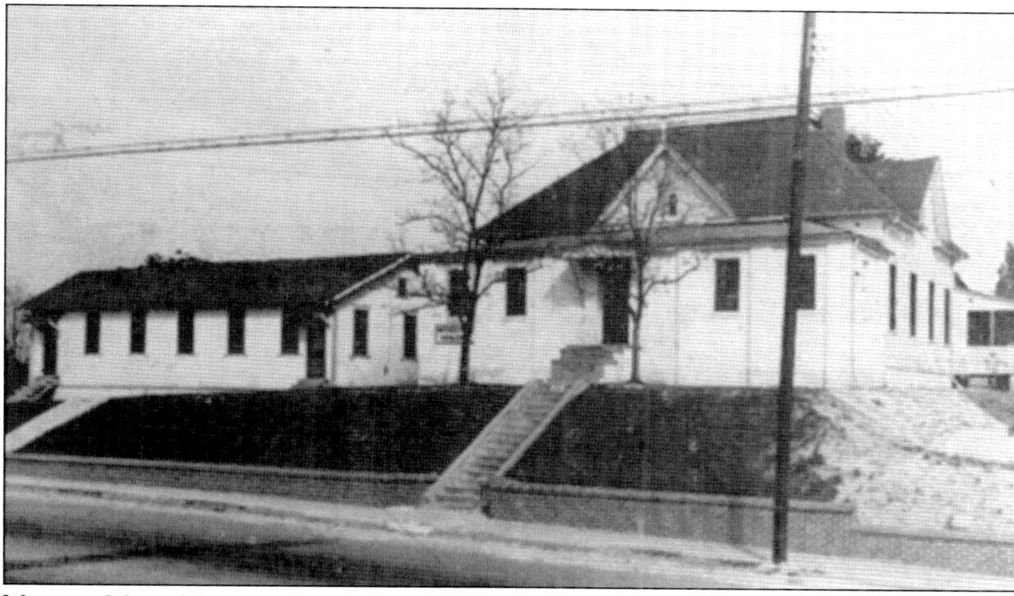

Mother Mary Mission. Founded in 1939 by Fr. Harold Purcell as a center for the religious, charitable, educational, and industrial advancement of the African American community in the South Girard section, Mother Mary was patterned after the City of St. Jude, which Purcell had established in Montgomery, Alabama. It featured a health and dental clinic, a chapel, and an auditorium that hosted social functions. The original mission house is pictured here. (Courtesy Columbus Public Library.)

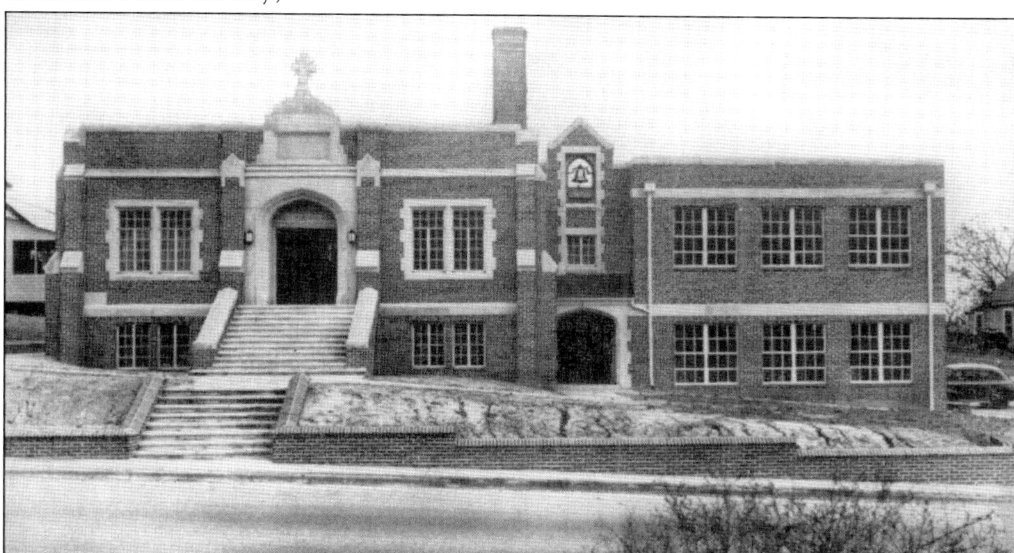

Mother Mary Mission School. In 1940, the Vincentian Sisters of Charity from Pittsburgh, Pennsylvania, joined the mission. Mother Mary Mission School opened September 8, 1941. The inaugural class of 60 students in four grades quickly grew to 90 by October. For the first five years, the students and sisters operated in tight quarters and received instruction in the mission house, which doubled as a clinic until the brick building pictured was constructed. (Courtesy Kenneth Thomas.)

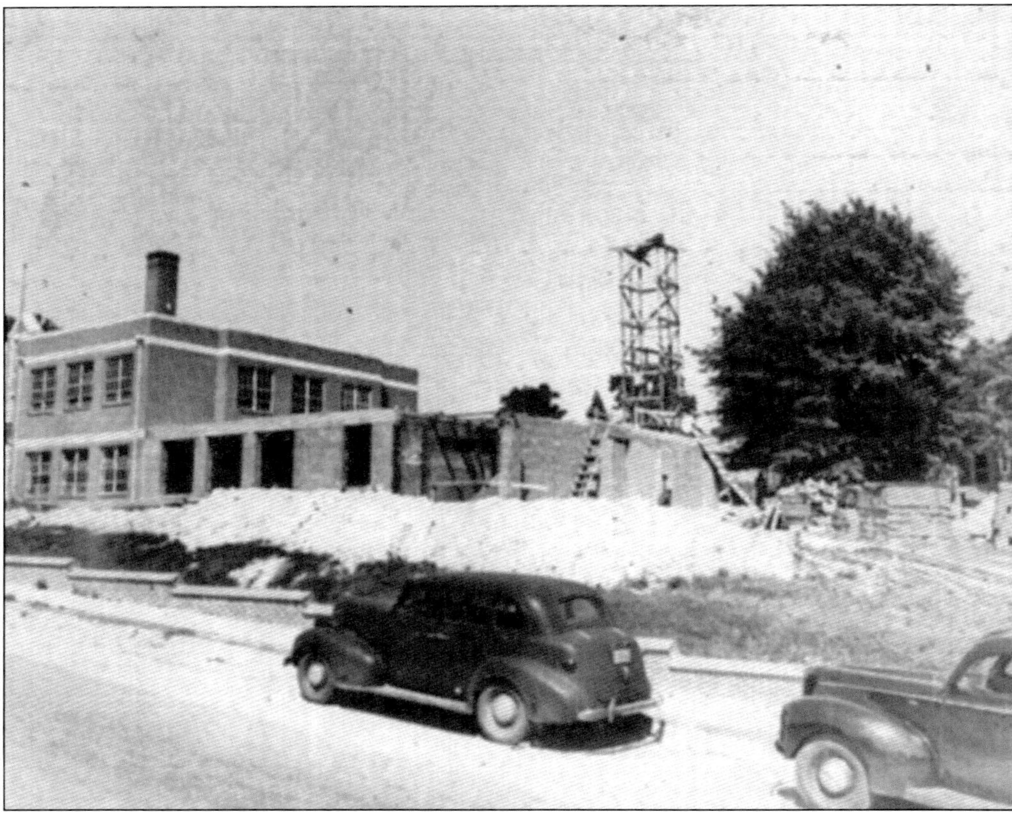

Mother Mary Mission Addition, 1946. The mission operated a clinic that provided health care to African Americans, whether Catholic or not. In 1942, Drs. M. H. McAdoo and W. G. McAdoo established the clinic and provided care once a week. (Courtesy Columbus Public Library.)

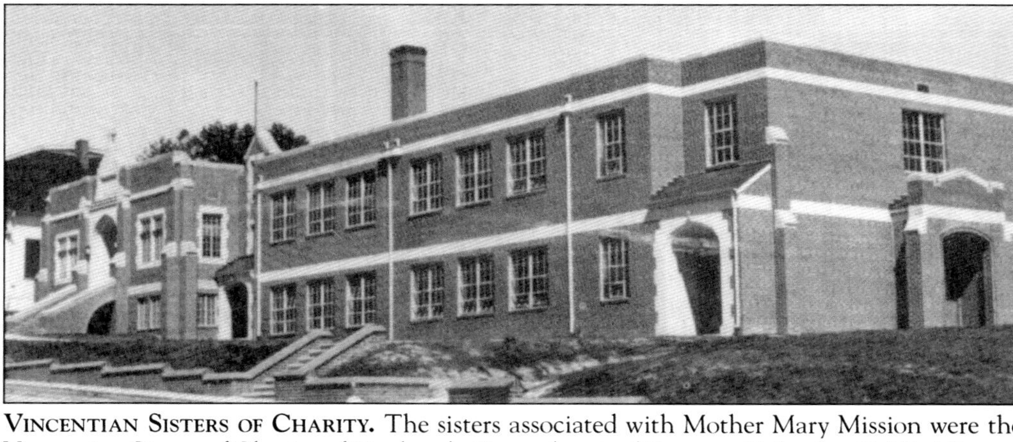

Vincentian Sisters of Charity. The sisters associated with Mother Mary Mission were the Vincentian Sisters of Charity of Pittsburgh, Pennsylvania. (Courtesy Columbus Public Library.)

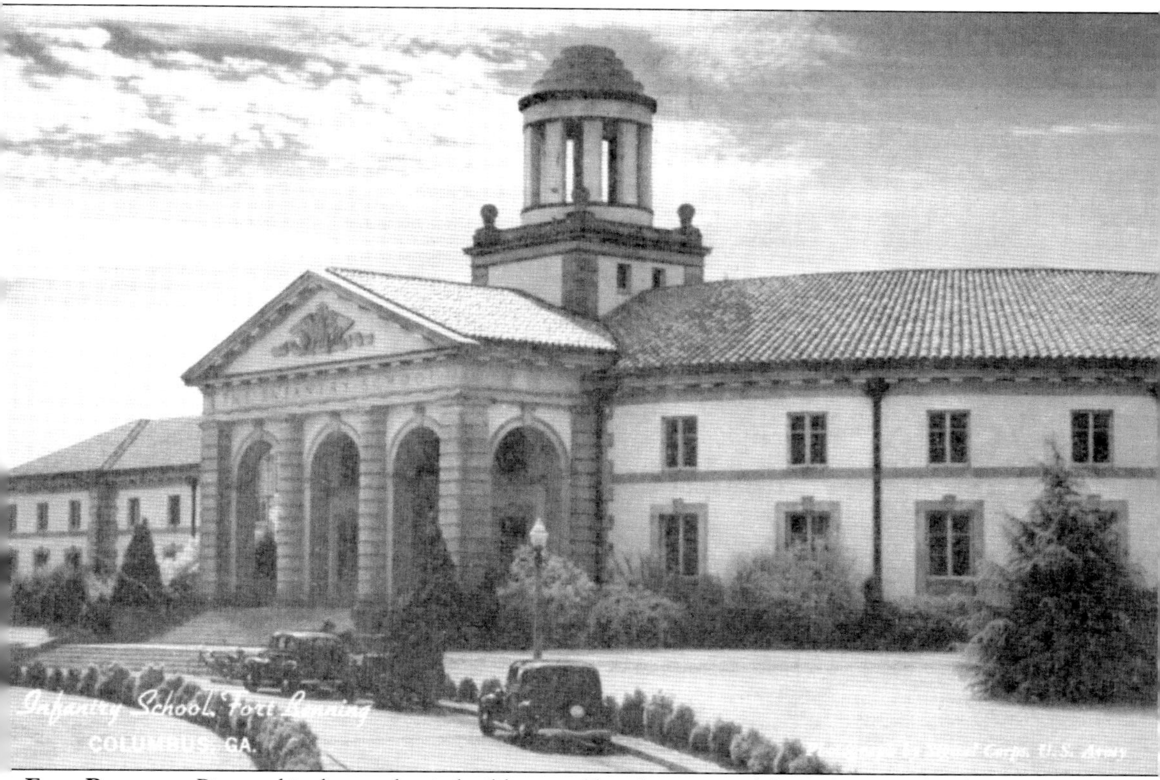

FORT BENNING. Pictured is the academic building and headquarters of the Infantry School at Fort Benning. Camp Benning was established in 1918, when a temporary location was established on Macon Road. The camp was moved in June 1919 southeast of Columbus, in parts of Chattahoochee and Muscogee Counties. By 1922, funds were authorized for a permanent construction, Fort Benning. The fort has greatly contributed to the region's economy. By the 1940s, its impact helped move Phenix City out of receivership. (Courtesy Dennis Jones.)

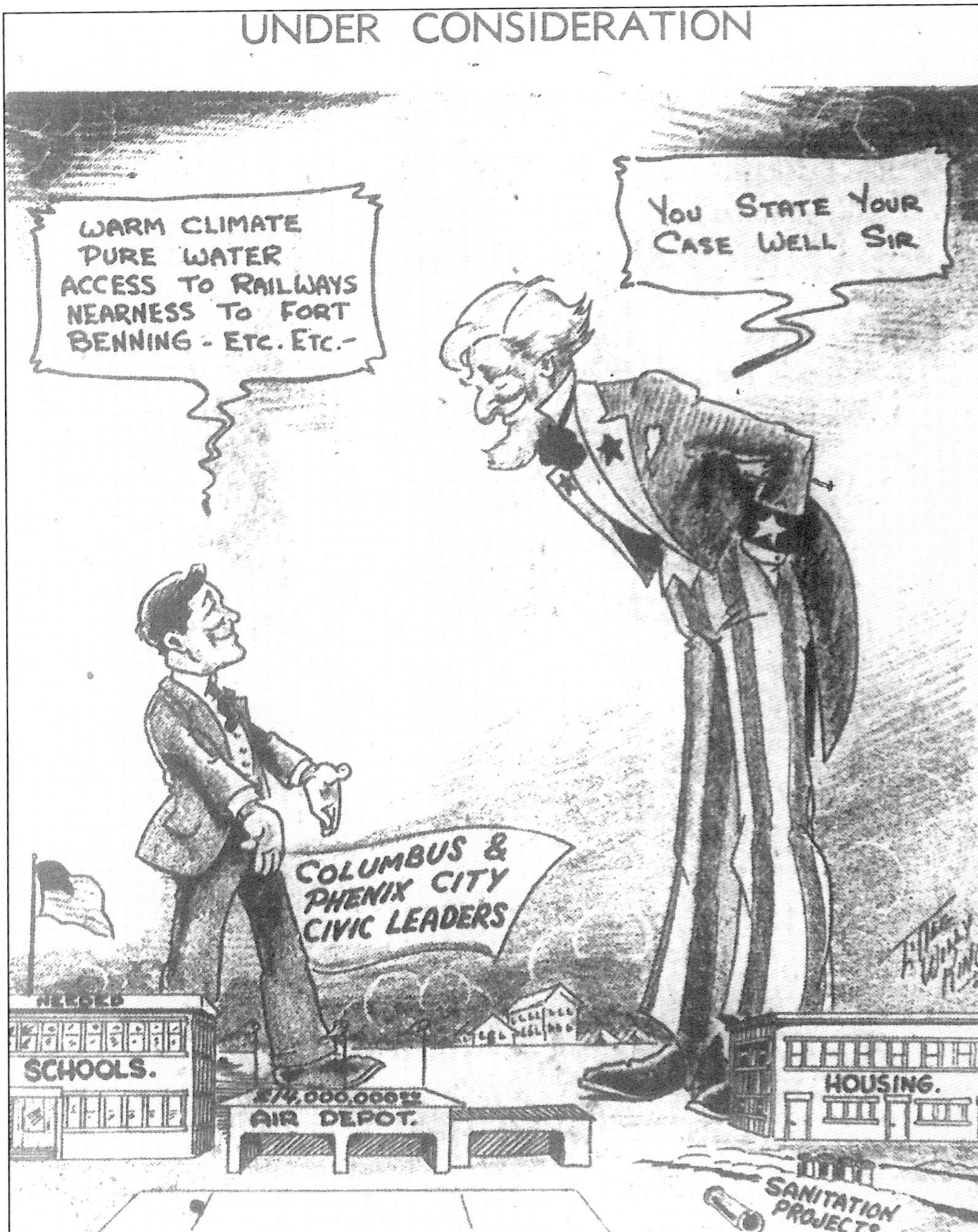

Under Consideration. Cartoonist Little Willy King captured the bi-city's civic leaders' penchant for obtaining federal funding during World War II. In addition to the economic benefit derived from Fort Benning, both cities obtained numerous governmental contracts. (Courtesy Columbus Public Library.)

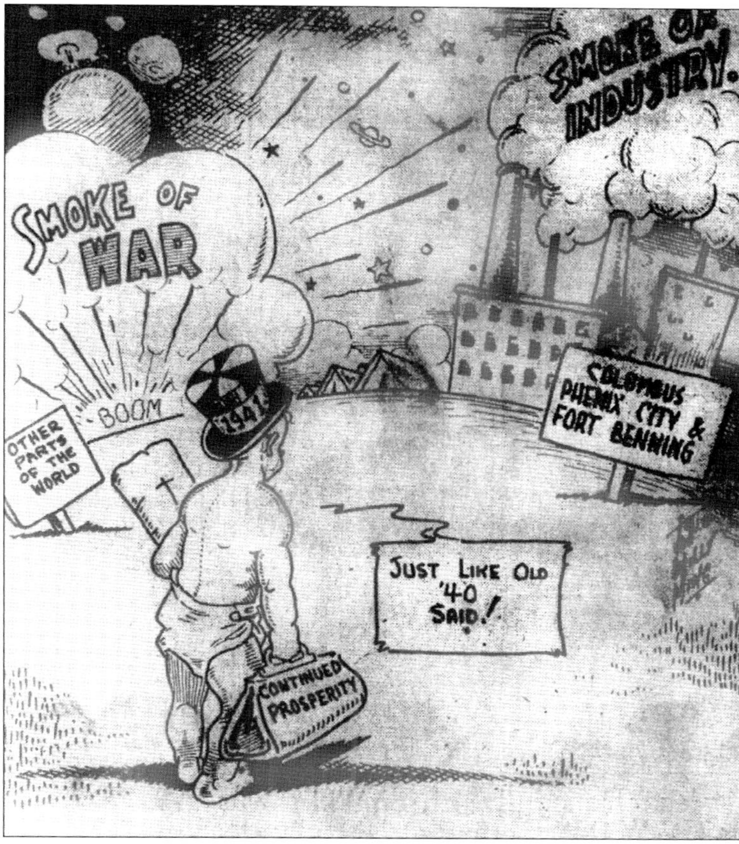

SMOKE OF WAR, 1941. The economic impact of Fort Benning and wartime mobilization is illustrated in Little Willy King's New Year's sketch. King depicts Baby New Year arriving with a satchel full of continued prosperity. Wartime expansion of Fort Benning necessitated the acquisition of 11,722 acres of Russell County farmland, and $15 million was spent on construction and development. In addition to land sales and building costs, Phenix City's prosperity came from gambling, prostitution, alcohol, and narcotics. (Courtesy Columbus Public Library.)

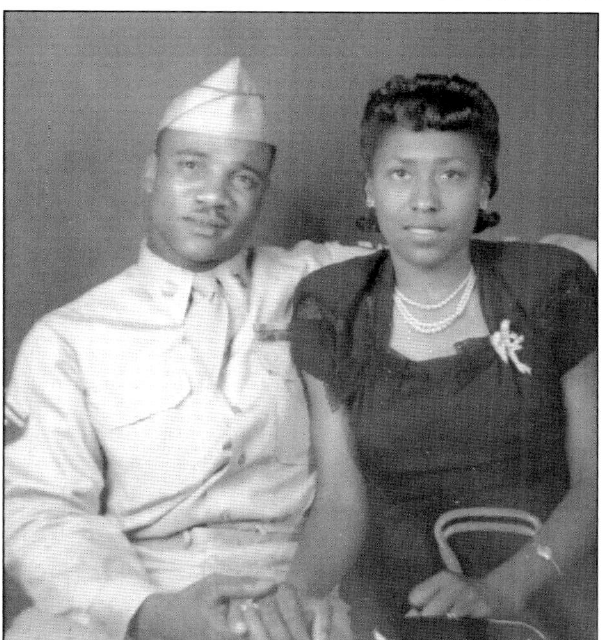

WAR MARRIAGES. World War II and Fort Benning had an additional impact on Phenix City. Among the changes faced by both black and white Phenix City families were the hundreds of marriages entered into by servicemen and the women of the community. Here a Fort Benning soldier poses with his fiancée. Notice the engagement ring. (Courtesy Columbus Black History Museum.)

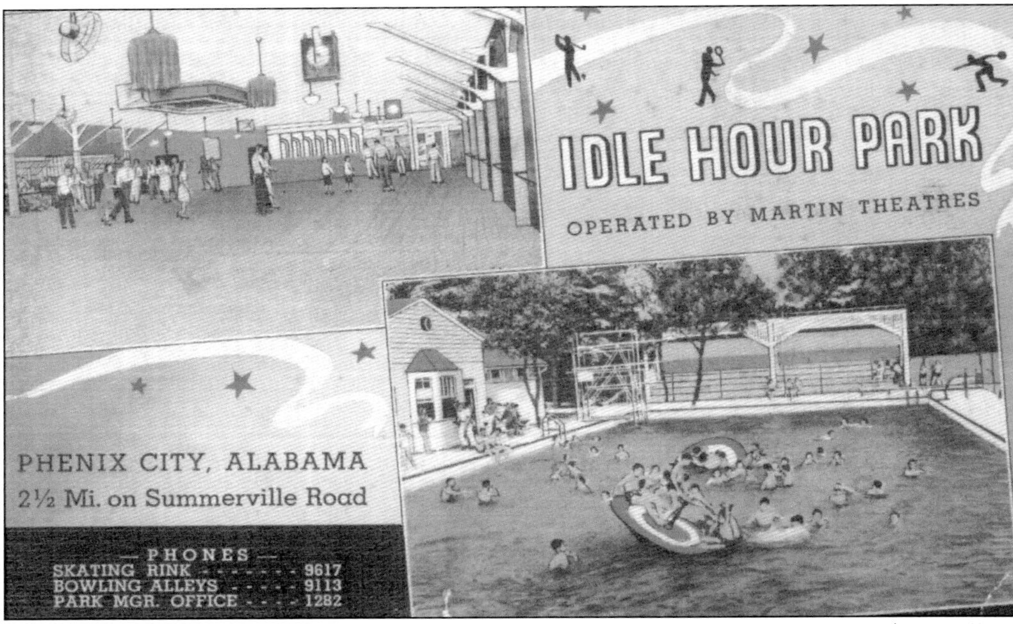

IDLE HOUR PARK. Roy E. Martin developed Idle Hour Park at an estimated cost of $2.5 million. The movie theater magnate's hobby was once Phenix City's premiere family recreational facility. In January 1950, Phenix City purchased the park from Martin's estate. Although the park was city owned and operated by a park board, the city commission did not allocate funds for its operation. (Courtesy Dennis Jones.)

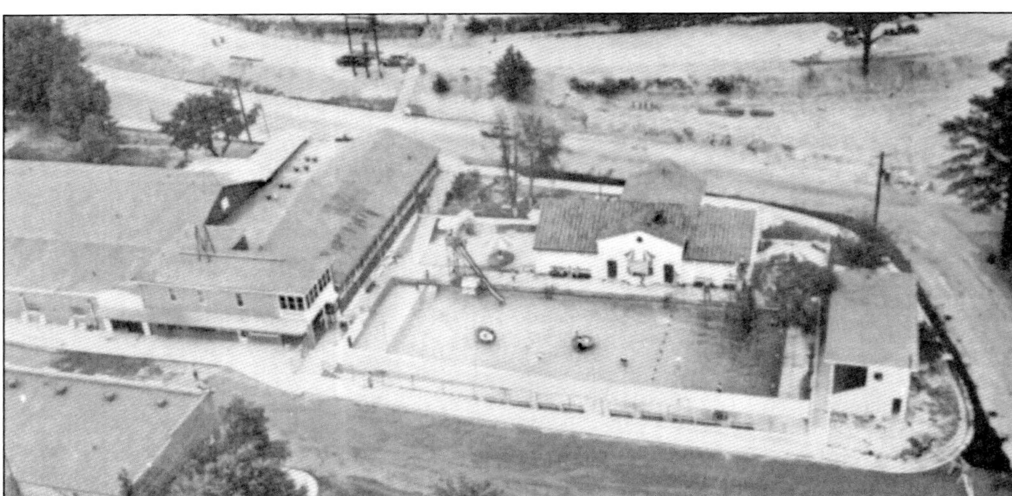

IDLE HOUR SWIMMING POOL. Seen in this aerial view, the swimming pool's 265,000 gallons of water were pumped from the lake and filtered by the park's water plant. The pool has since been filled with sand and now serves as a volleyball court. (Courtesy Columbus Public Library.)

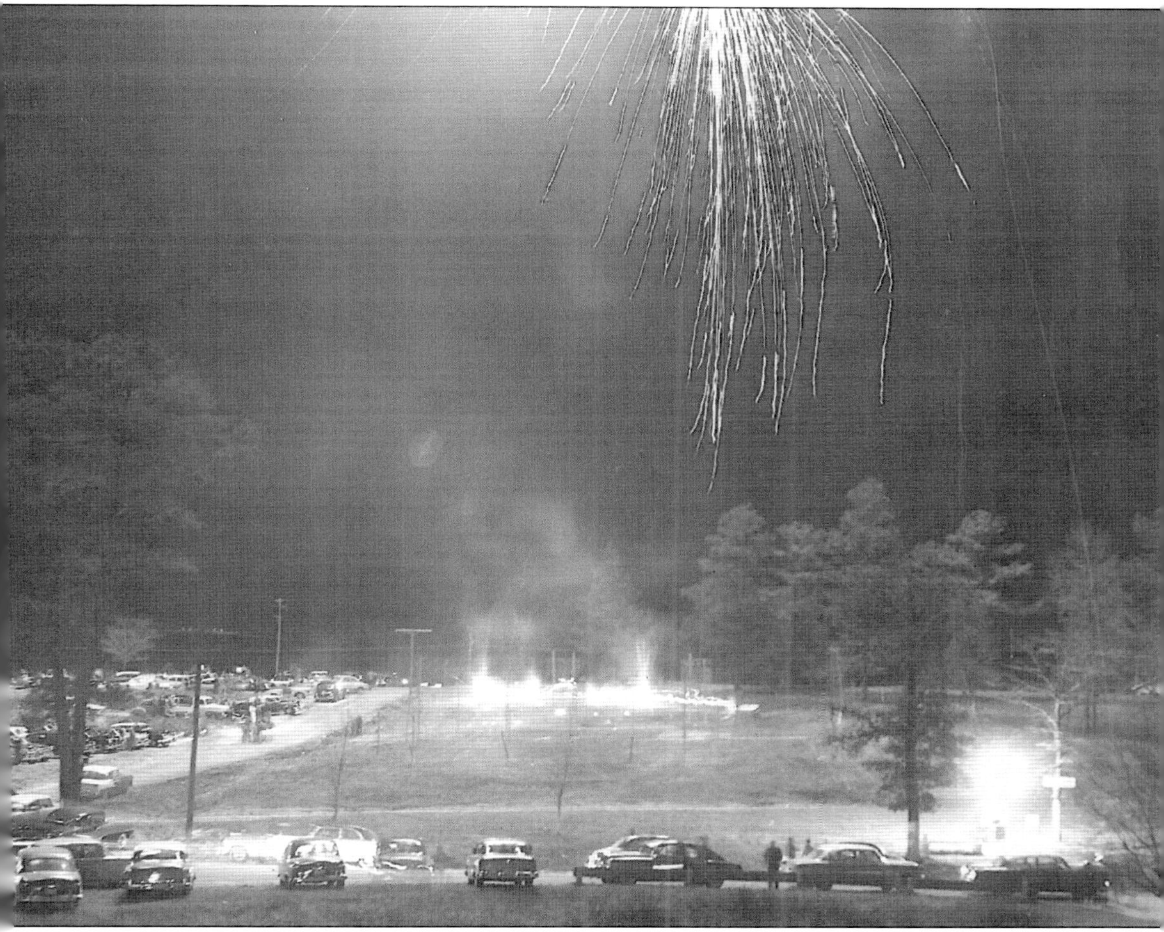

Idle Hour Fireworks. The 240-acre park featured a 25-acre spring-fed lake, swimming pool, clubhouse, dance hall, bowling alley, skating rink, shooting gallery, football stadium, baseball field, picnic areas, and zoo. Idle Hour provided a pleasant background to view the fireworks. (Courtesy Sean Driggers.)

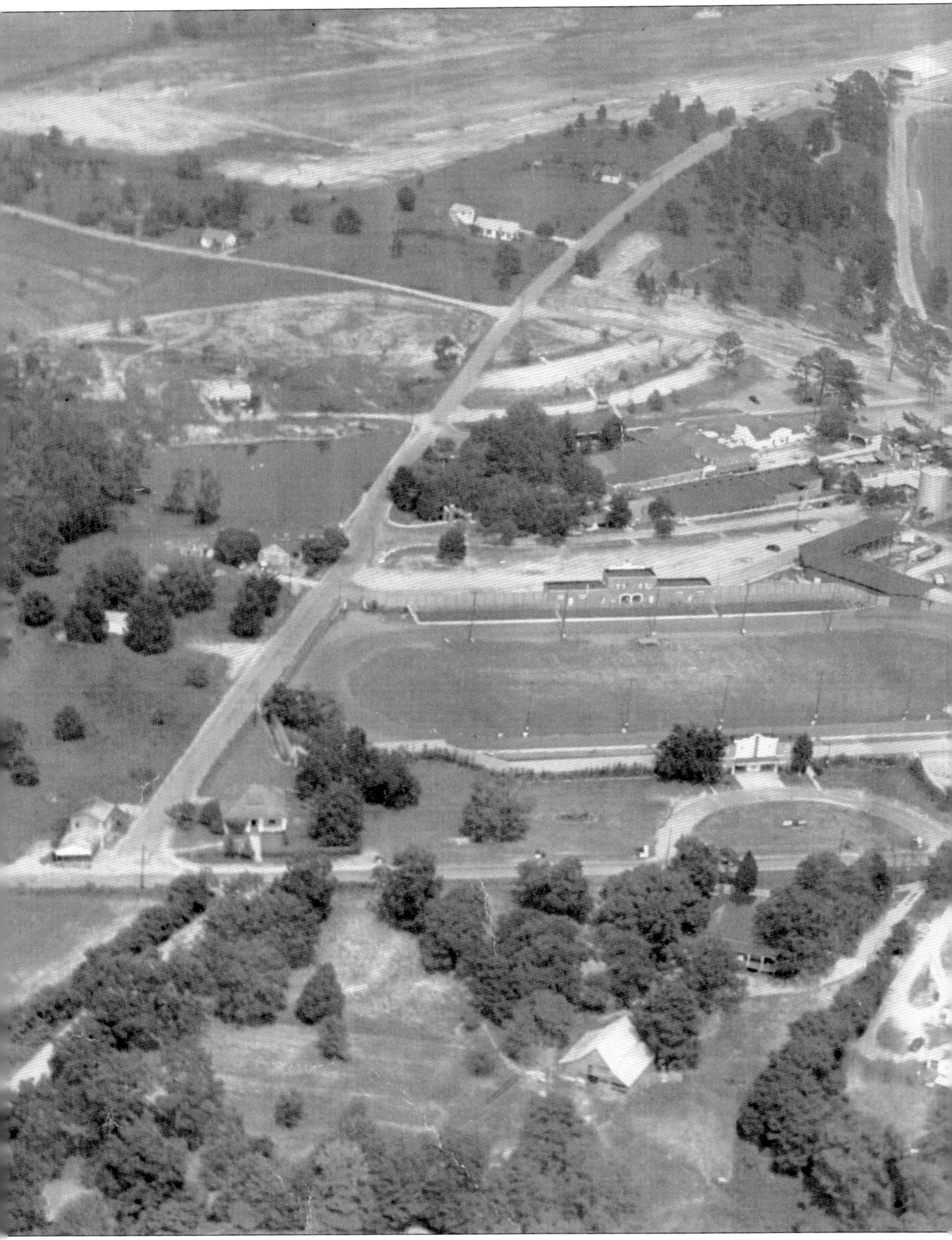

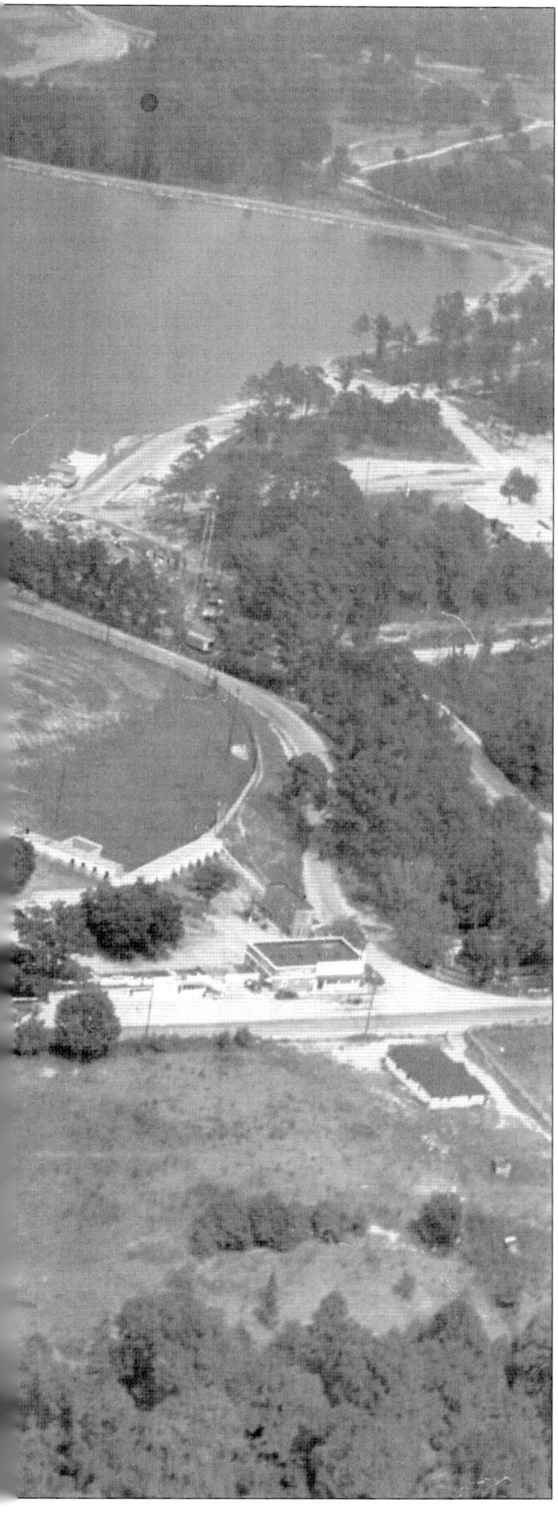

IDLE HOUR PARK AERIAL VIEW. The enormity of the Idle Hour Park complex is displayed in this aerial view. The park consisted of 240 acres. Roy E. Martin also developed the municipal airport seen in the distance. (Courtesy Columbus Public Library.)

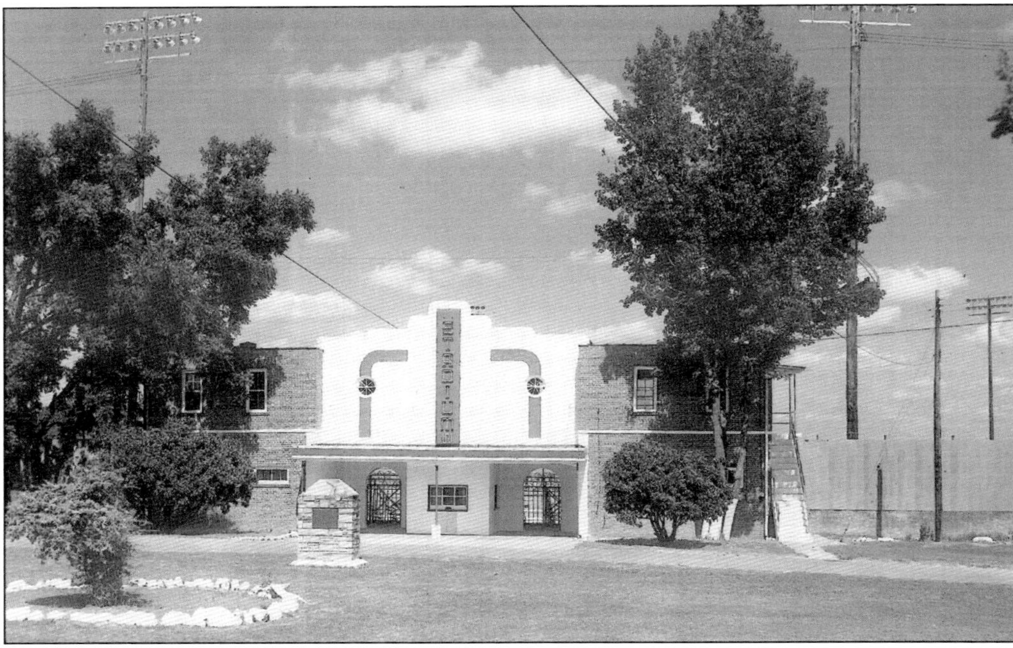

Stadium Entrance. Pictured is the entrance to the football field at Idle Hour Park. Construction of the stadium began in 1941. Roy Martin envisioned Phenix City and the stadium hosting teams from Alabama and Georgia. Martin was no doubt influenced by the economic impact of the Auburn-Georgia rivalry, played in Columbus from 1920 to 1958 (with the exception of 1929). (Courtesy Sean Driggers.)

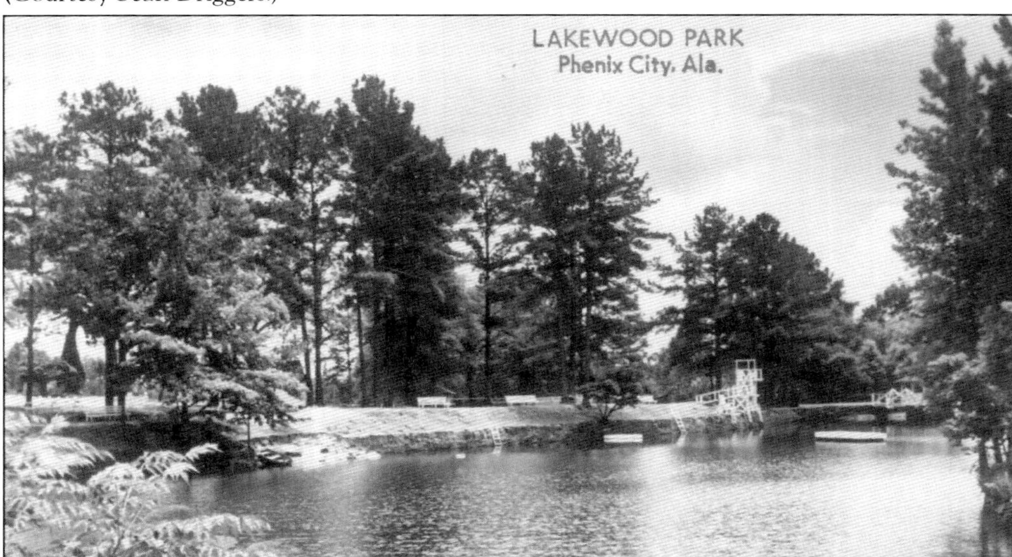

Lakewood Park. The "Lake Waluhiyi" Project was a community recreation development designed by the junior chamber of commerce. The project sought to make the two lakes of the old waterworks reservoir on Holland Creek the centerpiece of a 600-acre park. *Waluhiyi* is Cherokee for "beautiful place." But no matter how beautiful, the name did not take. The lake was segregated. African Americans used Rosemont Park. (Courtesy Dennis Jones.)

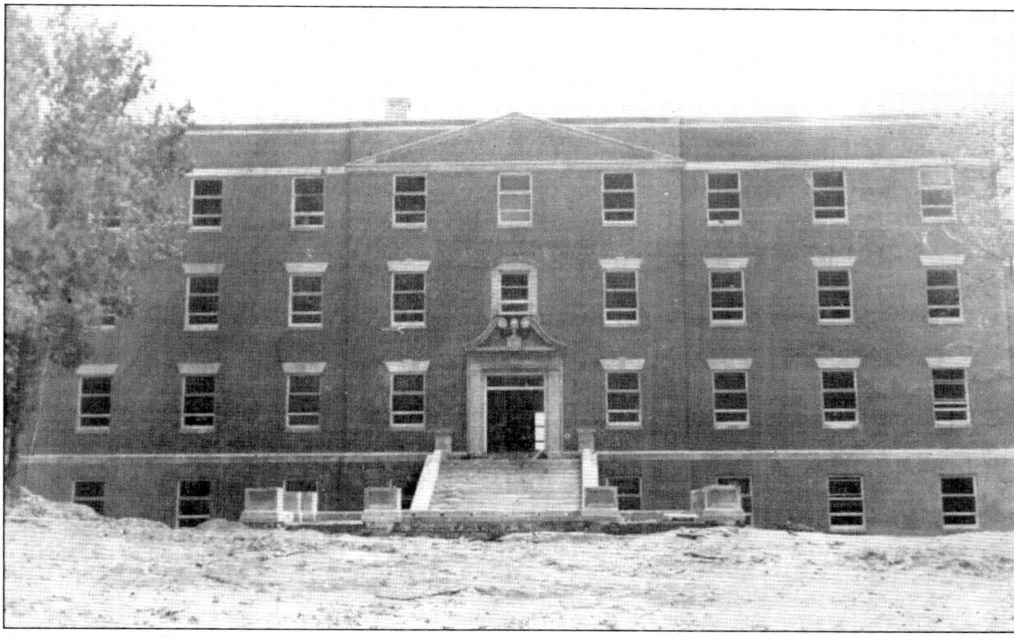

PHENIX CITY HOSPITAL. Constructed at a cost of $350,000 in 1947, the hospital is located on the site of Fort No. 5, a Civil War defense bastion. The four-story hospital had 52 beds for white patients and 18 for non-whites. The first floor featured laboratories, service operations facilities, and segregated dining rooms; the second floor, offices and the "colored" ward. The white ward was located on the third floor, and the surgery unit occupied the fourth. Pictured is the hospital under construction in 1946. (Courtesy Columbus Public Library.)

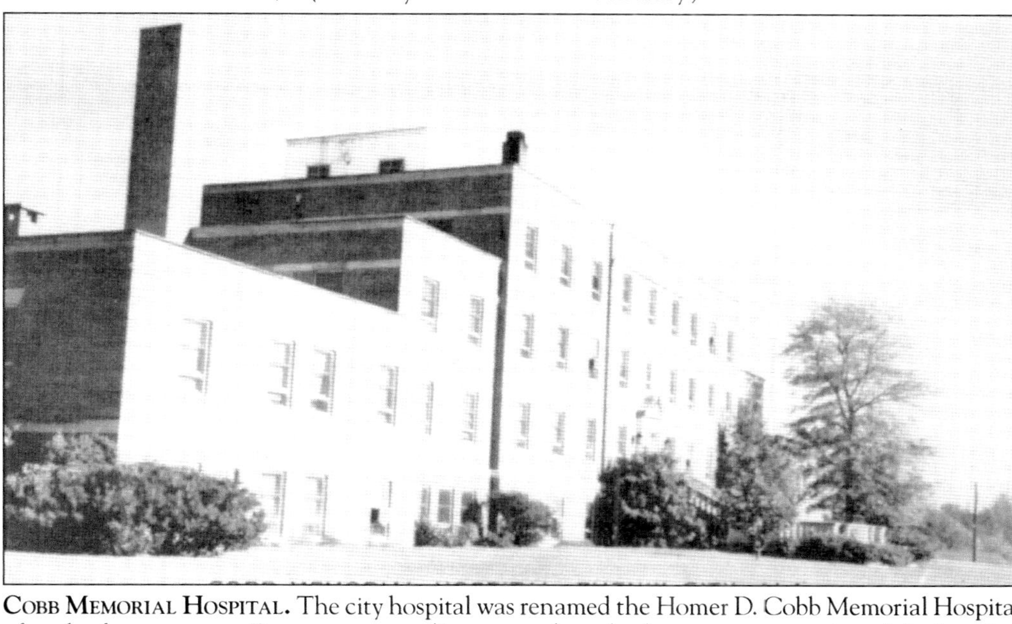

COBB MEMORIAL HOSPITAL. The city hospital was renamed the Homer D. Cobb Memorial Hospital after the former mayor. Due to overcrowding, ground was broken on an expansion of the hospital in 1956. Two wings were built on the north and south ends of the hospital, adding 50 beds and an emergency room. (Courtesy Columbus Public Library.)

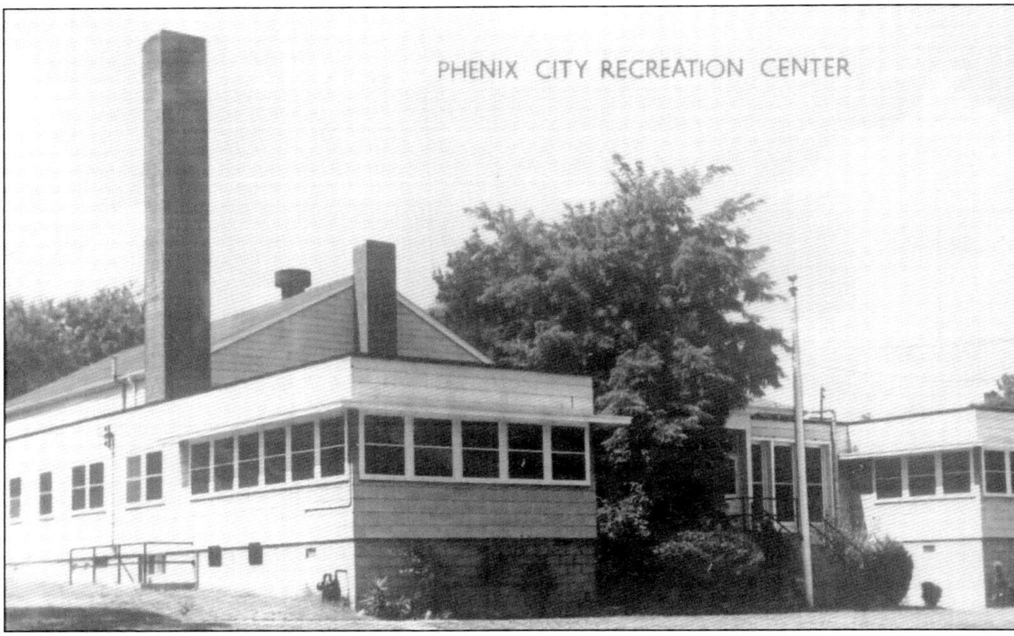

USO Building. Erected in 1942 at a cost of $75,000 (not including the land), the USO served both local citizens and World War II military personnel at Fort Benning. After the war, the building housed the chamber of commerce and the city's recreation department. The USO was located at Third Avenue and Sixteenth Street. (Courtesy Dennis Jones.)

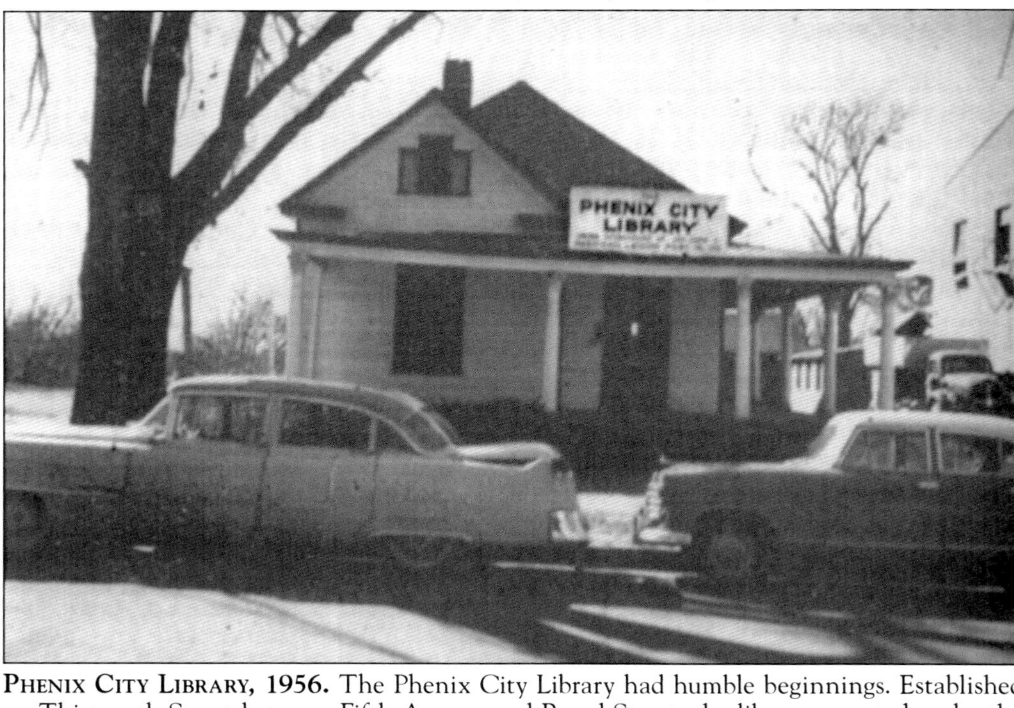

Phenix City Library, 1956. The Phenix City Library had humble beginnings. Established on Thirteenth Street between Fifth Avenue and Broad Street, the library operated under the sponsorship of the Jaycees and American Legion Post 135. (Courtesy Columbus Public Library.)

Six

Sin City 1954–1956

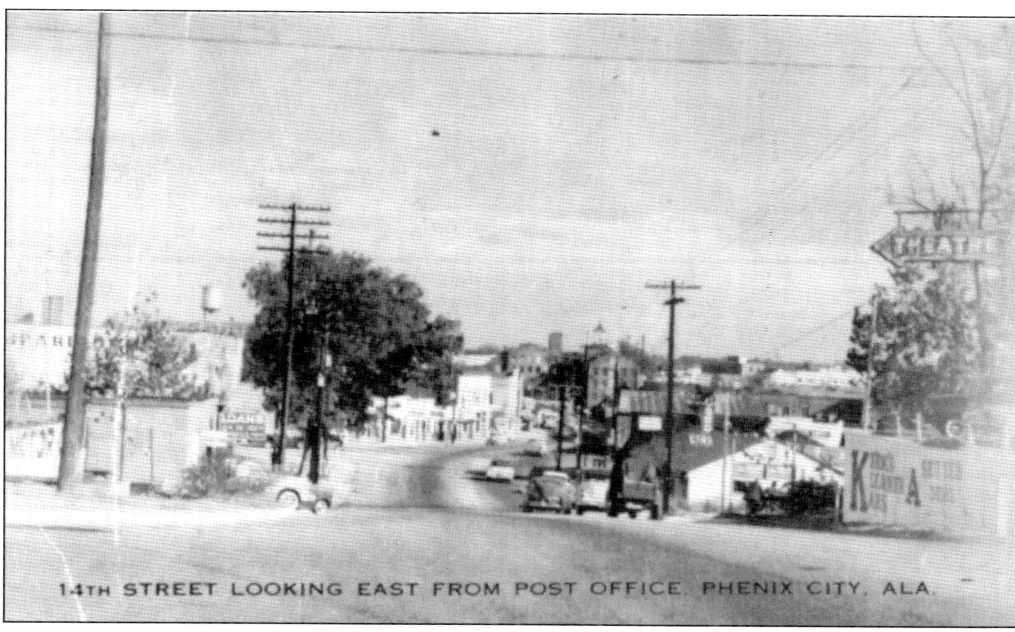

Looking East Down Fourteenth Street from Post Office. By the 1950s, Phenix City was well known as the "bad boy" among Alabama municipalities. Its main industries were gambling, prostitution, racketeering, and allied vices. Dillingham and Fourteenth Streets were the main corridors for illicit activity. (Courtesy Dennis Jones.)

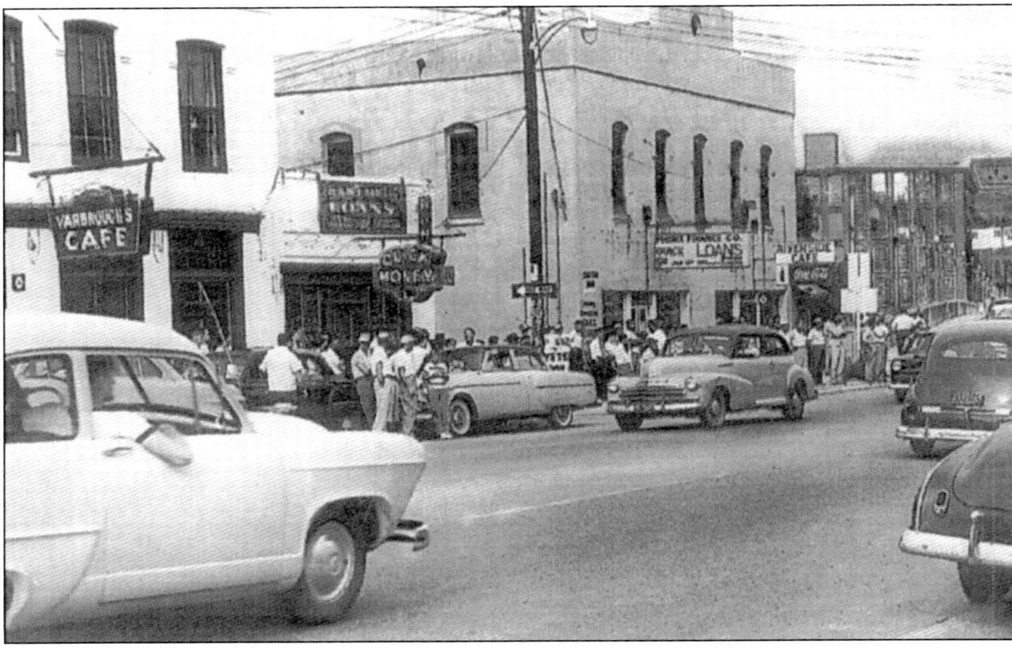

NORTH SIDE OF FOURTEENTH STREET. Establishments such as Riverside Café, Oyster Bar, Boone's Café, the Maytag, Golden Rule Café, the Silver Slipper, Silver Dollar, and the Blue Bonnet Café operated on Fourteenth Street and offered a cornucopia of gambling, prostitution, drugs, and alcohol. In all, Fourteenth Street housed 12 gambling joints, 8 loan companies, 1 sporting goods pawnbroker, 3 short-term loan companies, 2 service stations, and 1 drugstore. (Courtesy Columbus Public Library.)

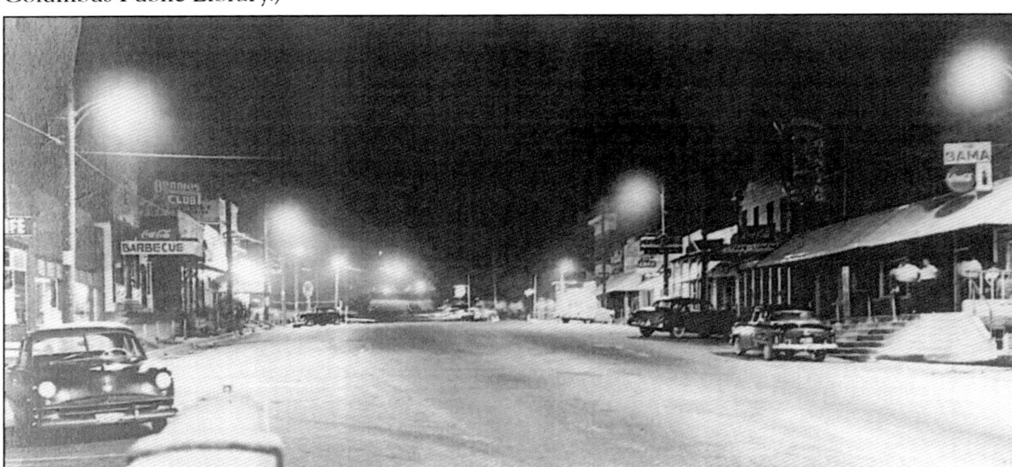

NIGHT VIEW OF FOURTEENTH STREET, PHENIX CITY. Pictured is a partial view of Fourteenth Street at night. Gambling and prostitution were not limited to Fourteenth Street. Dillingham Street had fewer establishments than Fourteenth Street but recorded higher gross profits. The Bridge Grocery, New Bridge Grocery, Ritz Café, 602 Club, Bama Club, Yellow Front Café, 514 Club, and Girard Cleaners offered gambling, alcohol, prostitution, and lottery. When crime was at its peak, it was estimated that as many as 500 prostitutes, or B-Girls, could be found in Phenix City on any given day. (Courtesy Sean Driggers.)

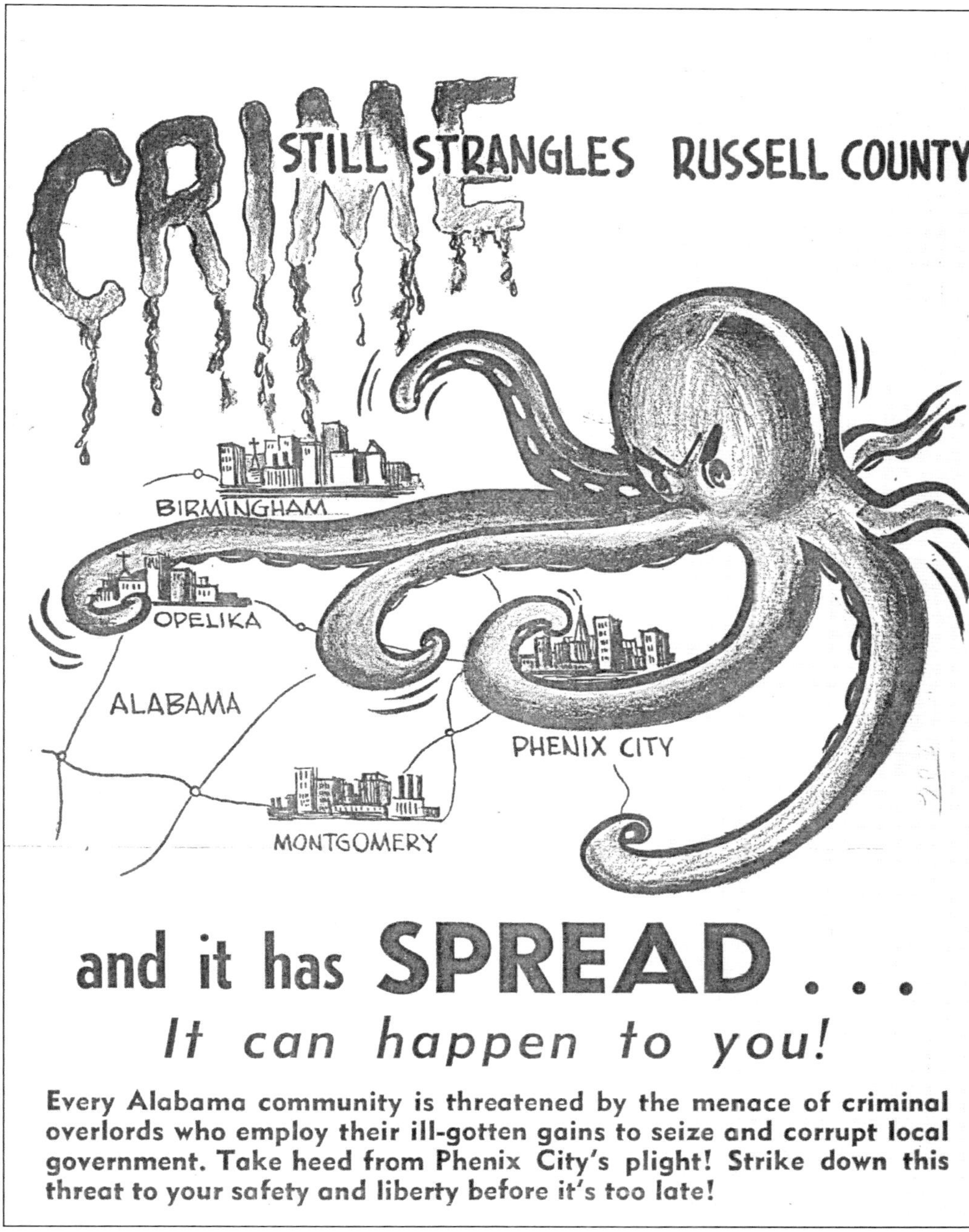

CRIME STILL STRANGLES RUSSELL COUNTY. The Russell Betterment Association distributed these fliers as a warning against the tentacles of organized crime. (Courtesy Columbus State University Archives.)

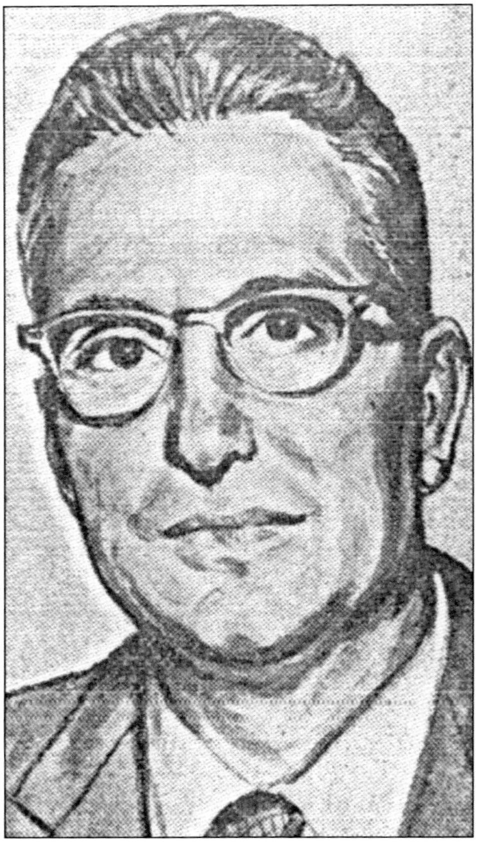

HUGH BENTLEY. Sporting goods merchant Hugh Bentley led numerous reform movements to fight organized crime in Phenix City. Bentley formed the Christian Laymen's Association and the Good Government League. Neither developed beyond discussion groups. In 1951, Bentley organized the Ministers Alliance. It collected and presented evidence of organized crime to the Russell County Grand Jury. City commissioner Elmer Reese opined that "our preachers are wonderful, as long as they preach and stick to the Bible." The grand jury agreed and dismissed the evidence. With the assistance of Howard Pennington and Hugh Britton, Bentley formed the Russell Betterment Association (RBA). (Courtesy Columbus State University Archives.)

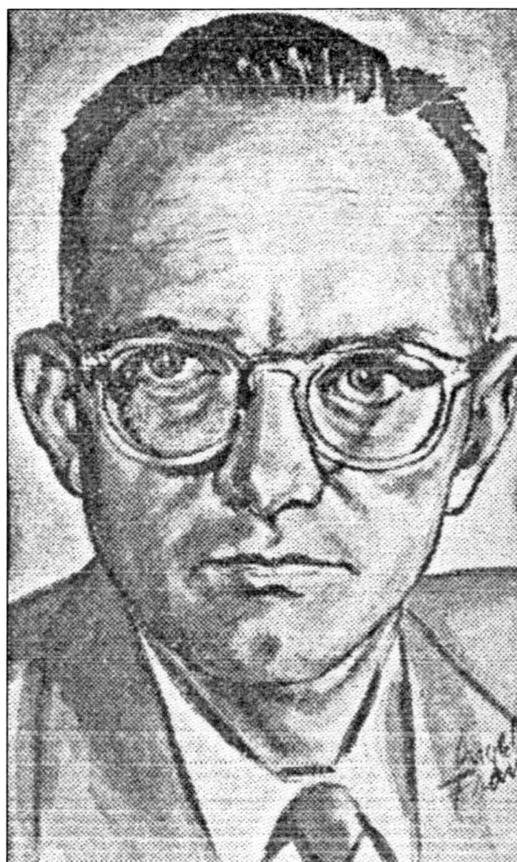

HUGH BRITTON. RBA's intelligence officer and vice president, Hugh Britton, pushed efforts to improve the quality of life in Phenix City. The RBA collected much of the evidence used to indict gangsters during the cleanup of Phenix City and Russell County. (Courtesy Columbus State University Archives.)

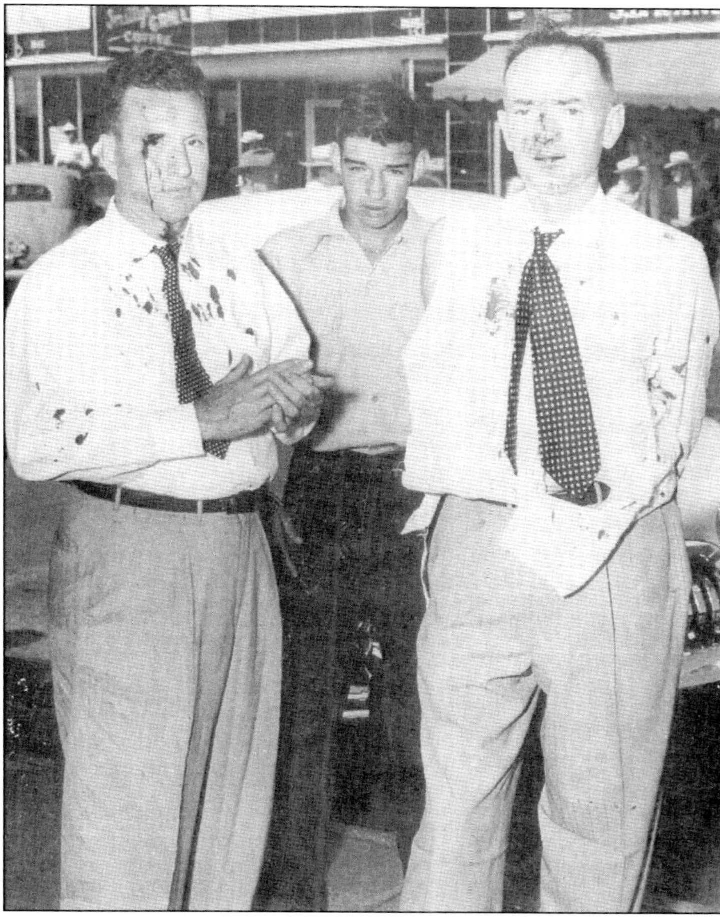

BEATEN AT THE POLLS. Beaten, bloodied, and battered, from left to right, Hugh Bentley, Hubo Bentley, and Hugh Britton are photographed after being attacked at the polls. (Courtesy Columbus State University Archives.)

JIMMIE PUTNAM'S. The reverse of the Putnam's Tourist Court postcard assured tourists that the motel was not one of the famous Phenix City brothels. It reads, "WE DO NOT SERVE LOCAL PEOPLE, WE ARE STRICTLY TOURIST ONLY." Jimmie Putnam was the city clerk of Phenix City and a friend of Arch Ferrell. (Courtesy Dennis Jones.)

"Jimmie" PUTNAM'S TOURIST COURT

Approved Member American Motel Association, Inc.

Located on U. S. Highway 80, West of Phenix City, Alabama. 1 Mile West of Intersection of U. S. Highways 241 and 80, First Filling Station beyond this point West. TELEPHONE NUMBER 8-9519 DAY OR NIGHT.

Large roomy cabins with plenty of ventilation, each cabin has window exhaust fans making hot nights unknown to our customers. We have a nice bedroom suit in each cabin with inner spring mattress, venetian blinds, curtains, radio, tiled floors, plenty of towels, wash rags and hot water, large roomy showers and modern bath room. *WE DO NOT SERVE LOCAL PEOPLE, WE ARE STRICTLY TOURIST ONLY.* We also have two room cabins designed to accommodate four people. We have cabins with twin beds. We guarantee absolutely clean, up to date, quiet cabins with conveniences equal to any first class hotel. Our cabins are heated with steam radiators controlled with thermostats. Give us a trial and you too will be recommending our cabins to your friends. A home away from home.

RING BELL ON SIGN POST

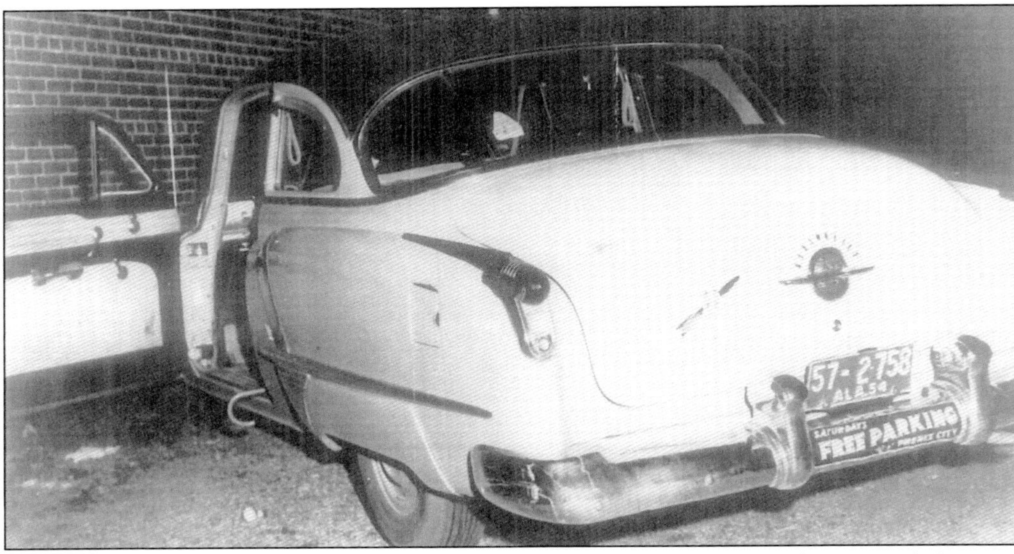

Albert Patterson's Assassination. Southern cities were still reeling from the May 1954 *Brown v. Board of Education* decision when Phenix City's foundation was shaken. On June 18, 1954, Albert Patterson was assassinated in an alley near his downtown Phenix City law office. Patterson had won the Democratic nomination for Alabama attorney general, and his campaign was built upon purging Phenix City of vice. His murder was the catalyst for a cleanup of the city. Pictured is Patterson's car in the alley between the Coulter Building and the Elite Café. (Courtesy Alabama Department of Archives and History.)

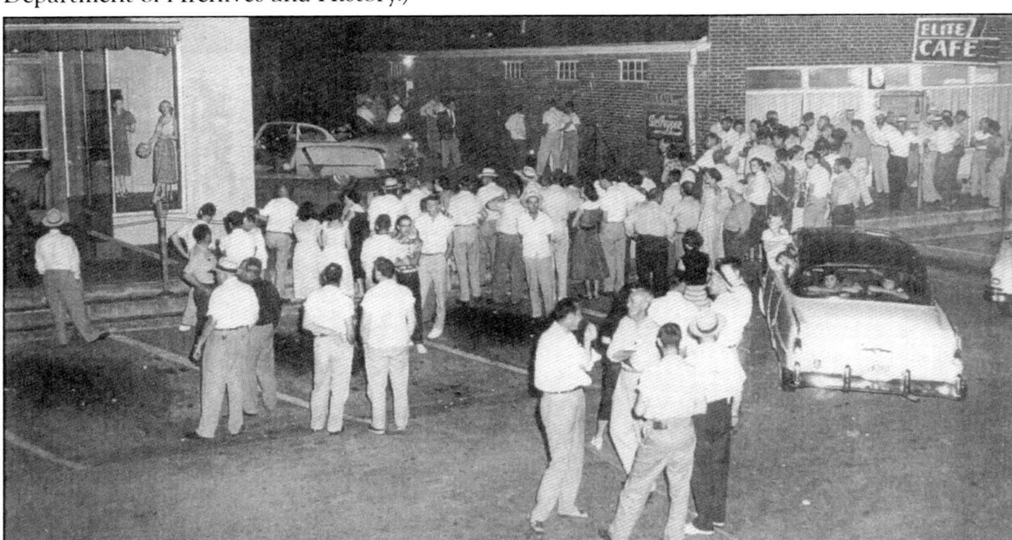

Crowd near the Albert Patterson Murder Site. Phenix City had financial motives in turning a blind eye to crime. It was estimated that vice furnished around $300,000 a year, or 60 percent of the city's income, through fines and licenses. Columbus citizens viewed Phenix City as a civic asset. "No shady operator in his right mind would establish a joint on the Georgia side when the climate is so much better across the bridge," stated a 1951 magazine article. The murder of Albert Patterson proved to be the spur needed to effect the eradication of organized crime. (Courtesy Alabama Department of Archives and History.)

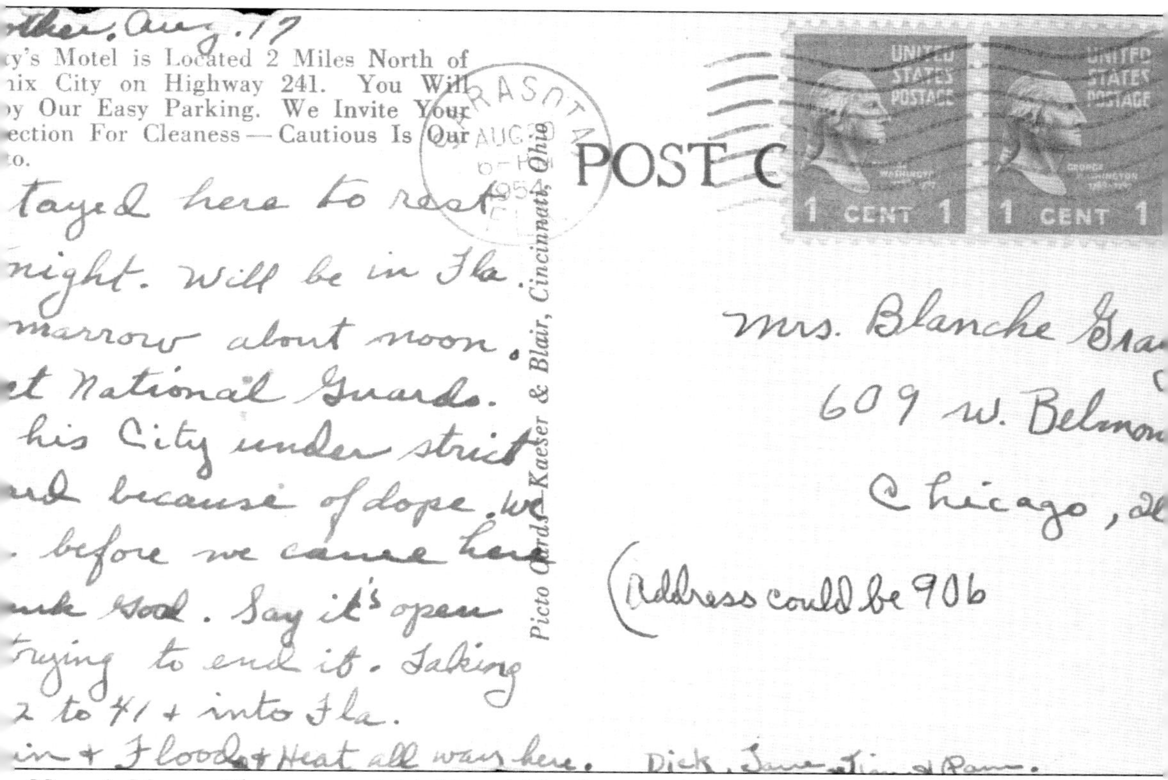

NEATY'S MOTEL. The reverse of this Neaty's Motel postcard captures a visitor's impression of Phenix City. Writing to his mother, on August 17, 1954, the traveler states, "Stayed here to rest tonight. Will be in Fla. tomorrow about noon. Met National Guards. This city under strict guard because of dope. We ate before we came here thank God. Say it's open but trying to end it." (Courtesy Dennis Jones.)

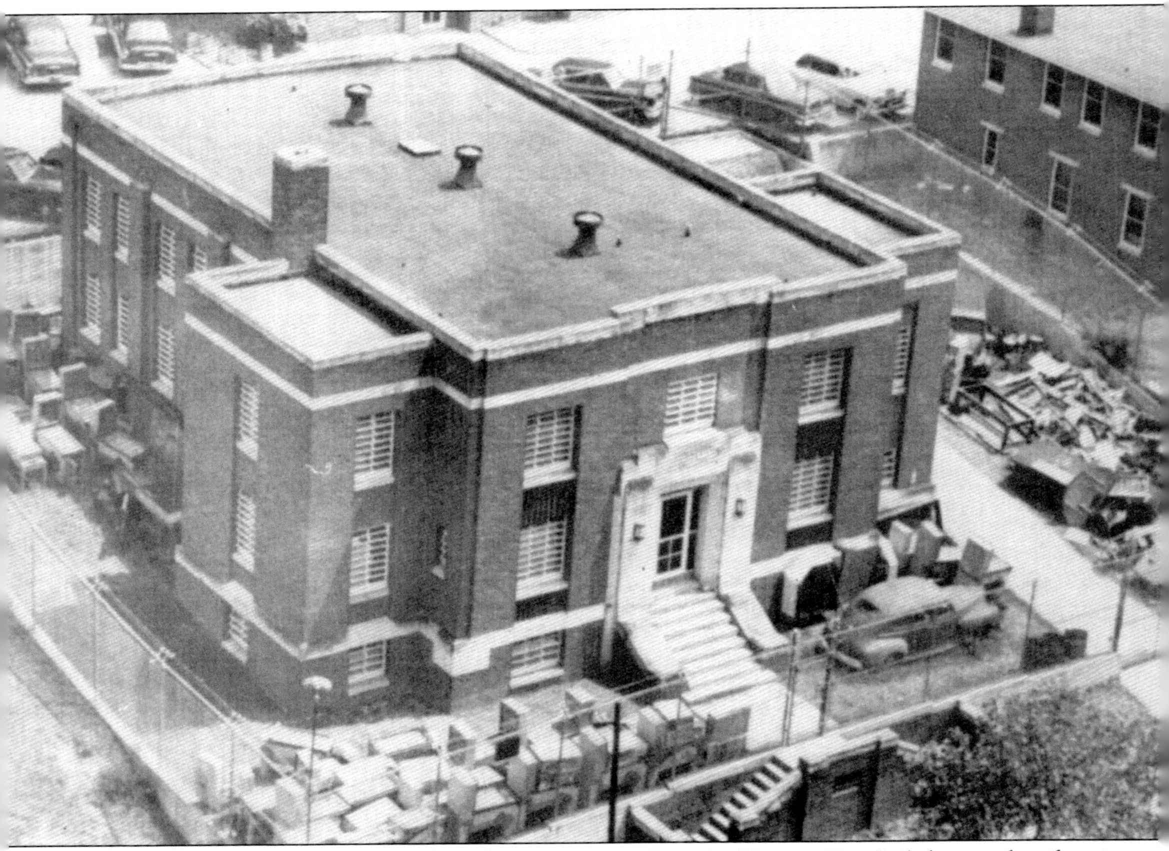

Phenix City Jail. The gambling devices surrounding the Phenix City Jail show only a fraction of gaming paraphernalia confiscated and collected by the National Guard. Guardsmen estimated the value of the slot machines and craps tables to be around $5 million. (Courtesy Columbus Public Library.)

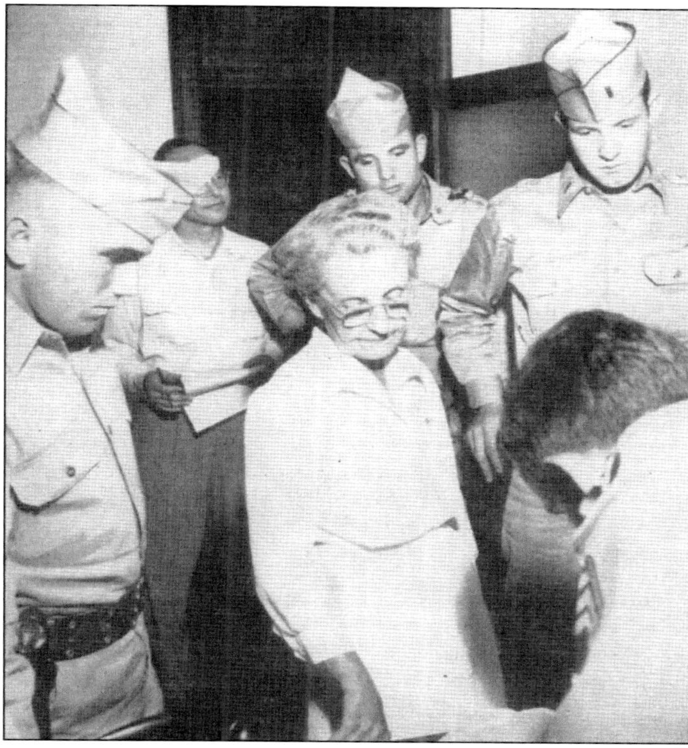

Ma Beachie. Beachie Howard, known as Ma Beachie, operated Beachie's Swing Club. Ma Beachie's club offered strippers, gambling, and liquor. The onetime garish honky-tonk later became home to Revival Center. (Courtesy Columbus Public Library.)

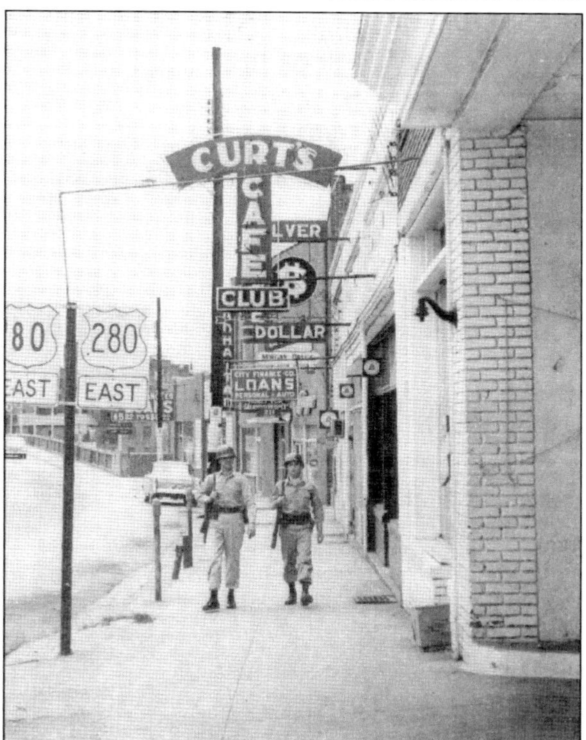

Phenix City under Martial Law. The Alabama National Guard patrols Fourteenth Street after Gov. Seth Gordon Persons placed Phenix City under martial law and sent in 75 guardsmen under the command of World War II veteran Gen. Walter J. Hanna. The guardsmen performed patrols and round-the-clock raids on nightclubs, warehouses, and gambling institutions. Fort Benning declared Phenix City off limits to its soldiers. (Courtesy Columbus Public Library.)

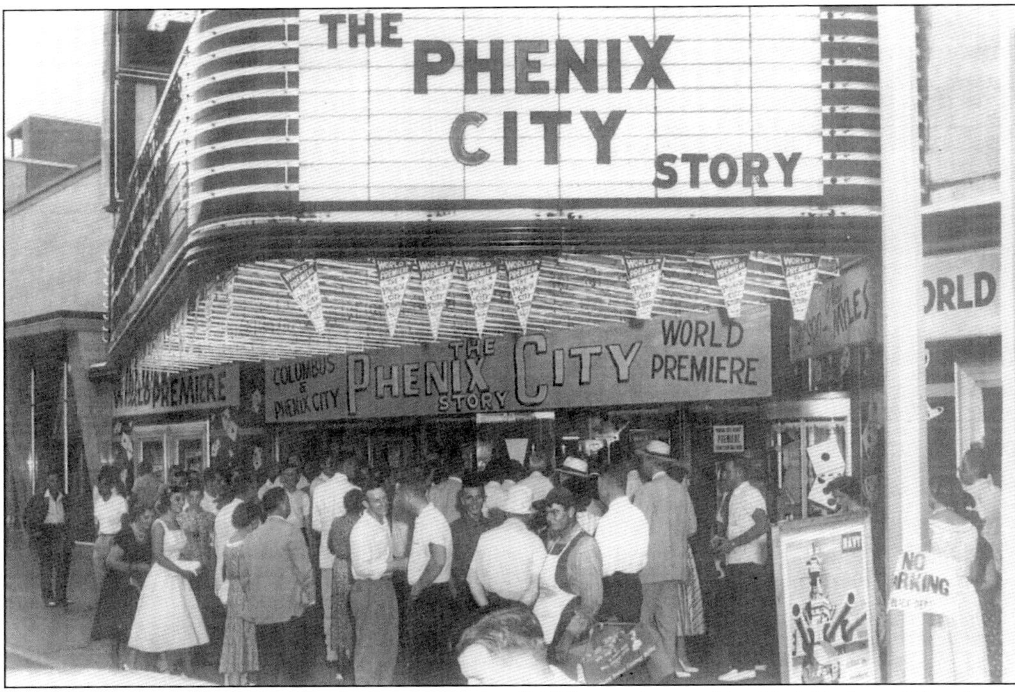

THE PHENIX CITY STORY. *The Phenix City Story* (1955) was directed by Phil Karlson. The drama depicts the 1954 assassination of Alabama attorney general Albert Patterson. The film debuted on August 14, 1955, at the Palace Theater. (Courtesy Columbus Public Library.)

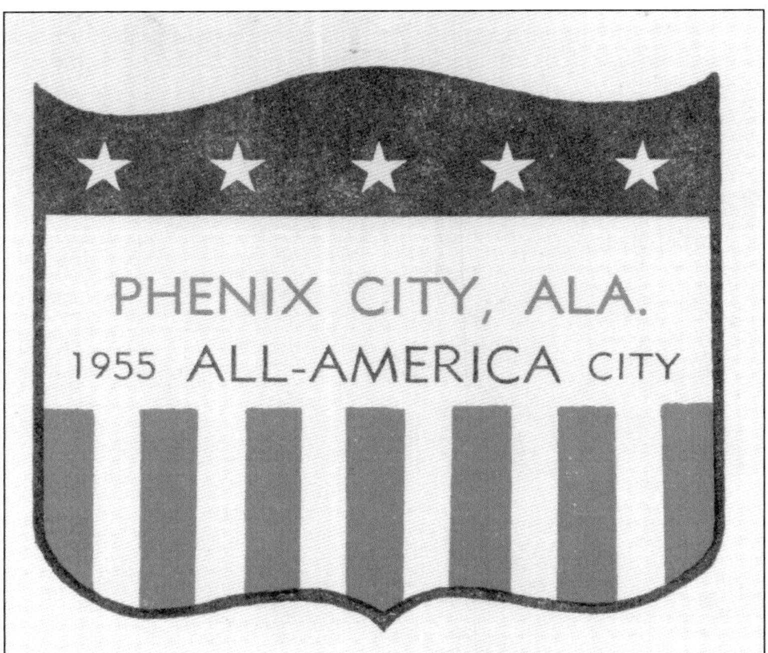

ALL-AMERICA CITY. Phenix City was honored in 1955 as one of 11 cities designated an All-America City. Efforts to eradicate organized crime no doubt played a factor in winning this distinction. All-America City Day was observed on January 7, 1956. (Courtesy Columbus State University Archives.)

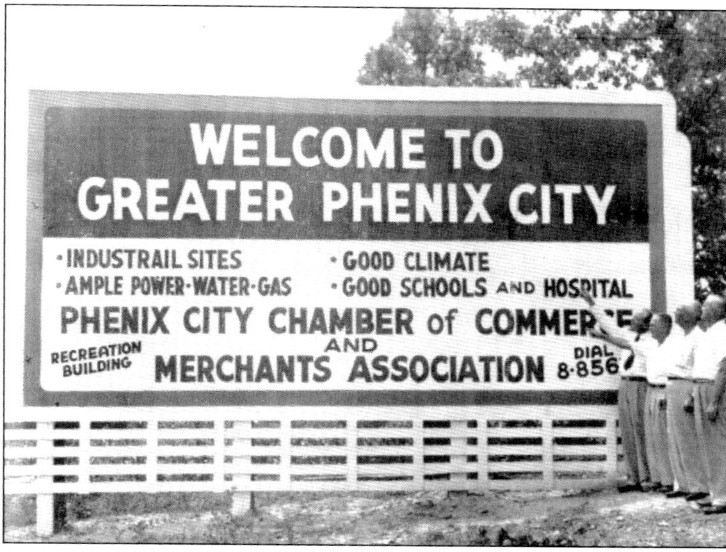

Welcome to Greater Phenix City, 1956. After the city's cleanup, the Phenix City Chamber of Commerce and Merchants Association conducted industrial promotional drives to secure industry and make up a budget shortfall caused by the cleanup costs. Standing from left to right are Leland Jones, W. W. Hunt, O. L. Randall, and C. C. Slocumb. (Courtesy Columbus Public Library.)

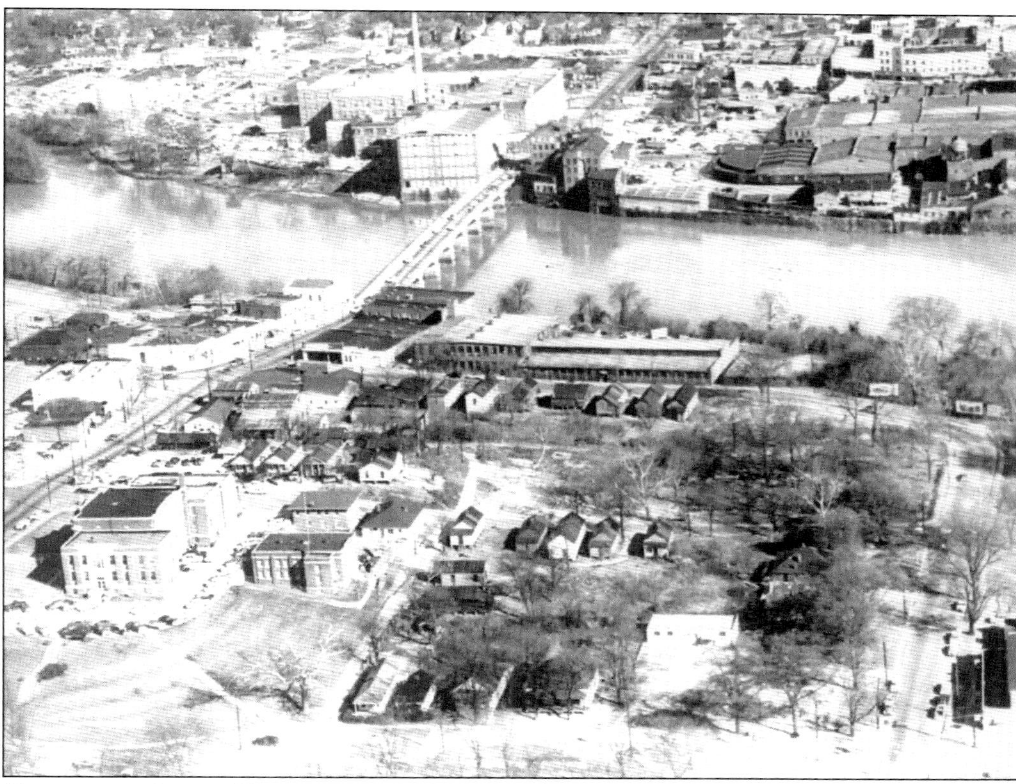

Commercial Center Redevelopment Project. The Phenix City Housing Authority's bulldozer revolution transformed the city center into a commercial district. The bulldozer swept away shacks and made way for shopping malls. Of the 68 buildings demolished in the project, 59 were deemed substandard. The Greater Phenix City Redevelopment Corporation purchased the tract for $270,000. (Courtesy Columbus Public Library.)

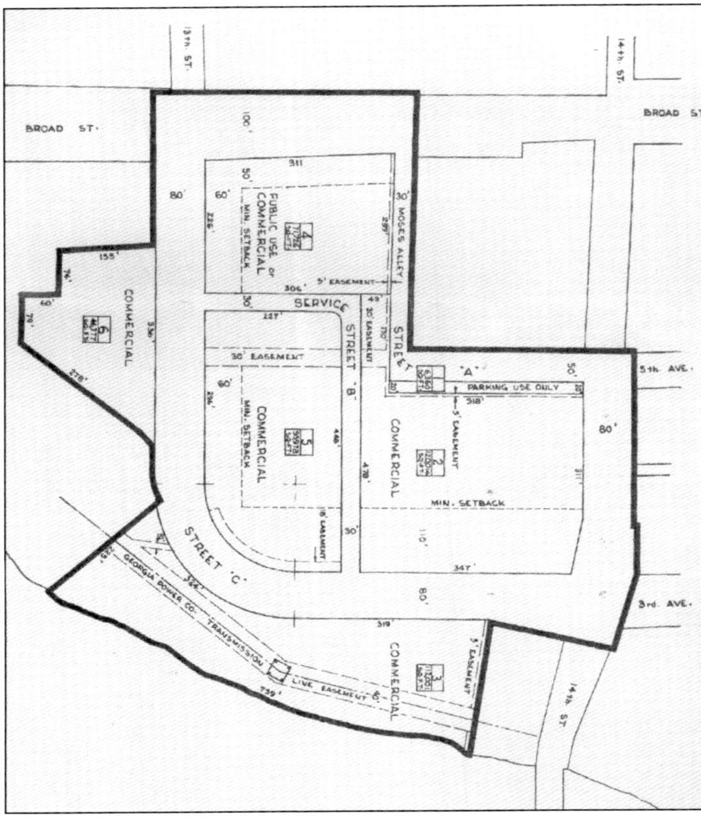

Phenix Plaza. Phenix Plaza Shopping Center was Phenix City's first modern shopping district. The 16-acre plaza was built at an estimated cost of $1.5 million and featured over 24 stores. (Courtesy Columbus State University Archives.)

Artist Rendering of Phenix Plaza. This artist rendering of Phenix Plaza proposes a detached shopping center. This differed from the actual construction of a connected L-shaped center. (Courtesy Columbus State University Archives.)

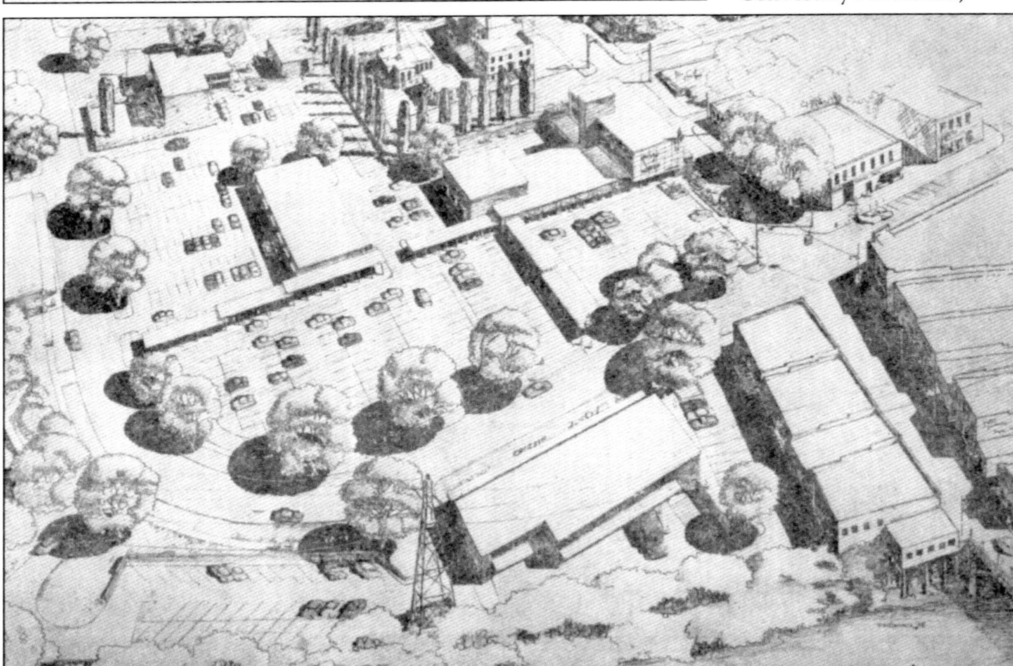

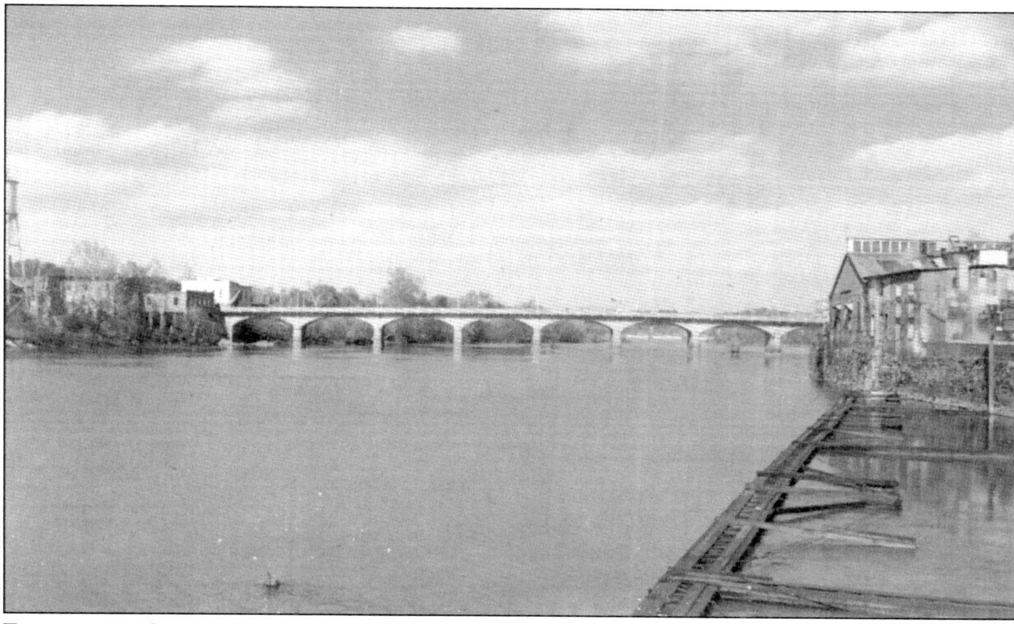

Fourteenth Street Bridge Viewed from Columbus. This view of the Fourteenth Street Bridge reveals the once thriving section of town as a shell of its former self. (Courtesy Dennis Jones.)

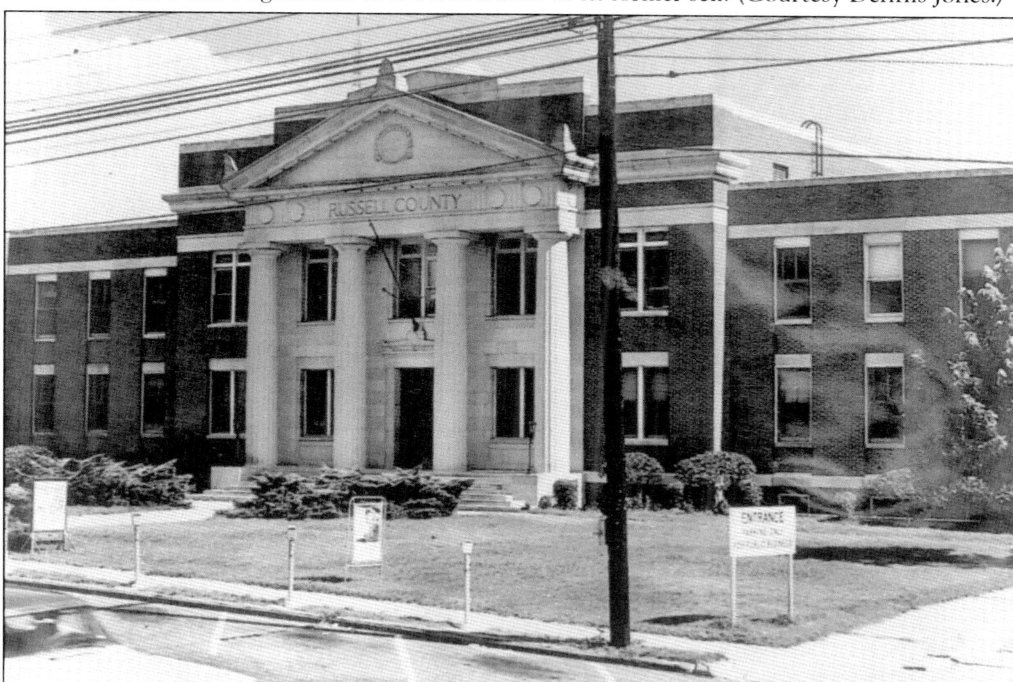

Russell County Courthouse. The Russell County Courthouse was erected in 1938. It stands as a symbol of the progress made by the city. (Courtesy Dennis Jones.)

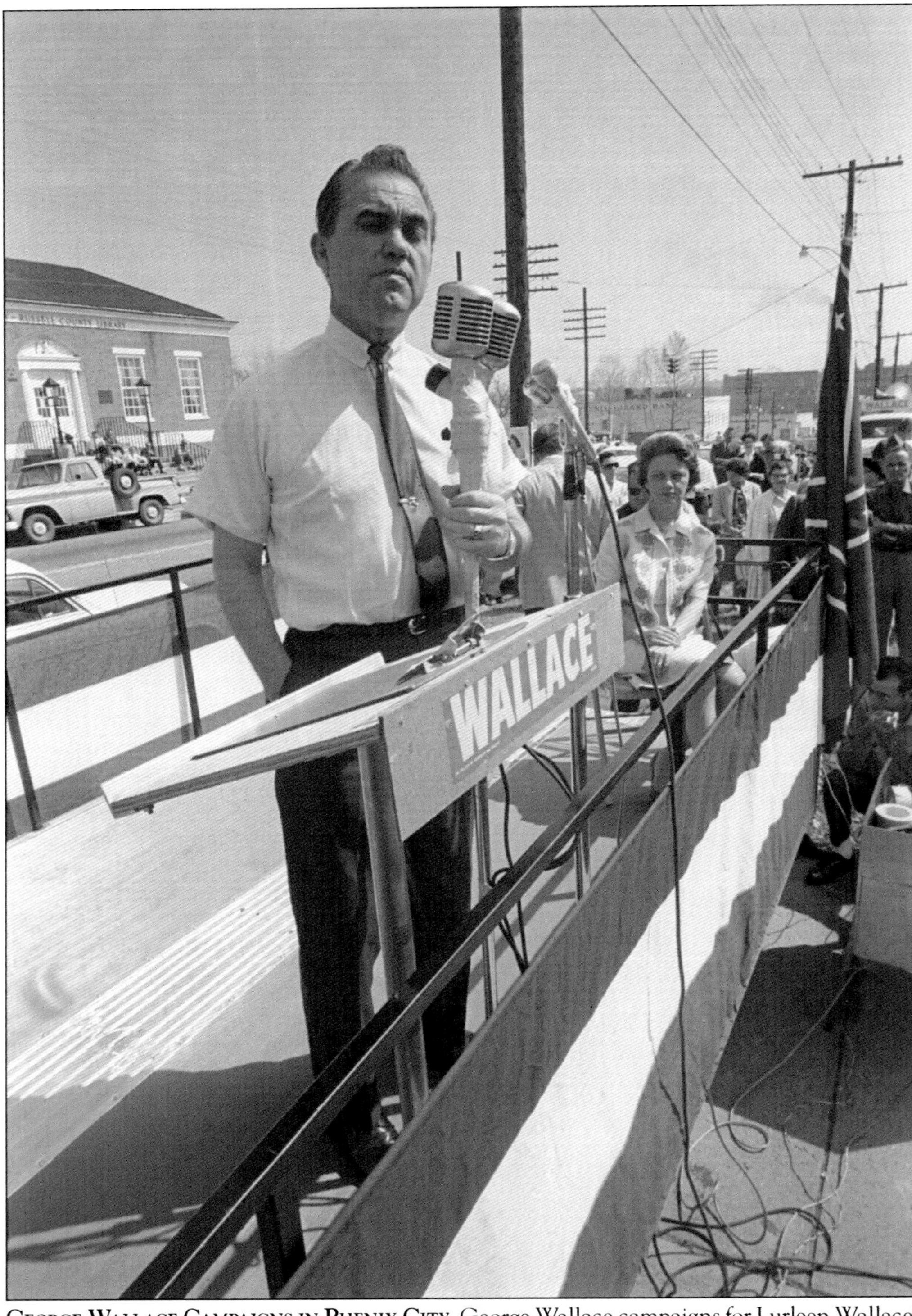

George Wallace Campaigns in Phenix City. George Wallace campaigns for Lurleen Wallace's candidacy for governor in 1966. (Courtesy Atlanta History Center.)

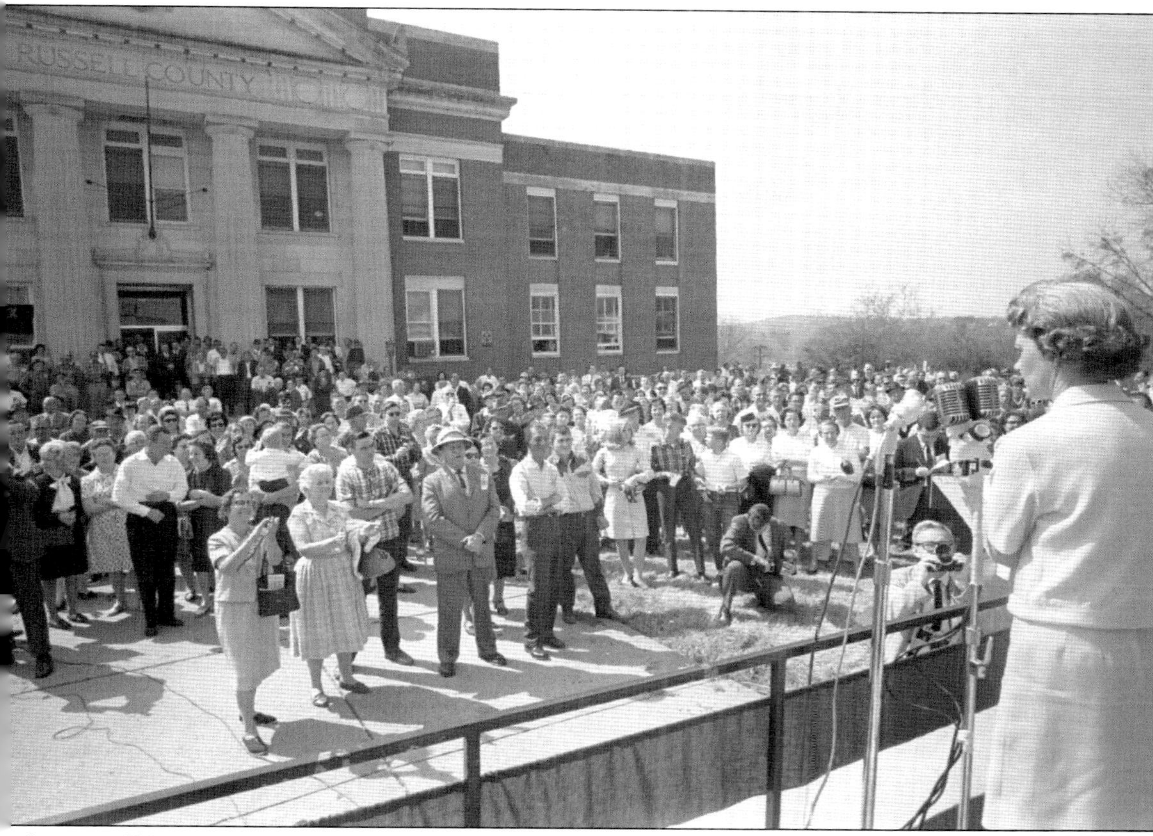

LURLEEN WALLACE CAMPAIGN IN PHENIX CITY. In 1966, after failing to get the Alabama legislature to amend the constitution to allow governors to serve consecutive terms, Wallace announced the candidacy of his wife, Lurleen. She won the May Democratic primary with 54 percent of the vote, which—in those days when the Democratic party–dominated Alabama politics—assured her election in November. (Courtesy Atlanta History Center.)

Consistent with our mission to preserve history on a local level, this book was printed in South Carolina on American-made paper and manufactured entirely in the United States. Products carrying the accredited Forest Stewardship Council (FSC) label are printed on 100 percent FSC-certified paper.

MADE IN THE USA